BTEC FIRST

TRAVEL AND TOURISM

endorsed for
BTEC

ALWAYS LEARNING

PEARSON

Published by Pearson Education Limited, Edinburgh Gate, Harlow, Essex, CM20 2JE.

www.pearsonschoolsandfecolleges.co.uk

Text © Pearson Education Limited 2013
Typeset by Thomson Press
Original illustrations © Pearson Education Limited 2013
Illustrated by Adrian Barclay/KJA-artists.com and Thomson Digital
Cover design by Pearson Education Limited and Andrew Magee Design
Cover photo/illustration © Shutterstock.com: Manuel Fernandes
Indexing by Sophia Clapham

The rights of Nicola Appleyard, Rachael Aston, Gillian Dale, Malcolm Jefferies, Andy Kerr, Christine King, Tom Rock and Carol Spencer to be identified as authors of this work have been asserted by them in accordance with the Copyright, Designs and Patents Act 1988.

First published 2013

16 15 14
10 9 8 7 6 5 4 3 2

British Library Cataloguing in Publication Data
A catalogue record for this book is available from the British Library

ISBN 978 1 446906 27 9

Printed in Slovakia by Neografia

Websites
There are links to relevant websites in this book. In order to ensure that the links are up to date and that the links work we have made the links available on our website at www.pearsonhotlinks.co.uk. Search for this title BTEC First Travel and Tourism Student Book or ISBN 978 1 446906 27 9.

Copies of official specifications for all Pearson qualifications may be found on the website: www.edexcel.com

A note from the publisher
In order to ensure that this resource offers high-quality support for the associated BTEC Pearson qualification, it has been through a review process by the awarding organisation to confirm that it fully covers the teaching and learning content of the specification or part of a specification at which it is aimed, and demonstrates an appropriate balance between the development of subject skills, knowledge and understanding, in addition to preparation for assessment.

While the publishers have made every attempt to ensure that advice on the qualification and its assessment is accurate, the official specification and associated assessment guidance materials are the only authoritative source of information and should always be referred to for definitive guidance.

BTEC examiners have not contributed to any sections in this resource relevant to examination papers for which they have responsibility.

No material from an endorsed book will be used verbatim in any assessment set by BTEC. Endorsement of a book does not mean that the book is required to achieve this BTEC qualification, nor does it mean that it is the only suitable material available to support the qualification, and any resource lists produced by the awarding organisation shall include this and other appropriate resources.

Contents

About this book		v
How to use this book		vi
Study skills		x

Unit 1	The UK Travel and Tourism Sector	2
Unit 2	UK Travel and Tourism Destinations	40
Unit 3	The Development of Travel and Tourism in the UK	64
Unit 4	International Travel and Tourism Destinations	96
Unit 5	Factors Affecting Worldwide Travel and Tourism	124
Unit 6	The Travel and Tourism Customer Experience	140
Unit 7	Travel and Tourism Business Environments	174
Unit 8	Promotion and Sales in Travel and Tourism	208
Unit 9	Travel and Tourism Employment Opportunities	236
Unit 10	Organising a Travel and Tourism Study Visit	260

Answers to Assessment Practice Questions		279
Glossary		283
Index		287

The following units are available on the Pearson Education website.

Unit 11	Delivering the Travel and Tourism Customer Experience	www.pearsonfe.co.uk/btecfirsttravelunit11
Unit 12	Marketing in Travel and Tourism	www.pearsonfe.co.uk/btecfirsttravelunit12
Unit 13	Airports and Airlines	www.pearsonfe.co.uk/btecfirsttravelunit13

Acknowledgements

The publisher would like to thank the following for their kind permission to reproduce their photographs:

(Key: b-bottom; c-centre; l-left; r-right; t-top)

Alamy Images: Adrain Sherratt 84, Chris HOwes / Wild Places Photography 48, David Pearson 53, Dmitry V1. Smirnov 222, G P Bowater 75, Ian Dagnall 114, Ingram Publishing 249, Mark Hamel FAP 187, Peter Titmus 152; **Bananastock:** 139; **Corbis:** Michael Kappeler / EPA 273, Ocean 237, Ocean RF 175, Zero Creatives 151; **Courtesy of VisitBritain:** 26; **DK Images:** Brent Madison 94, Nigel HIcks 263, Terry Carter 108, Tim Draper 214; **Fotolia.com:** Andreas Rodriguez 168, Andrew Bayda 211, ARochau 52, Crok Photography 233, deviantART 195, Elnur 24, Jenny Thompson 51, Kadmy 174, 250, 255, Looby-Lou 115, M.W. 127, Max Topchii 209, Michael Mill 58, Neale Cousland 110, NJ 83, Oleg Zhukov 147, Patryk Kosminder 143, photomic 197, Picture-Factory 245, pwollinga 217, Roy Pedersen 155, sfmthd 200t, vesper8590 216, vetal1983 71cr, Zechal 243; **Getty Images:** AFP 86, Jerry Driendl / The Image Bank 116, Mark Broussely / Redferns 54; **In Association with Haven Holidays:** 16; **Big Pit: National Coal Museum**: 87; **Pearson Education Ltd:** Studio 8 2, 40, 64, 208, Jon Barlow 57, 259, Gareth Boden 89, 140, 260, Jörg Carstensen 236, Jules Selmes 96; **Photolibrary.com:** Kevin Arnold 71cl, Warren Faidley / Corbis 128; **Plainpicture Ltd:** Johner 268; **Rex Features:** David Pearson 35, Tim Brooke 23; **Shutterstock.com:** Curioso 97, Jule Bern 43, Justin Black 46, TonyV3112 239; **SuperStock:** The Francis Frith Collection 69; **Veer/Corbis:** AigarsR 150, AlexanderShalamov 125, Alexey Kirillov 184, Andresr 246, Antikainen 203, Ariwasabi 118, Barney Boogles 74, Brian Jackson 154, CandyBoxImages 161, cla78 219, Corepics 60, DaveAllenPhoto 190, Deklofenak 186, Dmitry Kalinovsky 200b, f9photos 99, 199, fyle 266, haveseen 105, I L Photography 3, ilolab 165, Ivan Synieokov 71r, Jan Novak 106, Joshua Haviv 225, Karramba Production 119, lightpoet 276, majaPHOTO 275, Matthew Bird 200c, Miran Buric 102, Monkey Business Images 9, 124, naumoid 252, newleaf 137, noblige 185, pab_map 79, Perseomedusa 261, phillipminnis 67, Piccia Neri 41, PiLens 136, Pinwheels 229, rbouwman 103, ribeiroantonio U1-Banner, russwitherington 65, Segrey Galushko U7-Banner, .shock 141, 248, timack 62, Vladislav Moiseev 71l, warrengoldswain 12, 235, wavebreakmediamicro 180, Wong Sze Fei 224, Zee 251; **www.imagesource.com:** 271; **YHA (England & Wales):** 19t, 19b

Cover images: *Front:* **Shutterstock.com:** Manuel Fernandes

All other images © Pearson Education

The author and publisher would like to thank the following individuals and organisations for their approval and permission to reproduce their materials:

p.2 UK Tourism Statistics 2012 – The Tourism Alliance; **p.5** Mintel: Oxygen Domestic Tourism Sept 2012; **p.6** The Conservation Volunteers; **p.7** National Parks England; **p.10** World Travel & Tourism Council, 2013; **p.10** Figure 1.4 – Visitor Economy Facts, VisitBritain; **p.11** Table 1.2 – England Fact Sheet, VisitEngland; **p.11** Great Britain Tourism Survey, VisitEngland; **p.12** Office for National Statistics licensed under the Open Government Licence v.1.0; **p.13** Case study artwork from 'Business demands an airline policy to boost economy', *The Times*, 29/03/2011, page 9; **p.13** Table – International Passenger Survey 2011, Office for National Statistics licensed under the Open Government Licence v.1.0; **p.15** Neilson holiday brochure extract, Thomas Cook UK & Ireland; **p.16** Table 1.3 – Experian Hitwise; **p.16** Haven Holidays; **p.19** Youth Hostel Association website; **p.20** Butlin's website; **p.21** Table – adapted from Survey of Visits to Visitor Attractions 2011, VisitEngland; **p.21** Key term – Survey of Visits to Visitor Attractions 2011, VisitEngland; **p.22** Nation Brands Index 2009, VisitBritain; **p.23** USA: Market and Trade Profile 2012, VisitBritain; **p.30** English Heritage; **p.30** The National Trust; **p.40** The UK Tourist 2010, VisitBritain; **p.46** gatwickairport.com; **p.47** Port of Dover; **p.51** Association of Leading Visitor Attractions (ALVA); **p.51** Merlin Entertainment; **p.54** Association of Leading Visitor Attractions (ALVA); **p.73** Thomas Cook UK & Ireland; **p.87** Big Pit: Amgueddfa Lofaol Cymru / National Coal Museum; **p.88** Merlin Entertainment and Themed Entertainment Association and AECOM; **p.95** World Travel & Tourism Council, 2013 and BBC News Website; **p.95** World Travel & Tourism Council, 2013; **p.146** European Commission; **p.152** Office for National Statistics licensed under the Open Government Licence v.1.0; **p.178** European Commission on Enterprise and Industry SBA Fact Sheet 2010 – 2012; **p.183** House of Commons Library Standard Note on Youth Unemployment Statistics, contains Parliamentary information licensed under the Open Parliament Licence v1.0; **p.183** Inbound tourist update April 2013, VisitBritain; **p.187** The *Caterer and Hotelkeeper* magazine; **p.188** Barmy Army Ltd; **p.190** Figure 7.2 – International Passenger Survey (IPS), Office for National Statistics licensed under the Open Government Licence v.1.0; **p.190** Table 7.1 – Survey of Visits to Visitor Attractions 2011, VisitEngland; **p.191** Table 7.2 – Survey of Visits to Visitor Attractions 2011, VisitEngland; **p.192** Figure 7.3 – International Passenger Survey (IPS), Office for National Statistics licensed under the Open Government Licence v.1.0; **p.194** Merlin Entertainment; **p.217** Sport Abroad, TUI Travel PLC Group; **p.266** English Heritage Handbook 2012.

Every effort has been made to trace the copyright holders and we apologise in advance for any unintentional omissions. We would be pleased to insert the appropriate acknowledgement in any subsequent edition of this publication.

About this book

This book is designed to help you through your BTEC First Travel and Tourism qualification and covers 13 units from the qualification.

▶ About your BTEC First Travel and Tourism

Choosing to study for a BTEC First Travel and Tourism qualification is a great decision to make for lots of reasons. The Travel and Tourism sector offers a wide variety of careers, from cabin crew to customer service assistant to operations officer, and there are also opportunities to work abroad. Your BTEC will sharpen your skills for employment or further study.

▶ About the authors

Nicola Appleyard began teaching in 2004 following a career working for P&O Ferries and working as a local travel agent. Since starting her teaching career she has taught BTEC Travel and Tourism, Business, WorkSkills and Public Service at a range of levels in the Further Education sector. Nicola has also set up a successful family business. She is currently working as a 14-16 Local Authority alternative provision co-ordinator at East Riding College.

Rachael Aston graduated with a Higher National Diploma in Business and Tourism and started her career in retail travel management working as an Assistant Manager for Going Places. She completed her teacher training qualification and has worked as a travel and tourism lecturer for 12 years and as a Programme Manager at Stourbridge College. Rachael recently moved into a quality and development role. Rachael also works as a freelance travel and tourism author and is due to complete her Masters in Education this year, specialising in mentoring, teaching and learning.

Gillian Dale taught travel and tourism in a college of further education for many years before starting her own business as an adviser working with colleges and work based training providers. She holds an MSc in Tourism Management and has written several text books for travel and tourism courses, including the BTEC National Pearson texts.

Malcolm Jefferies worked in the demanding airline industry managing the on-the-day operations to ensure that excellent customer service was provided to over 40,000 passengers a day. He has been an Open University Business School lecturer as well as a lecturer in UK colleges. Malcolm continues to lecture in the UK and overseas, primarily on customer service and international cultures. He has also co-authored a number of books on those subjects. Additionally, Malcolm provides consultancy on emergency planning and crisis management.

Andy Kerr holds an MA in Hotel and Catering Management and has worked in a number of country house hotels, in both food and beverage and general management. After this experience, Andy embarked on his teaching career and has taught a range of subjects, including business, hospitality and travel and tourism. He currently works at West Herts College in Watford. Andy is an experienced author and has been involved in the writing of several student books on travel and tourism. In his free time, Andy volunteers for the National Trust and can sometimes be found selling tickets and trips and advising customers at Dapdune Wharf on the River Wey Navigations.

Christine King has been involved in education for 30 years, initially teaching travel and tourism and then continuing her career as the Head of School for Hospitality, Leisure and Tourism at Guildford College. Subsequently, she has been involved in Equality and Diversity training and completed an MA in Education Management. Christine now acts as an education consultant.

Tom Rock worked in the leisure and arts and entertainment sectors for a number of years prior to becoming a teacher. He currently works at the Winsford East Academy in Cheshire as Lead Teacher for Travel and Tourism. Tom is an experienced author, having worked with Pearson on a number of projects.

Carol Spencer joined a major specialist tour operator as a graduate trainee and from there progressed to senior management positions in tour operations. After relocation to the north of England, Carol changed careers and began teaching in the Further Education sector. Carol has combined a 20 year teaching career at both Craven College and York College with a number of different roles, including working as a writer.

How to use this book

This book is designed to help you use your skills and knowledge in work-related situations, and assist you in getting the most from your course.

These introductions give you a snapshot of what to expect from each unit – and what you should be aiming for by the time you finish it.

How this unit is assessed.

Learning aims describe what you will be doing in the unit.

A learner shares how working through the unit has helped them.

▶ Features of this book

There are lots of features in this book to help you learn about the topics in each unit, and to have fun along the way!

Topic references and learning aim labels show which parts of the BTEC you are covering.

You will find an introduction at the start of each topic with a short activity to help you get started.

Key terms boxes give definitions of important words and phrases that you will come across. Key terms appear in blue, bold text and are defined on the page or in the glossary at the end of the book.

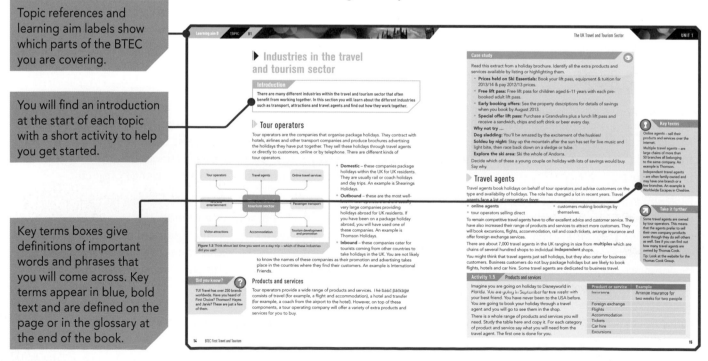

Activity 4.2　Escaping to an European city

Imagine you have been asked to put forward proposals for a residential study visit to a European city. Carry out a poll to find out which city would be the most popular and why.

Activities will help you learn about the topic. These can be completed in pairs or groups, or sometimes on your own.

Assessment practice 1.1

Which of the following is an example of inbound tourism to the UK? [1]

A A family from Amsterdam visiting France.

B A woman from Africa attending a conference in Manchester.

C A girl from London going on a gap year.

D A couple from Leicester holidaying in Wales.

A chance to practise answering the types of test questions that you may come across in your examination. (For Unit 1 and Unit 7 only.)

Assessment activity 9.2　2B.P3 | 2B.P4 | 2B.P5 | 2B.M2 | 2B.M3 | 2B.D1

You are looking for a job in the travel and tourism industry. You should look at contrasting job options.

Select two jobs, one at entry level and one at managerial level, within two different travel and tourism industries, four jobs in total. Compare and contrast each job and make a short presentation to show which job role you would consider applying for, you could also say what makes you suitable for that role.

For each job role you should consider the:

- job specification (requirements of the job role)
- person specification (skills and qualifications needed)
- statutory requirements (employer's responsibilities)
- contractual requirements (employee's responsibilities).

Tip

Make sure you check the spelling and punctuation in your presentation.

Activities that relate to the unit's assessment critera. These activities will help you prepare for your assignments and contain tips to help you achieve your potential. (For all units **except** Unit 1 and Unit 7.)

Just checking ✔

1 What was the Grand Circular Tour?

2 Why did many British seaside resorts suffer decline during the mid to late 20th century?

3 What is the difference between horizontal and vertical integration?

4 Why do some customers prefer to use the internet over high street travel agents to book products and services?

Use these to check your knowledge and understanding of the topic you have just covered.

Someone who works in the travel and tourism industry explains how this unit of the BTEC First applies to the day-to-day work they do as part of their job.

WorkSpace

▶ Jessica Shaw

Tour Manager for AdventuringUK

I work as a tour manager for AdventuringUK. I am responsible for:

- developing domestic package holidays to a wide range of UK 'adventure' destinations
- designing exciting, flexible tour packages that meet the needs of our customers
- exploring and researching new destination opportunities
- communicating itinerary instructions to customers
- responding to queries and dealing with problems that may arise during a tour.

I find my job really rewarding and exciting. I love the research part of my job; one of my main roles is visiting different places in the UK and finding suitable destinations. It's great being able to accompany the holidaymakers on the trip; it means that I am there to help if anyone has any problems, but I also get to join in with the fun activities too!

AdventuringUK is a small tour operator that was established about 15 years ago in response to the demand for more active, adventurous holidays. When they first began operations, AdventuringUK employed four staff. I've been working here for five years and I have seen the business grow; we now employ 18 staff. Customers are really positive about their experiences; they often tell me that they would much prefer to be doing something active and exciting on a holiday rather than just lounging around in the sun.

To work in this industry you need to be highly motivated and flexible. When you are working away from home on a tour, you are effectively on call for 24 hours a day so you need to have good stamina! You also need to be friendly and good with people. Most of the customers are great, but when you do get the occasional customer moaning you have to be able to deal with them in a calm and considerate manner.

Think about it

1 Why do you think that demand for adventure holidays has increased over the last few years?

2 Can you think of any other types of holiday that have grown in demand over the last few years?

3 What would be the main demands of working such flexible shift patterns?

89

This section gives you the chance to think more about the role that this person does, and whether you would want to follow in their footsteps once you've completed your BTEC.

▶ BTEC Assessment Zone

You will be assessed in two different ways for your BTEC First in Travel and Tourism. For most units, your teacher/tutor will set assignments for you to complete. These may take the form of projects where you research, plan, prepare, and evaluate a piece of work or activity. The table in the BTEC Assessment Zone explains what you must do in order to achieve each of the assessment criteria. Each unit of this book contains a number of assessment activities to help you with these assessment criteria.

Assessment and grading criteria		
Level 1	Level 2 Pass	Level 2 Merit
Learning aim A: Explore the developments that have helped shape the UK travel and tourism sector		
1A.1	**2A.P1**	**2A.M1**
Outline four key developments that have helped shape the UK travel and tourism sector.	Describe key developments that have helped shape the UK travel and tourism sector.	Explain key developments that have helped shaped the UK travel and tourism sector.
	See Assessment activity 3.1, page 82	**See Assessment activity 3.1, page 82**

The table in the BTEC Assessment Zone explains what you must do in order to acheive each of the assessment criteria, and signposts assessment activities in this book to help you to prepare for your assignments.

For Unit 1 and Unit 7 of your BTEC, you will be assessed by a paper-based examination. The BTEC Assessment Zones for these units helps you to prepare for your examinations by showing you some of the different types of questions you may need to answer.

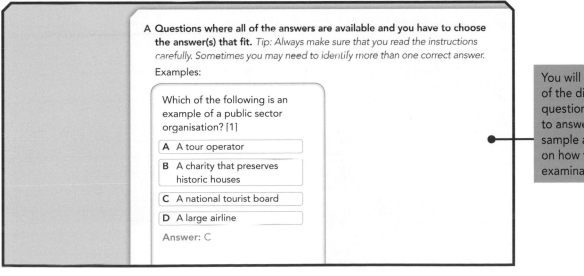

A Questions where all of the answers are available and you have to choose the answer(s) that fit. *Tip: Always make sure that you read the instructions carefully. Sometimes you may need to identify more than one correct answer.*

Examples:

Which of the following is an example of a public sector organisation? [1]

A A tour operator

B A charity that preserves historic houses

C A national tourist board

D A large airline

Answer: C

You will find examples of the different types of questions you will need to answer, as well as sample answers and tips on how to prepare for the examination.

Study skills

▶ Planning and getting organised

The first step in managing your time is to plan ahead and be well organised. Some people are naturally good at this. They think ahead, write down commitments in a diary or planner and store their notes and handouts neatly and carefully so they can find them quickly.

How good are your working habits?

Improving your planning and organisational skills

1 Use a diary to schedule working times into your weekdays and weekends.

2 Also use the diary to write down exactly what work you have to do. You could use this as a 'to do' list and tick off each task as you go.

3 Divide up long or complex tasks into manageable chunks and put each 'chunk' in your diary with a deadline of its own.

4 Always allow more time than you think you need for a task.

▶ Sources of information

You will need to carry out research to complete your BTEC First assignments, so it's important to know what sources of information are available to you. These are likely to include the following:

Take it further

If you become distracted by social networking sites or texts when you're working, set yourself a time limit of 10 minutes or so to indulge yourself. You could even use this as a reward for completing a certain amount of work.

Key term

Bias – People often have strong opinions about certain topics. This is called 'bias'. Newspaper or magazine articles, or information found on the internet, may be biased to present a specific point of view.

Remember

Store relevant information when you find it – keep a folder on your computer specifically for research – so you don't have to worry about finding it again at a later date.

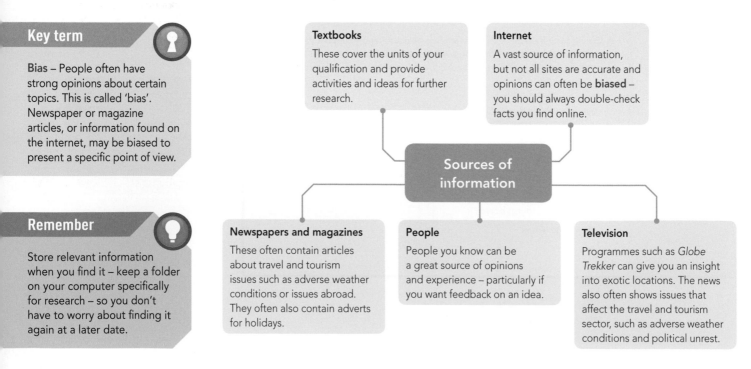

Textbooks
These cover the units of your qualification and provide activities and ideas for further research.

Internet
A vast source of information, but not all sites are accurate and opinions can often be **biased** – you should always double-check facts you find online.

Sources of information

Newspapers and magazines
These often contain articles about travel and tourism issues such as adverse weather conditions or issues abroad. They often also contain adverts for holidays.

People
People you know can be a great source of opinions and experience – particularly if you want feedback on an idea.

Television
Programmes such as *Globe Trekker* can give you an insight into exotic locations. The news also often shows issues that affect the travel and tourism sector, such as adverse weather conditions and political unrest.

▶ Organising and selecting information

Organising your information

Once you have used a range of sources of information for research, you will need to organise the information so it's easy to use.

- Make sure your written notes are neat and have a clear heading – it's often useful to date them, too.
- Always keep a note of where the information came from (the title of a book, the title and date of a newspaper or magazine and the web address of a website) and, if relevant, which pages.
- Work out the results of any questionnaires you've used.

Selecting your information

Once you have completed your research, re-read the assignment brief or instructions you were given to remind yourself of the exact wording of the question(s) and divide your information into three groups:

1 Information that is totally relevant.

2 Information that is not as good, but which could come in useful.

3 Information that doesn't match the questions or assignment brief very much, but that you kept because you couldn't find anything better!

Check that there are no obvious gaps in your information against the questions or assignment brief. If there are, make a note of them so that you know exactly what you still have to find.

▶ Presenting your work

Before handing in any assignments, make sure:

- you have addressed each part of the question and that your work is as complete as possible
- all spelling and grammar is correct
- you have referenced all sources of information you used for your research
- that all work is your own – otherwise you could be committing **plagiarism**
- you have saved a copy of your work.

🔑 Key term

Plagiarism – If you are including other people's views, comments or opinions, or copying a diagram or table from another publication, you must state the source by including the name of the author or publication, or the web address. Failure to do this (so you are really pretending other people's work is your own) is known as plagiarism. Check your school's policy on plagiarism and copying.

Introduction

This unit will introduce you to the travel and tourism sector. You will discover how important this large sector is to our economy, bringing revenue from both UK residents and foreign tourists who spend their money in the UK. You will also find out how the sector provides many interesting types of jobs, over 2.5 million of them (Source: UK Tourism Statistics 2012 – The Tourism Alliance).

You will find out about the different types of tourism and the reasons for travel. You will see how technology is changing the way travel and holiday experiences are offered to a variety of customers from holidaymakers to business travellers.

All the industries that make up the sector are introduced in this unit so that you can see what their role is and how they depend on each other. Think about this now. For example, how does a hotel depend on the passenger transport industry? What organisations does the hotel use to promote its services? And how does it relate to visitor attractions?

Assessment: This unit will be assessed externally using a 60-minute paper-based examination.

Learning aims

In this unit you will:

A understand the UK travel and tourism sector and its importance to the UK economy

B know about the industries, and key organisations, within the travel and tourism sector, their roles and interrelationships

C understand the role of consumer technology in the travel and tourism sector.

> We did this unit first. It was a good way of seeing what travel and tourism was all about and made me feel excited about the rest of the course. I was really surprised to find that many travel companies all belong to one organisation even though they have different names.
>
> Harry, *15-year-old Travel and Tourism student*

The UK Travel and Tourism Sector

1

Types of tourism

Introduction

It is useful to the travel and tourism sector, and to government, to know how much money is spent on tourism within the UK and how much is spent on travelling abroad. Learn the special terms we use for different types of tourism and think of some examples for each one.

According to the World Tourism Organization, tourism is about people travelling to, and staying in, places outside their usual environment for less than a year for leisure, business and other purposes. It includes people who stay overnight and visitors who just go for a day trip. Tourists may be people who live in the UK or people who have come from other countries. When we go abroad on holiday we too are tourists.

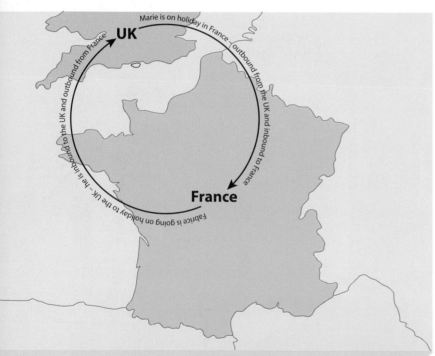

Figure 1.1 Diagram of inbound and outbound travel.

Domestic tourism

You are a domestic tourist whenever you go on holiday in the country in which you live or go on a day trip to another town or place of interest. For statistical purposes tourists take an overnight stay and those who are on a day trip are called day visitors.

Outbound tourism

This term includes anyone who travels from the UK to another country for a holiday (or other type of visit).

Inbound tourism

People who travel to the UK for tourism purposes are inbound tourists. They are outbound from their own country.

Activity 1.1   Type of tourism

What kind of tourism is each of these?

1 Patrick is travelling from his home in Birmingham to Austria for a skiing holiday.
2 Sergio is from Moscow. He is visiting his brother in the UK.
3 Sally lives in Liverpool and is going to visit to her daughter in Australia.
4 Christopher is Polish but has been living in Portsmouth for four years. He is going on a day trip to London.

TOPIC A2

▶ Types of travel

Introduction

The terms we use for travel relate to the purpose of the visit. You might think that tourism is all about holidays, but it also covers travel for business and other specialist types of travel. If people are not travelling for holidays what might be the purpose of their trip? Think of at least five reasons for a trip.

▶ Leisure travel

Pleasure is the usual motivation for leisure travel and includes day trips, short breaks, holidays, visiting friends and relatives, staycations and special events.

These are some of the categories that The Office for National Statistics suggests for surveys on leisure travel:

- holidays, leisure and recreation
- visiting friends and relatives (VFR)
- shopping.

▶ Business travel

There are many different kinds of business travel as shown in Figure 1.2.

Meetings are essential for business people to discuss issues or projects face to face. When people do not work in the same place they may have to travel to a convenient location to attend a meeting, possibly in a meeting room in a hotel.

Incentive travel is offered as a reward for good performance in business or to persuade customers to buy something.

Conferences are larger gatherings where specialists from different industries or the whole department or staff of an organisation come together. These are held less often than meetings and take place in venues such as hotels with conference facilities. These are often expensive for businesses due to costs for travel, conference facilities and accommodation and food for people attending.

Events are more general activities such as awards evenings or product launches. They require a venue, food and often entertainment.

Discussion point

There has been a rise in people taking domestic holidays in the UK with 1 in 3 people saying they plan to take one (Source: Mintel: Oxygen Domestic Tourism Sept 2012). The weather in the UK is very unpredictable – in 2012 it rained all summer. What do you think holiday companies can do to persuade people to take a staycation despite the weather?

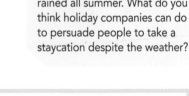

Figure 1.2 The acronym MICE will help you remember the different types of business travel.

▶ Specialist travel

Some travel and tourism companies cater for specific markets.

Table 1.1 – Examples of specific markets that companies cater for.

Type of tourism	Example
Adventure tourism	Outdoor activities (often in remote places)
Health	Visiting a health spa
Education	Going on a trip to study a language
Cultural heritage	Discovering places that relate to a country's history
Dark tourism	Visiting a place where a disaster has happened
Voluntary work	Combining a holiday with charity activity
Conservation	Combining a trip with conservation activity
Eco-tourism	A type of tourism that conserves the environment

Assessment practice 1.1

Which of the following is an example of inbound tourism to the UK? [1]

A A family from Amsterdam visiting France.

B A woman from Africa attending a conference in Manchester.

C A girl from London going on a gap year.

D A couple from Leicester holidaying in Wales.

Case study

The Conservation Volunteers is a charity that aims to conserve or reclaim the UK's green spaces. The organisation offers lots of activities, including volunteer holidays.

Their holidays in the UK are quite reasonably priced from £150 for a few days in Sussex to £550 for a week in the Isles of Scilly.

Of course, you have to work. For example, at the coast you would probably be carrying out a beach sweep. This means collecting litter and marine waste from the beaches. The waste is surveyed before disposal to provide information for the Marine Conservation Society's waste survey.

Prices include travel, accommodation and food. Accommodation is often quite basic, but volunteers have the satisfaction of helping conserve nature as well as spending time in some beautiful places.

1 What type of volunteering would you be prepared to do?

2 What kind of people would go on a volunteer holiday?

3 Choose a volunteer holiday and present it to someone in your group selling the benefits of the holiday.

To access the website for Conservation Volunteers, visit Pearson hotlinks. You can access this by going to www.pearsonhotlinks.co.uk and searching for this title.

Principles of sustainable tourism

Introduction

If you practise sustainable tourism you are someone who thinks about the impact of your visits on your travel destination. You can do this yourself as a responsible traveller, but travel and tourism industries are always trying to think of ways in which they can promote tourism without harming the environment. Discuss ways that you are environmentally responsible in your school, college or place of work.

There are many terms which relate to sustainable tourism that mean very similar things. You may hear the terms responsible tourism and **eco-tourism**.

Principles

The main principles of **sustainable tourism** are to:

- minimise negative environmental impacts in a destination
- create economic benefits, including future employment, for local people
- conserve local culture
- promote links and respect between tourists and local communities.

Key terms

Eco-tourism – resorts that have been developed in a sustainable way.

Sustainable tourism – meets the needs of tourists and local communities while protecting the natural, historical and cultural environment for the future.

Case study

There are ten national parks in England, each with a National Park Authority. Each Authority has a duty to conserve and enhance the natural beauty of the park and to promote understanding and enjoyment of the parks by the public. The authorities are also committed to the principles of sustainable tourism.

This means they have to consider:

- access to the public versus conservation
- vehicle emissions from visiting cars and buses
- parking issues
- loss of peace and quiet for people who live in or near the parks
- what building should be allowed

- erosion of paths and landscape
- loss of local shops to tourist-type shops
- high housing costs for local people.

Work in small groups and choose one English National Park per group. Use the list at the end of this case study to help you and find out what is being done in your chosen park to promote sustainable tourism. Present your findings to the other groups. Do not forget to give a brief introduction to the park and its location.

The ten English National Parks are: The Broads, Dartmoor, Exmoor, The Lake District, The New Forest, Northumberland, The North York Moors, The Peak District, The South Downs and The Yorkshire Dales.

SAVE OUR PLANET!

Dear Guest:

Every day tons of detergent and millions of gallons of water are used to wash towels that have been used only once.

PLEASE DECIDE FOR YOURSELF.

A towel on the rack means "I'll use it again."

A towel on the floor or in the tub means "please exchange."

Figure 1.3 Research other ways that hotels try to reduce energy consumption.

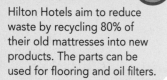

Did you know?

Hilton Hotels aim to reduce waste by recycling 80% of their old mattresses into new products. The parts can be used for flooring and oil filters.

▶ Benefits of sustainable tourism

Look at the WorkSpace in this unit. You will note that Stonehenge needs to be conserved to protect it for future generations to visit. It is in danger as, until very recently, people have been allowed to visit at will and have even taken pieces of stone away. Sustainable tourism would have prevented such destruction.

Environmental protection

Conservation organisations such as English Heritage, the National Trust and National Parks work to preserve historic buildings and the environment. Any fees charged to enter a house or park are invested in further protection.

Urban areas are often regenerated to make places available for leisure or recreation which attract tourists.

Links with the local community

Urban regeneration is not just for tourists. Facilities are attractive to local people and sometimes local residents are offered cheaper rates to visit attractions or attend events. A good example is Salford Quays which is well known for arts and culture; the BBC has relocated much of its business there.

Reduced energy consumption

In some countries, extreme measures are taken to conserve energy. For example, on safari in Kenya, guests may find that electricity is turned off for a few hours in their accommodation to restrict energy use. You will often see notices in hotel bathrooms asking guests to re-use towels to save energy on washing.

Reducing waste

Recycling is the most important way of reducing waste. Water can be recycled with treatment plants and all sorts of materials can be recycled. Look at what you recycle at home.

Cost savings

Businesses can cut costs by recycling, either by buying fewer new materials or by selling old materials. Using less energy is also a cost saving.

Competitive edge and image

Having a 'green' reputation is good for a company's image and business. Customers who care about the environment choose travel and tourism businesses that they know have policies on sustainability. For instance, some airlines offer carbon offsetting for flights.

Activity 1.2	Sustainable tourism and organisations

Choose one of the following organisations:

- a National Park Authority
- the National Trust
- Tourism Concern
- Earthwatch.

Work with a partner and find out about one current project the organisation is involved with. Prepare a short leaflet or flyer with the key points of sustainable tourism from that project.

WorkSpace

▷ Nico Rodriguez

Visitor Operations Site Supervisor

I work for a heritage organisation. I am responsible for:

- welcoming visitors and providing information about the site
- solving any problems that arise for visitors
- making sure health and safety requirements are met.

The ancient monument is prehistoric and consists of a circle of stones. I really enjoy working here and welcoming the thousands of tourists who visit every year. We can get thousands of visitors on a busy day in the summer and we still have to give the same standard of service. These visitors bring in millions of pounds a year in revenue and soon more jobs will be created as we are building a new visitor centre. Nearby roads will be closed so that the site will be quieter and less polluted. Visitors are not allowed within the circle of stones but can walk around them. Sometimes we allow special access visits. These are restricted to a few people at a time and I have to watch to make sure they don't touch the stones.

To be successful in this job, you have to be outgoing, sociable and able to work under pressure. It's very important to support the rest of the team and, as supervisor, I carry out their reviews so I want them to do well. I speak Spanish, as well as English, which is an advantage when we have Spanish-speaking visitors.

Think about it

1 Why do you think visitors are not allowed to walk near or touch the stones?

2 What experience do you have so far that would help you get a job within a heritage organisation such as English Heritage?

3 What might happen to Nico's job if, in order to conserve the site, tourists were prevented from visiting?

The importance of the travel and tourism sector to the UK economy

Introduction

The travel and tourism sector is very important to the UK economy. It provides employment and brings in revenue. In fact the sector is growing much faster than the wider economy – 1.3 per cent in 2012 whereas the UK economy overall is almost static. It is estimated that 1 in 13 jobs in the UK are in travel and tourism industries (Source: World Travel and Tourism Council (WTTC)).

What do we mean when we say a sector is growing? Why do you think travel and tourism is growing faster than other sectors?

Gross Domestic Product (GDP)

Gross Domestic Product is the most important economic statistic as it tells us the state of the UK economy in one number. If the GDP measure goes up, the economy is growing. If GDP is negative the economy is falling.

We are in recession if the measure is negative for two consecutive 3-month periods.

Travel and tourism helps GDP as it brings in revenue to the economy. It brings in at least £115 billion per year which is 8.9 per cent of GDP.

Direct contribution is money that is spent on travel and tourism products and services. Indirect contribution is the re-spending of money earned from travel and tourism. This is known as the multiplier effect and is discussed later.

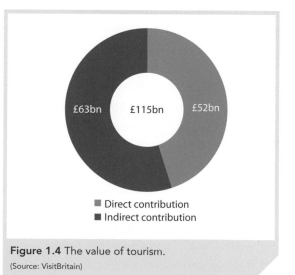

£63bn   £115bn   £52bn

■ Direct contribution
■ Indirect contribution

Figure 1.4 The value of tourism.
(Source: VisitBritain)

So how does the travel and tourism sector produce this contribution to the economy? It does so through attracting inbound tourists to the UK and through UK residents taking day trips or holidays in the UK.

Value of inbound tourism

The Office for National Statistics calculates numbers of inbound tourists through the International Passenger Survey.

Key term

Gross Domestic Product (GDP) – this can be thought of as the value of a country's economy. It measures the specific value of all goods and services over a specific time period (usually one year). Domestic and inbound tourism contribute to the UK's GDP but not all outbound tourism does as this involves outbound tourists spending money in another country.

Did you know?

Tourism is the UK's third highest export earner. The top two are Chemicals and Financial Services.

Table 1.2 – Headline trends in inbound tourism to the UK (2001–2011).

Year	Number of visits (millions)	Spend (£ billions)	Average spend per visit
2001	22.835	£11.306	£489
2002	24.180	£11.737	£481
2003	24.715	£11.855	£475
2004	27.755	£13.047	£466
2005	29.971	£14.248	£471
2006	32.713	£16.002	£486
2007	32.778	£15.960	£487
2008	31.888	£16.323	£511
2009	29.889	£16.592	£554
2010	29.803	£16.889	£563
2011	**30.798**	**£17.998**	**£584**

Source: England Fact Sheet (access from VisitEngland website)

The table tells us how many visitors come into the UK and how much money they spend. It does not have figures for 2012 but there were important events in 2012 that attracted visitors such as the Golden Jubilee and London 2012.

Value of domestic tourism

Remember that people taking holidays and trips within the UK also contribute to GDP. We know how many visitors there are from the **Great Britain Tourism Survey**.

The survey shows that in 2011, £22.7 billion was spent by British residents on 127 million overnight trips in Great Britain.

Day trips are calculated separately.

> **Take it further**
>
> Go to the VisitBritain website and find information about the latest statistics for inbound tourism. Add the figures to the table above and make three key points about the trends. To access the website for this, visit Pearson hotlinks. You can access this by going to www.pearsonhotlinks.co.uk and searching for this title.

> **Key term**
>
> **Great Britain Tourism Survey** – takes place every year and gives information about tourism by residents of Great Britain. It excludes Northern Ireland.

Activity 1.3   Great Britain Tourism Survey

Go to the VisitEngland website to find the Great Britain Tourism Survey. To access the VisitEngland website, visit Pearson hotlinks at www.pearsonhotlinks.co.uk and search for this title.

Find the tables for 2011, or later if available. You will find tables as follows:

- overall
- holidays
- visiting friends and relatives (VFR)
- business.

Create a pie chart for **expenditure** only for the 2011 (or latest) figures for holidays, business and VFR.

Which category accounts for most spend? Explain why you think this is.

Key terms

Direct employment – jobs where employees are in direct contact with tourists and provide the tourism experience.

Indirect employment – jobs in companies that supply the direct employment companies such as aircraft suppliers and hotel laundry suppliers.

Primary research – original research – carried out for the first time.

Secondary research – using information already produced by someone else.

Multiplier effect – the additional revenue, income or employment created in an area as a result of spending on tourism.

Employment

You have seen how spending from tourism contributes to the economy.

The travel and tourism sector is also important because it provides jobs.

In 2011 2.7 million jobs were in travel and tourism or related sectors. This was 9.1 per cent of all employment; 30 per cent of these jobs were in London and the South East (Office for National Statistics).

Take a look at a local map and pick out the travel and tourism organisations.

Some of these jobs are **direct** which means they are in travel and tourism organisations. Others are **indirect**, which means they are in industries that support travel and tourism, for example, construction of hotels.

Activity 1.4   Local jobs in tourism

Carry out a survey of jobs in travel and tourism in your town or region.

Part One: Primary research

Work in small groups and choose an area of the town for each group. You will need a map of your area.

First of all walk around the area and decide which organisations provide direct employment in travel and tourism. Examples might be hotels or bus tours or visitor attractions.

Make notes on the kind of jobs provided. Mark the organisations on your map.

Part Two: Secondary research

For this part you need to find statistics on the internet for employment in your town or region. Find out how many jobs are in travel and tourism.

Make some tables or charts showing this information.

Present your results to the rest of your group.

Economic multiplier effect

When tourists spend money in a destination or on a day trip, this provides income for the company or people it is spent with. These companies, or people, then spend money in turn on further goods and services. For example, if you go to a hotel, you pay for your room and food. The hotel then uses its income to buy more supplies of food, to pay for laundry, maintenance of the hotel and business services such as accountancy. Staff will also receive wages, which they can spend. The **multiplier effect** is expressed as a ratio.

The multiplier also applies to jobs. You saw earlier that jobs in travel and tourism may be as a result of direct or indirect employment. Those indirect jobs are caused by the multiplier effect.

Infrastructure development

The tourism sector in the UK is growing. Campaigns by VisitBritain have attracted more international tourists and events such as the London 2012 Olympics have made the country more popular. To continue to attract tourists, the government must decide what infrastructure is needed to support growth. This means that the services and facilities that tourists need must be in place. An example is an efficient and easily accessible airport. Keep an eye out for updates on whether London will have a new airport or whether Heathrow's third runway plans will be accepted.

Did you know?

A new museum attracts tourists who pay to enter. They also spend money in the museum café and shop. This brings in revenue of £10 million per annum. The museum management then buy supplies, and pay staff who spend in the area. Tourists also visit other shops and restaurants in the museum. This all creates additional spending of £25 million giving a multiplier of 1.25.

Case study

You have learnt that infrastructure development is important to the growth of travel and tourism. In England there has been a lot of debate on whether we should have a new airport to serve London. This is because Heathrow and Gatwick are almost at capacity. Stansted is not at capacity, but is not as popular as other airports in terms of access. With proposed high speed rail links, Manchester and Birmingham might increase in popularity for international travellers. The potential site for a new London airport is in the Thames estuary. This would be expensive to build and there are some environmental arguments against it.

Divide the group into two smaller groups. Carry out some research and produce arguments for and against the development of a new airport in the Thames estuary.

Your teacher will explain the rules of debating to you.

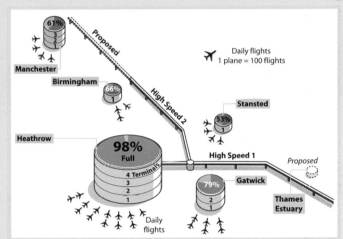

Assessment practice 1.2

Study the information and answer the questions below.

Sector	Visitor numbers (m)	Spend (£bn)
Business	6.8	4.0
Leisure	11.5	6.6
VFR	8.4	3.6
Study	0.5	1 4
Other	2.4	1.2

Source: International Passenger Survey 2011

1 What does Gross Domestic Product mean? [1]
2 Which sector contributes the most money to GDP? [1]
   A Business
   B Leisure
   C Study
   D VFR

▶ Industries in the travel and tourism sector

Introduction

There are many different industries within the travel and tourism sector that often benefit from working together. In this section you will learn about the different industries such as transport, attractions and travel agents and find out how they work together.

▶ Tour operators

Tour operators are the companies that organise package holidays. They contract with hotels, airlines and other transport companies and produce brochures advertising the holidays they have put together. They sell these holidays through travel agents or directly to customers, online or by telephone. There are different kinds of tour operators.

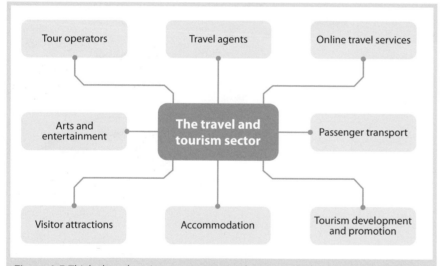

Figure 1.5 Think about last time you went on a day trip – which of these industries did you use?

- **Domestic** – these companies package holidays within the UK for UK residents. They are usually rail or coach holidays and day trips. An example is Shearings Holidays.

- **Outbound** – these are the most well-known tour operators and are usually very large companies providing holidays abroad for UK residents. If you have been on a package holiday abroad, you will have used one of these companies. An example is Thomson Holidays.

- **Inbound** – these companies cater for tourists coming from other countries to take holidays in the UK. You are not likely to know the names of these companies as their promotion and advertising takes place in the countries where they find their customers. An example is International Friends.

Products and services

Tour operators provide a wide range of products and services. The basic package consists of travel (for example, a flight and accommodation), a hotel and transfer (for example, a coach from the airport to the hotel). However, on top of these components, a tour operating company will offer a variety of extra products and services for you to buy.

Case study

Read this extract from a holiday brochure. Identify all the extra products and services available by listing or highlighting them.

- **Prices held on Ski Essentials:** Book your lift pass, equipment & tuition for 2013/14 & pay 2012/13 prices.
- **Free lift pass:** Free lift pass for children aged 6–11 years with each pre-booked adult lift pass.
- **Early booking offers:** See the property descriptions for details of savings when you book by August 2013.
- **Special offer lift pass:** Purchase a Grandvalira plus a lunch lift pass and receive a sandwich, chips and soft drink or beer every day.

Why not try ...

Dog sledding: You'll be amazed by the excitement of the huskies!

Soldeu by night: Stay up the mountain after the sun has set for live music and light bite, then race back down on a sledge or tube.

Explore the ski area: Ski the whole of Andorra.

Decide which of these a young couple on holiday with lots of savings would buy. Say why.

Travel agents

Travel agents book holidays on behalf of tour operators and advise customers on the type and availability of holidays. The role has changed a lot in recent years. Travel agents face a lot of competition from:

- **online agents**
- tour operators selling direct
- customers making bookings by themselves.

To remain competitive travel agents have to offer excellent advice and customer service. They have also increased their range of products and services to attract more customers. They will book excursions, flights, accommodation, rail and coach tickets, arrange insurance and offer foreign exchange services.

There are about 7,000 travel agents in the UK ranging in size from **multiples** which are chains of several hundred shops to individual **independent** shops.

You might think that travel agents just sell holidays, but they also cater for business customers. Business customers do not buy package holidays but are likely to book flights, hotels and car hire. Some travel agents are dedicated to business travel.

Key terms

Online agents – sell their products and services over the internet.

Multiple travel agents – are large chains of more than 50 branches all belonging to the same company. An example is Thomson.

Independent travel agents – are often family-owned and may have one branch or a few branches. An example is Worldwide Escapes in Cheshire.

Take it further

Some travel agents are owned by tour operators. This means that the agents prefer to sell their own company products even though they do sell others as well. See if you can find out how many travel agents are owned by Thomas Cook.

Tip: Look at the website for the Thomas Cook Group.

Activity 1.5   Products and services

Imagine you are going on holiday to Disneyworld in Florida. You are going in September for two weeks with your best friend. You have never been to the USA before. You are going to book your holiday through a travel agent and you will go to see them in the shop.

There is a whole range of products and services you will need. Study the table here and copy it. For each category of product and service say what you will need from the travel agent. The first one is done for you.

Product or service	Example
Insurance	Arrange insurance for two weeks for two people
Foreign exchange	
Flights	
Accommodation	
Tickets	
Car hire	
Excursions	

▶ Online travel services

There has been significant growth in the use of the internet to purchase goods and services, therefore nearly all travel and tourism companies now have an online service as well as selling their products and services in retail shops. It is a way of being competitive.

Many smaller companies that might not have been able to compete by opening shops or huge call centres can gain business through a website. An online search by a customer using key words such as 'holidays in Greece' will bring up many results and not just those from well-known companies.

Table 1.3 – Some examples of the most popular travel websites.

Travel agencies	Aviation	Destinations and accommodation
www.thomson.co.uk	www.easyjet.com	www.tripadvisor.co.uk
www.thomascook.com	www.ryanair.com	www.booking.com
www.expedia.co.uk	www.britishairways.com	www.laterooms.com
www.lastminute.com	www.monarch.co.uk	www.tripadvisor.com
www.travelrepublic.com	www.flybe.co.uk	www.travelodge.com

Source: Experian Hitwise

What kind of online services are there?

Experian Hitwise publishes information on the most popular travel websites.

Advice sites

These might be online versions of books, for example, Lonely Planet Guides, or sites which give tourists information and reviews on destinations and hotels, such as Tripadvisor.com.

Consolidators

Lastminute.com was probably the first successful **consolidator**, selling a wide range of travel and tourism products. There have been a number since. Some specialise, for example:

- booking.com – in hotels
- holidayautos.com – in cars
- flight-checker.com – in flights.

Passenger transport

Road

Most domestic tourism takes place using road transport. People taking day trips usually go by car. This is still true in spite of rises in fuel costs. Coach holiday companies also plan their holidays using major road routes. Holidaymakers can use scheduled coach services to travel from home to their destination.

Table 1.4 – Road travel.

Advantages	Disadvantages
Can drive and stop at will	Fuel is expensive
Can take a lot of luggage	Traffic
We have few toll roads such as the M6 and the Dartford crossing	Difficult for inbound tourists to drive on the left with right-hand drive cars
Can listen to your own music – as loud as you want!	Takes a long time
	Have to concentrate carefully as there are more road accidents than with other modes of transport.

Activity 1.6　　Planning a trip

You will need a road map of the UK for this activity for reference.

Plan a route from your home to Lands End. Work out what roads you will take, and when and where you will stop for refreshments or even overnight. State how long the journey will take and the length of each stop.

Present your findings on a blank map of the UK.

Rail

All of our **national** rail network is owned and maintained by Network Rail. However, this company does not run trains. These services are run by Train Operating Companies. The government decides which train companies are given permission, known as a franchise, to run trains in a particular area. There are 24 different train operating companies in the UK, for example First Capital Connect and East Coast. Network Rail is responsible for maintaining the infrastructure including tracks. You will often see maintenance taking place at night and on Sundays when the network is less busy. Train fares are not fixed and you can usually get cheaper fares by booking ahead. Eurostar provides services to France and Belgium.

Passenger Focus is a consumer association that make sure that rail and bus passengers get a good deal.

There are many proposed developments in the UK for rail services. In 2017 work starts on the new railway project Highspeed 2. It will provide a high speed rail line between London and Birmingham and on to Manchester and Leeds. The first services should start in 2025. Building the network will provide jobs and improve connections between major cities. Another rail project is Crossrail, a new suburban rail service for London and the South-East. It will connect the City, Canary Wharf, the West End and Heathrow Airport to commuter areas east and west of the capital.

Key term

National – means operating within the UK.

Table 1.5 – Rail travel.

Advantages	Disadvantages
Very comfortable (especially first class)	Expensive
Almost everywhere is accessible by rail	Fare structures are very confusing
Can sleep, read, work en route	Changes can be difficult for foreign travellers
High safety record	
Products such as food and drink are available, often in a restaurant car	

Air travel

Air services are provided by a range of airlines. These may offer **domestic** routes or **international** routes. Domestic travel is not as important in the UK as in, for example, the US. This is because our country is small and it is often as easy to travel by rail and road as by plane. However, business people often travel from outlying areas to London and then on to other destinations. Health and safety in air travel is strictly regulated by the Civil Aviation Authority.

Types of airlines

- **Scheduled airlines:** the biggest examples in the UK are Virgin Airlines and British Airways. These are also known as full service airlines. This means that the price of the ticket includes a baggage allowance, food, drinks and entertainment onboard.
- **Low-cost scheduled airlines:** the main examples are Ryanair and easyJet. Ryanair is unusual as it is based in Ireland but it has many bases in the UK. On low-cost airlines the price of the ticket is low but extra fees are charged for each service. These extra fees are for services such as pre-booked seats, priority boarding, food and drinks and lottery tickets.
- **Charter airlines:** these are airlines that operate flights for holiday schedules, so are not as frequent.

Sea travel

Historically, sea travel is important as we live on an island. We are served by ferry companies linking us to the continent, particularly France and Belgium, to our island neighbours in Scotland, Ireland and the Channel Isles. The introduction of the Channel Tunnel and the growth in low-cost flights have lessened our dependence on sea travel to reach Europe.

Another form of sea travel is cruising. It is possible to join a cruise from a UK port or to fly and join elsewhere.

Key terms

Domestic – means operating within the UK.

International – means operating between countries.

Take it further

Visit the Ryanair website and choose a flight. Go through all the stages of booking, without actually booking. Look at the prices and note the extra fees. How much would it cost if you booked all the extras for one person?

Compare your prices with the rest of your group. Find this website by visiting Pearson hotlinks at www.pearsonhotlinks.co.uk and searching for this title.

Accommodation

Hotels

Some hotels are owned independently but most are likely to be part of a chain. Which of these hotel chains have you heard of?

- Novotel
- Hilton
- Holiday Inn
- Radisson.

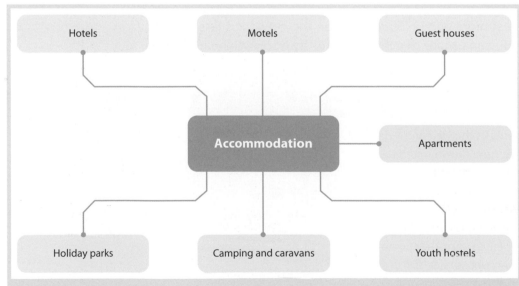

Figure 1.6 The different types of accommodation that tourists can choose from when visting the UK.

All of these offer a full range of facilities to guests and cater for holiday and business customers. You would expect luxury rooms, restaurants and conference facilities and often spa facilities and pools.

The fastest growing hotel sector is the budget sector which has grown even in the recession as people look for cheaper accommodation. Well-known budget chains include Premier Inn and Travelodge.

Guest houses and bed and breakfast

Some tourists prefer to experience some 'local colour' and choose to stay in a guest house. These are often large houses converted to provide rooms for tourists by their owners. These are not always an inexpensive option as there is a trend for boutique-style bed and breakfasts promoted by companies such as Mr and Mrs Smith.

Apartments

Apartments are self-catering. Many families choose these or self-catering houses. They provide cooking facilities and families have the freedom to eat what and when they please.

Youth hostels

These are owned and run by the Youth Hostel Association (YHA) and began as low priced accommodation for hikers and young travellers.

Remember

- Non-serviced accommodation offers only the accommodation, just the room or apartment.
- Serviced accommodation will include cleaning, changes of towels and sheets as necessary and may include food and hotel facilities such as a spa, a gym and entertainment.

Take it further

Hotels in the UK are usually graded from 1 to 5 stars. This system is managed by VisitEngland, VisitScotland, VisitWales, the Northern Ireland Tourist Board and the AA who all use the same criteria for assessment. Find out what you should expect for each grade. What kind of customer do you think each grade appeals to?

Case study

The YHA is a charity that started out in 1930. Its role is to provide accommodation primarily for young people, although all are welcome. The Association has 200 different youth hostels in rural, coastal and city locations in England and Wales. It runs a charitable scheme called Breaks for Kids, which offers thousands of disadvantaged young people a break every year. Some of the hostels are in cities like Manchester. This is the description of the Manchester hostel. You can see it has a restaurant and a bar yet a room might be as little as £36 per night.

This buzzing canal-side backpackers hostel has been re-fitted, so your city break will be even more comfortable – great quality, cheap accommodation for a Manchester weekend break close to the city centre. Enjoy a pre-dinner drink in the bar, then people-watch from the restaurant window or terrace, while you enjoy a tasty evening meal.

(Source: Youth Hostel Association website)

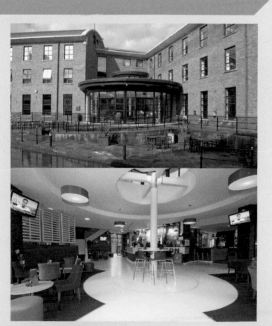

Choose a youth hostel in an area that you would like to visit. Say why it appeals to you. List the products and services on offer at your chosen hostel. Plan a day's activity while staying at the hostel.

Camping

We used to think of camping as arriving at a site with lots of equipment and putting up a small tent and cooking outside. While this option can still be found it is more likely that a campsite offers a range of accommodation from tents which are fully equipped and already set up to static caravans or chalets with full kitchens and proper bathrooms.

This range of accommodation might be found on a holiday park which not only offers a range of accommodation, restaurants, cafes and pools but also lots of entertainment.

Case study

Butlin's

The weather is getting warmer, summer's nearly here, there's a bank holiday and a week off school – all great excuses to get away for a few days with your family.

During our half-term breaks this May, you will have access to everything that Butlin's has to offer, like Splash Waterworld, our free funfair, arts and crafts, West-End quality shows and professional sports coaching. And because our half-term breaks are extra special, you will also be able to enjoy all of these exclusive activities and shows.

The accommodation includes
* early check in
* daily housekeeping
* bedrooms, a bathroom with shower and a lounge and kitchen
* widescreen TV.

Restaurants serve breakfast, lunch and dinner. The menu includes traditional fish and chips, a selection from the grill and lighter options. Children have their own menu to choose from and there's a play area.

(Source: Butlin's website)

1 What do you think Butlin's aims to provide for guests?

2 Why do you think families would choose this rather than traditional camping?

3 Is the accommodation serviced or non-serviced?

Assessment practice 1.3

Give one advantage and two disadvantages of using non-serviced accommodation for a family with three children under 7 years old. [3]

Advantage 1 _____

Disadvantage 1 _____

Disadvantage 2 _____

Visitor attractions

There are thousands of **visitor attractions** in the UK, bringing revenue from both domestic and inbound tourists.

Every year in England, VisitEngland undertakes a survey of visits to visitor attractions. From the survey we can see which are the most popular paying and non-paying attractions.

Key term

Visitor attraction – an attraction where it is feasible to charge admission for the sole purpose of sightseeing. The attraction must be a permanently established excursion destination.

(Source: Survey of Visits to Visitor Attractions 2011, VisitEngland)

Case study

Top ten paid attractions in England, 2011

	Attraction	Region	Category	2010	2011
1	Tower of London	London	Historic properties	2,413,214	2,554,746
2	Westminster Abbey	London	Places of worship	1,394,427	1,899,956
3	St Paul's Cathedral	London	Places of worship	1,892,467	1,819,925
4	Flamingo Land Theme Park and Zoo	Yorkshire and Humberside	Leisure and theme parks	1,268,619	1,427,193
5	Chester Zoo	North West	Wildlife	1,154,285	1,425,319
6	Windermere Lake Cruises, Bowness	North West	Other	1,312,423	1,350,081
7	Royal Botanic Gardens, Kew Gardens	London	Gardens	1,140,690	1,188,933
8	Stonehenge	South West	Historic properties	1,009,973	1,099,656
9	ZSL London Zoo	London	Wildlife	1,011,257	1,090,741
10	Houses of Parliament and Big Ben	London	Historic properties	967,317	1,054,151

(Source: Survey of visits to visitor attractions 2011, VisitEngland)

1 Where are most of the top attractions?

2 Why do you think this is?

3 Which attraction has the biggest rise in visitors between 2010 and 2011?

4 What percentage was the rise?

The survey also reports on the top free attractions. All of the top ten are London museums apart from the Royal Naval College in Greenwich (London) which is a historic property. Although entry is free to these attractions they can still gain income in a number of ways:

- Income from fees for special exhibitions
- Income from donations on entry
- Sales from merchandise in museum shops
- Sales in restaurants and cafes
- Hire of facilities
- Government funding
- Grants from the heritage Lottery Fund for special projects.

Take it further

Can you find out what the top attractions are in the rest of the UK? Look at the websites of VisitWales, VisitScotland and the Northern Ireland Tourist Board to find out what they are.

People go to visitor attractions for many different reasons. They may choose to go to a theme park for a day's fun and entertainment or to a museum to learn about culture or heritage. School trips take place to enhance the education of pupils, perhaps to learn about nature at the Eden Project or see animals in a zoo at ZSL London Zoo.

The management of visitor attractions needs to know what kind of products and services the customers would like to experience on a visit and provide these. We will look at some examples, but first, you need to be aware that visitor attractions are commonly categorised as:

- natural attractions
- purpose-built attractions
- heritage attractions.

Natural attractions

Examples are mostly in rural or coastal locations and include:

- beaches
- lakes and rivers
- caves.
- mountains
- forests

Many of these are protected, for example as National Parks or as Areas of Outstanding Natural Beauty. This does not mean that visitors are not allowed, but that they have to behave in a way that protects the environment.

Activity 1.7   Visiting a natural attraction

Choose a natural attraction you have visited or would like to visit.

1 What was your purpose in going there?

2 What sources of revenue were at the attraction?

3 What products and services were on offer? Think about entry fees, cafes, lockers for changing at the beach, deckchairs, shops.

Purpose-built attractions

By purpose-built we mean built especially to attract tourists and to provide them with fun, entertainment and sometimes education. This category includes:

- theme parks
- rides such as the London Eye
- museums and galleries
- venues like the O2 arena or Wembley.
- resorts such as Disneyland Paris or Center Parcs

Heritage

Heritage attractions inform us about our history, allowing us to find out how people lived in the past. Heritage attractions may be natural or built. For example, Stonehenge was built, although not originally for tourism.

Some of the top attractions are heritage attractions. In the case study you can see that the top three were the Tower of London, Westminster Abbey and St Paul's Cathedral.

Britain is seen as a world-class destination in terms of its built heritage, ranked fourth out of 50 nations in the Nation Brands Index (2009) (Source: VisitBritain).

The Royal Yacht Britannia is a popular tourist attraction in Edinburgh. What other nautical attractions can you think of?

Discussion point

What attracts tourists to the top three heritage attractions? Should tourists be allowed to visit places of worship? Who benefits, the tourist or the attraction? Why should people pay to enter a church?

Did you know?

The popular TV drama *Downton Abbey* was filmed at Highclere Castle in Berkshire. Film locations are popular attractions for tourists.

Case study

The USA is Britain's third most important market for number of visitors and top for the amount spent by visitors.

Visiting castles, churches and monuments is an activity enjoyed by at least 43 per cent of visitors from the USA. Many Americans are interested in their ancestry and want to visit places where their ancestors lived.

US inbound visitors to the UK

	2011	Share of total
Visits (000s)	2,846	9.2%
Nights (000s)	23,333	9.9%
Spend (£m)	2,362	13.1%

Top towns visited by US visitors (000s)

London	1815
Edinburgh	190
Manchester	70
Glasgow	63
Oxford	58

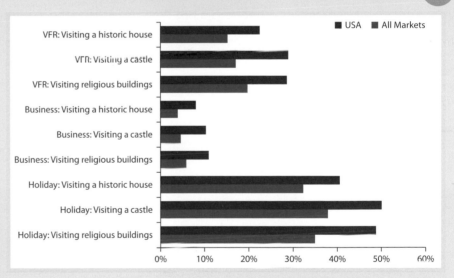

Answer the following from the graph and charts in this case study.

1 Are US holiday visitors more likely to visit a castle or a historic house?
2 Which category of US tourists is least likely to visit a castle?
3 Why is the number of nights much greater than the number of visitors?
4 Why is the percentage total of spend greater than the total of visits?
5 Why do you think London is the most visited place for US tourists?

(Source: USA: Market and Trade Profile 2012, VisitBritain)

▶ Arts and entertainment

You have learnt that attractions may be natural such as beaches and mountains, or built such as theme parks, or related to our heritage in castles and historic houses. In addition, both domestic and inbound tourists are attracted to see art exhibits or attend entertaining events. These may be one-off events, festivals or theatre.

Special events

These may be national, regional or local.

One-off examples in the last few years:

- London 2012 Olympics and Paralympics
- Queen's Diamond Jubilee.

Some events are annual:

- Wimbledon
- Chinese New Year
- Ascot
- Edinburgh Tattoo.

There are lots of festivals that attract tourists:

- Music – Glastonbury, T in the Park, Leeds and Reading festivals
- Cultural – Edinburgh Festival.

Theatre is a big draw. In London the West End theatres attract many visitors.

Key terms

Primary products and services – the main purpose of the visit, for example to see rock bands.

Secondary products and services – add appeal and give extra revenue to the event organisers, for example T shirts, posters, refreshments, parking and camping.

Activity 1.8   Events poster

Choose one of the events mentioned above.

Carry out some research and produce a poster that illustrates the event including text on the role of the event, the **primary product** or service and the **secondary products** and services.

Case study

Perhaps the most famous thing about London's West End is its theatre scene. Alongside Broadway in New York, West End theatre represents the highest quality commercial theatre in the world. There are around 40 theatres in London's 'Theatreland'. Theatre performances in the West End tend to be musicals, classic plays and comedies. At any time you can choose from a wide range of West End shows such as musicals like *Wicked, Billy Elliot, Les Miserables* and *The Phantom of the Opera*, to plays like *War Horse, The Woman in Black* and *The Mousetrap*. Find out more about London theatres. To research what

is currently playing look at the VisitLondon website; this can be found by visiting Pearson hotlinks, www.pearsonhotlinks.co.uk, and searching for this title.

Besides going to see a show, tourists can have a backstage tour. You can do this at Drury Lane, the National Theatre or the Royal Opera House. A tour allows you to see costume departments, scene-building and how technology works.

In 2011, the West End enjoyed record box office sales with takings of over £525 million.

1 Choose a show that is currently on in the West End.
2 Find out how much it would cost for the four most expensive seats on a Saturday night. Compare the price with the cheapest seats. What is the difference?

Tourism development and promotion

There is a wide range of government-sponsored organisations at national, regional and local level whose role is to develop and promote tourism. Some of these can be seen in Table 1.6.

Table 1.6 – Role of tourist organisations.

Organisation type	Examples	Role
Government department responsible for tourism	Department for Culture, Media & Sport (DCMS)	To decide on policy for tourism Promote growth in tourism Encourage domestic tourism and its revenue
National tourist boards	VisitEngland, VisitScotland, VisitWales and the Northern Ireland Tourist Board	Market tourist companies and destinations Provide information on tourism products and destinations Promote special events Offer advice to local tourist bodies
Regional tourist boards	East of England Tourist Board VisitCornwall	Promote tourism to their region Promote events Offer advice to tourist businesses
Tourist information centres	VisitManchester	Provide information for tourists in the local area Give advice to local tourism businesses Promote local events

Activity 1.9   Tourist Information Centres

Tourist Information Centres were once a feature of every town. They provided a focal point where tourists could go to book accommodation, find out about local attractions and book tickets for attractions and events. Many tourists would come away armed with leaflets, maps and advice.

The centres used to be funded by the government, but with budget cuts, local authorities are having to make decisions about whether to keep the centres going. Many of them have closed and in their place you might find a tourist information point. This could be a person standing on a street corner.

Where there are Tourist Information Centres you will find that part of their premises is now a shop selling merchandise to bring in revenue to fund the centre.

Find out whether there is a tourist information centre in your town. If there is, see if you can organise a visit for your whole group. Find out what they do and all the products and services on offer.

If you do not have a centre, find out how a visitor would get information on what there is to do in the town and where to stay.

Case study

VisitBritain is Britain's national tourism agency, responsible for marketing Britain worldwide and developing Britain's visitor economy.

Our mission: Building the value of tourism to Britain, working in partnership with the industry and nations and regions to generate additional visitor spend.

Our vision: To inspire the world to explore Britain.

Our strategy:

- Inspire travellers from overseas to visit and explore Britain.
- Deliver a global network to support tourism promotion overseas.
- Advise Government and the industry on tourism, particularly on issues that affect our global competitiveness.
- Maximise public investment through partner engagement and commercial activity.

(Source: VisitBritain website)

1 What is the difference between VisitBritain and VisitEngland?

2 Who are the target markets for VisitBritain?

3 What is meant by partner engagement and commercial activity?

▶ Key organisations in the travel and tourism sector

Introduction

You have been introduced to most of the component industries of the travel and tourism sectors. However, there are still some key organisations and ancillary services to discuss. These are important as they offer support to the main industries by representing their interests or they offer products and services which add value to main products such as package holidays. Imagine you are going on holiday – what companies might provide products and services besides the tour operator and transport provider?

▶ Trade and professional bodies

The role of trade and professional bodies is to represent the interests of their members. This could be representation to the government to influence policy decisions or to the media to promote members in a positive way. Trade and professional bodies usually regulate their members providing rules or guidelines for how they operate.

We will look at some examples from different travel and tourism industries.

Civil Aviation Authority (CAA)

This organisation has the role of ensuring that UK airlines, airports and **National Air Traffic Services (NATS)** comply with regulations for aviation, particularly those relating

Key term

National Air Traffic Services (NATS) – the organisation responsible for air traffic control in the UK. It is a public/private partnership between the government, several airlines, Heathrow Airport Trust and an Employee Share Trust.

to health and safety. It also manages the UK's principal travel protection scheme known as the Air Travel Operator's Licensing (ATOL) scheme. This is similar to insurance where operators pay into a fund which can then be used to repatriate customers if a company goes bankrupt while they are away.

Office of Rail Regulation (ORR)

The Office of Rail Regulation is the independent safety and economic regulator for Britain's railways. It has to make sure that the industry meets regulations.

Association of British Travel Agents (ABTA)

This organisation represents travel agents and also provides a code of conduct for their operation. It has 1,200 members, many of whom are tour operators. ABTA represents these members' interests, particularly in terms of lobbying the government on their behalf and making sure their voice is heard when new laws are proposed. One of the organisation's important roles is to manage complaints from customers. People who have been on a holiday booked through an agent belonging to ABTA expect certain standards of service. If there is a complaint and the booking agent cannot resolve it, it will be passed on to ABTA, who will arbitrate.

Association of Independent Tour Operators (AITO)

This organisation represents independent, specialist tour operators. It provides a bond scheme, as does ABTA. Like the ATOL scheme, these provide funds to help customers if a tour operator goes bankrupt and they need to be brought home by another company.

UK Inbound

This body represents tour operators who are organising trips and holidays in the UK for inbound tourists. It represents the interests of its members to government and is funded by the subscriptions members pay. Examples of members are China Holidays and English Heritage.

▶ Ancillary organisations

These organisations provide supporting services for tourists or travellers. Some of them provide products that can also be bought from a tour operator, airline or a travel agent, for example car hire. You, as customer, can choose whether to buy direct from the ancillary organisation or to buy at the same time as you buy your holiday or flight. Sometimes the prices are very different, sometimes they are the same, so it is a good idea to check prices from a range of suppliers before booking.

Tour operators, travel agents and airlines receive commission for selling products and services on behalf of other companies.

Car hire

We have many car hire companies in the UK. They are all private companies and you can book a car in the UK or for a holiday abroad. Examples include Hertz and Europcar. In addition, there are consolidators such as Holidayautos. They only book car hire and do not actually own cars, but book one on your behalf with any one of the car hire companies. The customer will not know which one until they collect the car. The companies offer car hire as the primary product, but there are lots of related costs which have to be checked carefully.

Travel insurance

When you buy travel insurance you can choose to buy it from the tour operator, from the travel agent or direct from an insurance company, which you can do online. As well as deciding which of these is best, you need to decide whether to buy a policy for one specific trip or whether to buy an annual policy. Anyone who makes a few trips a year is better off buying an annual policy.

Activity 1.10 Finding the best deal on travel insurance

Gerald and Melissa are 29-years-old. They have three trips booked for next year:

Trip	Travel brochure insurance	Insurance company insurance	Annual policy
A ten-day skiing trip in February			
A weekend city break to Paris in April			
Two weeks on a Greek island in July			

Use the internet and travel brochures to find out how much insurance would cost. What is the best option?

Airport services

Airports make revenue from many sources besides the main business of looking after airlines using the airport. The airport indirectly provides a shopping experience for travellers as it provides outlets for retailers to rent. Cafes, restaurants, car hire companies and tour operators also rent outlets in the airport.

Car parks are a good source of revenue from passengers who want to leave their car while they are away. The car park may be run by the airport or subcontracted to a car park operator.

VIP lounges are available and give those who are happy to pay the entry fee somewhere quiet to sit and have a drink while they wait.

Event booking

There are many event-booking companies operating via the internet. For a commission they will sell you seats at the theatre, tickets for music tours or sporting events.

Did you know?

TKTS in London's Leicester Square sells tickets for the day's West End shows at discounted prices.

▶ Product comparison providers

These are websites like Flight Checker, Moneysupermarket.com and Go Compare. They operate over the internet and allow you to compare products and services.

▶▶ Types of organisation in the travel and tourism sector

Introduction

Organisations in travel and tourism are funded in different ways and have different aims and objectives depending on the type of organisation they are. Some have to make profits to pay shareholders, others are aiming to provide a service or educate and not so worried about making a profit. Others are funded by government and are there to protect our heritage or provide a public service. What do you think the difference is between public and private companies?

▶ Private

Most organisations in the travel and tourism sector are privately owned. This means they are owned by an individual or partners or by a group of people called shareholders. The main function of a private company is to make profits which can then be paid in dividends to the shareholders or retained by the owner. Profits can be made by selling more holidays, flights or other tourism products and services.

There are lots of examples of private companies in the sector. They include well known names such as Thomson Holidays, easyJet, Haven and Hilton. Theme parks, travel agents and tour operators are all privately owned.

▶ Public

Travel and tourism organisations in the public sector are funded and usually run by the government. They might make a profit, but more importantly they aim to provide services such as advice or promotion of our tourism sector. Many visitor attractions fall into this category.

▶ Voluntary

These organisations are often charities. Some are pressure groups who try to influence government policy and consumer thinking, for example, Tourism Concern. These organisations do not try to make a profit although they receive revenues which help fund their cause. They can get their revenue from merchandise, donations and grants. Some of them exist to educate the public about particular issues.

Remember

The Department of Culture, Media & Sport is the government department looking after tourism. It is in the public sector. VisitBritain is also in the public sector.

Activity 1.11 What's my type?

Find out which type of organisation each of these belongs to and complete the table. Choose from public, private and voluntary.

Virgin Atlantic	
National Trust	
Youth Hostel Association	
First Choice	
VisitScotland	
National Park Authority	
Butlin's	

Now find other examples of your own for public, private and voluntary.

Case study

The **National Trust** is a UK conservation charity. Its role is to protect historic places and green spaces and open them up to everyone, forever. The organisation is independent of government. Its income comes from membership fees, donations and **legacies**. It also receives revenue from entrance fees and other sales, for example, merchandise.

The Trust has over four million members and 67,000 volunteers. Over 350 historic houses, gardens and ancient monuments are looked after by the Trust. It also takes care of some forests, woods, beaches and even archaeological remains.

The Trust receives grants to support its work for special projects, for example to carry out nature conservation work at Orford Ness. Grants are awarded from Lottery funds and from organisations like the Arts Council and Natural England.

The Trust often works in partnership with other charities to work on projects.

English Heritage was set up through the National Heritage Act in 1983. Its role is to preserve ancient monuments and historic buildings. It also aims to educate and entertain the public with events, special heritage days and publications.

The organisation is sponsored by the government, via the Department for Culture, Media & Sport (DCMS). 65 per cent of funding comes from the DCMS. English Heritage looks after more than 400 sites.

The organisation itself gives grants and advises on preservation of heritage. English Heritage generates over a quarter of its income through commercial activities and fundraising. Most comes from membership, entry fees to English Heritage properties and from retail and catering.

Government is reducing the funding given to English Heritage so the organisation is trying to generate more income by itself. Some of the shortfall for special projects like Stonehenge comes from Lottery funding.

(Source: English Heritage website and the National Trust)

Complete the table below identifying similarities and differences between the National Trust and English Heritage. Research further on their websites.

Similarities	Differences

To access their websites, visit Pearson hotlinks. You can access this by going to www.pearsonhotlinks.co.uk and searching for this title.

Key term

Legacy – money or property left to someone in a will. An example is a historic house left in someone's will to the National Trust.

Assessment practice 1.4

A voluntary organisation such as the Youth Hostel Association provides accommodation primarily for young people.

1 Give two other products or services a voluntary organisation might provide. [2]
2 Give two sources of funding for a voluntary organisation. [2]

▶ The interrelationships between travel and tourism organisations

Introduction

Travel and tourism organisations often work together. This might be to share expertise and knowledge or to give customers a better service. Sometimes the organisations share resources. This would reduce costs as they would not need to invest in all the materials or equipment needed to run their business. Think of a travel and tourism business you know. What other businesses do you think it works with?

▶ Common ownership

You have seen that TUI Travel was a parent company for smaller companies or brands such as First Choice and Hayes and Jarvis. There are several examples of such an arrangement in travel and tourism although they are not obvious because the main (parent) company keeps the names of the companies it has bought or merged with.

Common ownership can be demonstrated in two main ways in the **chain of distribution**.

Key term

Chain of distribution – means of getting the product or service to the customer.

1 **Vertical integration** is when a business at one level of the chain of distribution buys or merges with a business at another level – higher or lower. For example, Thomas Cook package their own holidays, own their own airline and travel agents, are therefore are vertically integrated.

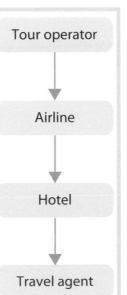

Tour operator → Airline → Hotel → Travel agent

2 **Horizontal integration** is when a business at one level of the chain of distribution buys or merges with a business at the same level. Thomas Cook are also horizontally integrated through their ownership of other brands such as Nelson Ski, Cresta, Escapades, and Manos, all tour operators specialising in different holidays and destinations. Another example of horizontal integration is British Airways buying BMI.

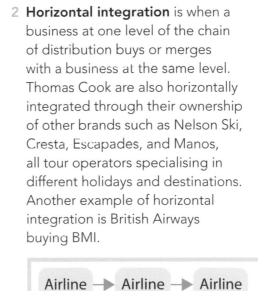

Airline → Airline → Airline

Link

You can learn more about the chain of distribution in Figure 8.1 in *Unit 8: Promotion and Sales in Travel and Tourism.*

▶ Commercial partnerships

Many visitor attractions, for example, have partnerships with transport companies. They can offer discounts to day trippers and tourists to enter an attraction if they take the transport on offer. This allows both to benefit; a train might fill up seats off peak and the attraction will get more visitors.

We have seen examples of all types of organisations working with consolidators to get their products to more customers.

Another type of partnership in travel and tourism is an implant. This is where a travel agent, for example, puts some small outlets within another company, usually a store, to sell its products with low overheads. An example is Virgin Holidays in Debenhams.

Activity 1.12 Who owns what?

Work in small groups and choose one of the following organisations.
- British Airways
- Merlin Entertainment
- ABTA
- Thomas Cook.

Find out which other organisations it owns and controls, if any. Find out which separately owned companies it has partnerships with.

Prepare a short presentation of your findings.

▶ Advantages and disadvantages

What do you think the reasons are for companies working closely with partners or buying other companies? Note the partners are not always in the travel and tourism sector.

Activity 1.13 Advantages and disadvantages

Add your own examples to the tables in this activity.

Advantage	Example	Your example
Shared marketing and promotion	A cereal manufacturer offers free entry for an attraction. The attraction is promoted on the cereal packs and they share the cost of the promotion.	
Increased sales and income	A multiple travel agent buys a small independent travel agent and takes its sales.	
Provide good customer care	An airline works with a ground services company at the airport to provide customer care and control baggage.	
Economies of scale	Two tour operators merge and share one head office cutting costs of rent, overheads and staff.	
Shared resources	Long-haul airlines sell seats for each other's flights but under their own airline brand – airlines can operate fewer flights this way.	
Wider customer base	Car hire companies working with airlines can reach more customers through the airline website.	

continued

Activity 1.13 (continued)   Advantages and disadvantages

Disadvantages	Example	Your example
Size of operation	The operation gets so big that it is difficult to control.	
Less customer choice	There are fewer holiday companies to choose from.	
Loss of personalised customer care	Sales people selling holidays online or via call centres don't get to know their customers.	
Inflexibility	Airlines have rules – for example on changing tickets – and don't take note of special circumstances.	

Case study

Study of the easyJet website shows that it works with the following partners: Allianz, Booking.com, Europcar, National Express, Holiday Extras.

Find out what each of these partners does. Can you find any others? To access the easyJet website visit

Pearson hotlinks. You can access this by going to www.pearsonhotlinks.co.uk and searching for this title.

For each partnership say what the advantages are to both easyJet and the partner.

Learning aim C   **TOPIC**   **C1**

The role of consumer technology

Introduction

The use of technology is increasing in all areas of our lives and has had a huge impact on travel. We are going to look at some examples of how it is used in different areas of travel and tourism. First, think of how technology impacts on travel agents. If you were going on holiday, would you book everything yourself on the internet or go to a travel agent?

Airports

Self-service check-in

Machines for self-service check-in are where passengers can enter their details and print their boarding pass. This means they can go straight to the gate to catch the plane or take their luggage to a bag-drop off point, if they have one. An alternative is to check

Key term

Interpretation – a means of giving information to visitors to help them understand and enjoy what they are looking at.

in at home and print the boarding pass there. These systems should save time for the passenger and also reduce costs for the airline as they don't need so many check-in staff.

Security

Strict security at airports aims to protect passengers from potential terrorist attacks and checks that people are not carrying illegal items. If you have travelled by plane, you will have seen X-ray machines checking your bags – and you. In some airports full body scanners check passengers. In addition, border controls are in place to check the identity of people travelling. The UK has been issuing 'biometric' passports since 2006. The passports include a microchip which stores a digitised image of the holder's passport photograph. If your passport was issued after 2006 you will have a biometric passport.

▶ Visitor attractions

Technology is often used for **interpretation**. Multimedia allows visitors to have a much more exciting experience. In museums people can have a hands-on experience rather than just looking at an object. Interactive technology allows the visitor to make things work, especially useful in a science museum.

Audio guides are very popular. They offer taped information through an individual headset. Visitors can choose their language and go round the exhibition at their own pace.

If you want to go to an attraction, you can make your booking online before you go. This is very useful as you might be going to a different town and unable to go there to book ahead. Often, you can print off electronic tickets so that you don't have to queue to get in when you arrive.

▶ Accommodation

Online bookings

Most things can be booked online and accommodation is no exception. You can book directly with a hotel's own website or with a consolidator such as laterooms. com or trivago. Once you have made the booking, you can often cancel or amend online if necessary. You will get an email and maybe a text message confirming your booking.

Entertainment and communication

In luxury hotels, guests are welcomed with an onscreen personal message. A touchscreen can be used to control all the amenities in the room, such as lighting, air conditioning and the television or music. The device will also let guests communicate with the front desk or restaurant.

Hotels can use technology to check guests in. Guests arrive and check in on a screen. It is possible to check in without staff but guests expect a welcome so most hotels still have staff ready to greet guests.

Most types of accommodation offer Wi-Fi. However, you usually have to pay for it and in some hotels it is very expensive at as much as £5 per hour.

Mobile applications

There are hundreds of travel applications available and of interest to travellers. Some allow bookings to be made such as airline applications, train ticket apps or hotel bookings. Others offer support or information. Examples are translation applications, language lessons and guides to destinations. Maps give 3-D images and directions which help when sightseeing.

| Activity 1.14 | Travelling to Majorca |

Imagine you are going on holiday to Majorca. Find out what mobile applications would help you plan and book your holiday on your phone or tablet. You need to think about:

- booking flights
- booking a hotel
- booking a hire car
- help with Spanish
- guides
- foreign exchange.

You might think of some others. Write the name of each application and say how it will be useful to you.

E-ticketing

Tickets can be sent straight to email when you have booked online for hotels, flights, trains and events. All you have to do is print and go. In fact, you might not even print but show the ticket on your phone screen using an m-ticket.

Websites

A lot of travel and tourism websites also come in the form of mobile applications. It is easier though to carry out your research and review destinations on a large screen and you can be inspired to visit a destination by having a virtual tour of the scenery and facilities. Of course, you can book through the website and you can also use review websites to find out what other tourists thought about a hotel or destination.

What are the benefits of using e-tickets for businesses?

Assessment Zone

This section has been written to help you to do your best when you take the examination. Read through it carefully and ask your teacher if there is anything that you are still not sure about.

How you will be assessed

For this unit you will be assessed through a one-hour written examination. The examination paper will have a maximum of 50 marks. The number of marks available for each part of a question will be shown in brackets, e.g. [2], with the total for each question being shown at the end of the question.

There will be different types of question in the examination.

A Questions where all of the answers are available and you have to choose the answer(s) that fit. *Tip: Always make sure that you read the instructions carefully. Sometimes you may need to identify more than one correct answer.*

Examples:

Which of the following is an example of a public sector organisation? [1]

A	A tour operator
B	A charity that preserves historic houses
C	A national tourist board
D	A large airline

Answer: C

Which statement best describes the role of sustainable tourism? [1]

E	Minimises negative environmental impacts in a destination
F	Makes high profits for shareholders
G	Attracts as many tourists as possible
H	Builds new holiday centres

Answer: A

B Questions where you are asked to produce a short answer worth 1 or 2 marks. *Tip: Look carefully at how the question is set out to see how many points need to be included in your answer.*

Examples:

Budget hotels are a type of accommodation.

State two products or services that are offered by a budget hotel. [2]

Possible answers: rooms, restaurants, breakfast, Wi-Fi, television.

Name two technological developments that have improved the visitor experience in historic houses. [2]

Possible answers: online booking, multimedia interpretation, interactive exhibits, audio guides.

C Questions where you are asked to provide a longer answer – these can be worth up to 8 marks.

Tips: make sure that you read the question in full, and answer all of the parts of the question. It is a good idea to plan your answer so that you do not forget anything. Remember to check your answer once you have finished.

Example:

The Drayton family are going to Paris for four days at half term. The family consists of parents and two teenage children. They will be staying with relatives when they get to Paris. They are travelling from their home in south London.

Evaluate the different modes of transport that the Drayton family could use to get to Paris, giving the advantages and disadvantages of each. [8]

Answer:

There are three different ways that the Drayton family could travel to Paris. They could travel by car, aeroplane or the Eurostar.

Travelling by car could be a good option for the family as they would not have to worry about the amount of luggage they could take and they could go direct to wherever their relatives live in Paris. However, as the family live in London they may not own a car or they may not even have a driving licence. Also, as they are only going on holiday for four days, driving and taking the ferry or Eurotunnel could use up a lot of that time.

The Eurostar would be a good option for the Draytons as they live in London and so it would be easy for them to get public transport to St Pancras International. There are many train services throughout the day so the Draytons would have lots of choice about the time they left, and the trip itself is under three hours. The Eurostar goes directly to the centre of Paris and the Gare du Nord station has good transport links. However, the Eurostar can be quite expensive if not booked far in advance and it is likely to be very busy over the half term holiday.

If the Draytons decided to fly it would be easy for them to book their flights online. There is a choice of airlines on the route and the flight is only an hour and a half in duration. Gatwick airport is a short journey from south London.

The disadvantages of travelling by air are that flights are more expensive at half term and they would have to buy four tickets. They may have to pay extra for reserved seats so that they can sit together and they might have to check-in baggage which may cost extra. They also wouldn't be able to take liquids over a 100ml on the plane if they chose to take hand luggage. They also have to consider how to get to the airport and add this to their travel costs. They could get public transport to the airport but they may have to pay for a taxi due to the time of the flight, and they would also have to think about how to get from the airport to their accommodation in Paris.

Looking at all the options I think the Eurostar is the best choice for the Drayton family. They will have to ensure that they book quite far in advance but that would be the same if they decided to travel by aeroplane. They will have more choice of travel times with the Eurostar and will not have to worry about navigating while driving. In terms of overall travel time, including check-in times, the Eurostar is the best option.

Hints and tips

- **Use the time before the test.** Make sure that you have got everything you will need. Check that your pen works and that you read the instructions on the front of your examination paper. Try to make yourself feel comfortable and relaxed.

- **Keep an eye on the time.** The examination will last one hour, and you should be able to see the clock in the examination room so that you know how long you have got left to complete the paper. As a rough guide, allow one minute for every mark on the paper. This means that a question worth five marks should take you around five minutes to complete.

- **Read the questions fully.** Make sure you read each question through enough times to make sure that you understand what you are being asked to do. It is easy to misread a question and then write an answer which is wrong. Check you are doing what you are being asked to do. This is where many students lose marks.

- **Plan your answers.** For longer questions it is worth spending a minute or two to write down the key points which you want to include in your answer. If you are being asked to evaluate, you will need to think about positive and negative points. Using a plan will allow you to make sure you include both in your answer.

- **Check your answers.** Once you have answered all of the questions on the paper, you will probably have a few minutes to spare. Use this time to check your answers and maybe fill in any blanks which you have left. You should try to answer every question on the paper.

- **Read through longer answers.** Read through your longer answers to make sure your answer makes sense, and you have answered the question fully.

- **Make sure you have completed the front of the paper.** Once the examination has ended, check that you have written your name and candidate number on the front of the paper. This is important so that you will gain the marks for your work.

How to improve your answer

Read the two student answers below, together with the feedback. Try to use what you learn here to improve your answers in your examination.

Question

> Travel and tourism organisations often work in partnership with other businesses in their sector. For example, train operation companies undertake joint promotions with visitor attractions. These are known as commercial partnerships.
>
> Explain two advantages and one disadvantage of a commercial partnership between travel and tourism organisations. [6]

Student 1's answer

Advantage 1 Lower costs

Advantage 2 Will get more customers

Disadvantage Higher prices for customers

Feedback:
Although the advantages are correct (1 mark each), there is no attempt to explain why or justify the answers (this would bring an additional mark for each advantage).

The learner needs to explain why costs might be lower, for example, by sharing the costs of a promotion. The learner identifies that the company could get more customers but does not say how. It is unlikely that a partnership leads to higher prices for customers unless very expensive promotions are undertaken and costs passed on to customers. This has not been explained (0 marks).

Overall the student has gained two marks for their answers.

Student 2's answer

Advantage 1:

Wider customer base as the partnership means that each partner can access the other company's customers. For example, with the joint promotion between train company and visitor attraction, customers find out about the visitor attractions which they may not have heard about before. They might decide to buy a ticket for the train and for the attraction.

Advantage 2:

Partners can achieve economies of scale as they can share resources such as staff or an office space. This will mean that they reduce their costs.

Disadvantage:

Loss of personalised customer care – if one partner receives an enquiry or complaint from the other partner's customers, they may not have enough knowledge or the resources to be able to deal with it. They would have to pass the customer to the other business which would be annoying for the customer.

Feedback:

The learner has identified advantage 1 and clearly explained why it is a benefit to both partners. (2 marks) The second advantage is explained as examples are given to illustrate the answer. (2 marks). A likely disadvantage has been identified and the learner has explained why this disadvantage might occur. (2 marks) Overall the student has gained six marks in total for their answers.

Assess yourself

Question 1

Which two of these are most likely to offer non-serviced accommodation? [2]

A Hotel

B Holiday park

C Campsite

D Guest house

Question 2

A travel agent sells products and services on behalf of tour operators and other travel and tourism companies. One product is a holiday.

Give two other products or services that travel agents provide. [2]

Question 3

Joe and Lily are going away to Scotland for a week's holiday. They are trying to decide whether to drive or go by train. They live in London and need to travel to Aberdeen.

Evaluate whether they should go by road or by train. [8]

Introduction

Have you been on holiday in the UK? Have you ever wondered what attracts so many people to the UK as a holiday destination, and which places/attractions they visit? Tourism is very important to the UK economy. In 2011 nearly 31 million trips were made to the UK by visitors from abroad. During these trips, visitors spent a combined total of £18 billion. It is not only people from abroad who choose to come to the UK on holiday; those who live in this country choose the UK as a holiday destination too. In 2011, UK residents spent £21 billion making 119 million trips to other parts of the country for at least one night (Source: VisitBritain).

In this unit you will look at how visitors travel to, and around, the UK. You will discover the huge variety of interesting destinations — from mountain and seaside resorts to historical sites — and consider why visitors choose where to go and what to do. You will also learn how to find information from a variety of sources to help you plan holiday itineraries to suit a range of customer types.

Assessment: This unit will be assessed through a series of assignments set by your teacher/tutor.

Learning aims

In this unit you will:

A know UK travel and tourism destinations and gateways

B investigate the appeal of UK tourism destinations for different types of visitors

C plan UK holidays to meet the needs of different visitors.

I live near a big theme park and have always enjoyed the 'buzzy' atmosphere. I was there on work placement and absolutely loved being able to help all kinds of people, from families with small children to older people out for the day. I'm looking forward to working in a busy attraction one day.

Tayla, *16-year-old Travel and Tourism student*

UK Travel and Tourism Destinations

2

BTEC
Assessment Zone

This table shows you what you must do in order to achieve a **Pass**, **Merit** or **Distinction** grade, and where you can find activities in this book to help you.

Assessment criteria

Level 1	Level 2 Pass	Level 2 Merit	Level 2 Distinction
Learning aim A: Know UK travel and tourism destinations and gateways			
1A.1 Locate four travel and tourism destinations, from each destination category, with support.	**2A.P1** Accurately locate four travel and tourism destinations, from each destination category. **See Assessment activity 2.1, page 50**	**2A.M1** Plan in detail one route of road travel, one route of rail travel and one route of air travel in and around the UK. **See Assessment activity 2.1, page 50**	
1A.2 Locate six UK gateway airports and four UK seaports, with support.	**2A.P2** Identify and accurately locate six gateway airports and four seaports in the UK, including a typical passenger route for each. **See Assessment activity 2.1, page 50**		
1A.3 Locate two motorways and two rail lines, identifying the destinations connected by them, with support.	**2A.P3** Accurately locate three motorways and three rail lines, identifying the destinations connected by them. **See Assessment activity 2.1, page 50**		
Learning aim B: Investigate the appeal of UK tourism destinations for different types of visitors			
1B.4 Outline how one UK town or city destination, one seaside resort and one countryside area can appeal to two different types of visitors.	**2B.P4** Describe how one UK town or city destination, one seaside resort and one countryside area can appeal to two types of visitors. **See Assessment activity 2.2, page 59**	**2B.M2** Recommend how one UK destination might be able to increase its appeal to different types of visitors. **See Assessment activity 2.2, page 59**	**2B.D1** Justify own recommendations as to how one UK destination might be able to increase its appeal to different types of visitors. **See Assessment activity 2.2, page 59**
Learning aim C: Plan UK holidays to meet the needs of different visitors			
1C.5 English Maths Use different types of sources of information to plan one UK holiday for a selected visitor, and produce an itinerary.	**2C.P5** English Maths Using at least two different information sources, plan two UK holidays, for alternative types of visitors, producing an itinerary for each. **See Assessment activity 2.3, page 63**	**2C.M3** English Maths Plan two UK holidays, for different types of visitors, producing a detailed itinerary for each, and justifying choices made. **See Assessment activity 2.3, page 63**	**2C.D2** English Maths Analyse ways in which the two planned UK holidays could be adapted to meet the needs of different types of visitors. **See Assessment activity 2.3, page 63**

English Opportunity to practise English skills

Maths Opportunity to practise mathematical skills

How you will be assessed

The unit will be assessed by a series of assignments set by your teacher/tutor. You will need to be able to identify and locate tourist destinations, gateways (with three-letter codes for airports) and transport routes on outline maps.

You will also need to demonstrate your understanding of the appeal of tourist destinations to different types of visitors, and use different sources of information to plan UK holidays, providing an itinerary suitable for a particular type of visitor.

Your assessment could be in the form of:

- map work
- booklets/leaflets
- presentations
- travel itineraries, including a bibliography of the sources you have used.

UK travel and tourism categories

Introduction

You will need to know about the range of different destinations within the UK and how they can be categorised. Think about the places you or your friends and family have visited. What kind of destinations were these? Can you put them into different categories?

The UK is made up of four countries – these are England, Scotland, Wales and Northern Ireland. These countries all have a vast range of tourist destinations which can be put into the categories shown in Figure 2.1.

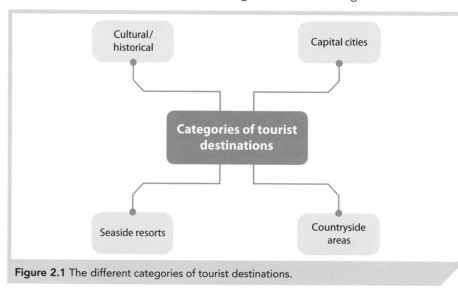

Figure 2.1 The different categories of tourist destinations.

Figure 2.2 Countries and capital cities of the UK.

Capital cities

Each country in the UK has a capital city. This is where their parliament or assembly sits and is the financial and cultural centre of the country. Look at Figure 2.2 and make sure you can locate all of the capital cities correctly.

Seaside resorts

Seaside **resorts** are often referred to as 'bucket-and-spade' beach destinations, as the beach is often the main attraction. There are seaside resorts on all of the UK coasts such as Brighton, Weston-Super-Mare and Scarborough. Many of these rely on visitors for their local economy to prosper.

Activity 2.1 — City and resort map work

Using a blank map:

- locate and name the countries and capital cities of the UK
- add at least eight resorts around the UK. Try to find at least one in every country and underline any that you have visited.

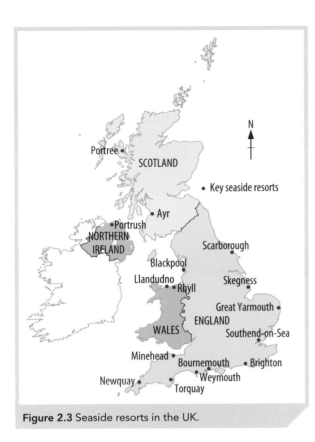

Figure 2.3 Seaside resorts in the UK.

▶ Countryside areas

The UK has a wide variety of countryside areas from dramatic mountain peaks and moorland such as those in Wales and Scotland to gentle rolling chalk downs such as the South Downs National Park. In such a densely populated country, it is important to preserve the countryside for the benefit of us all. One way of doing this is to control development and access by designating the area a National Park. Figure 2.4 shows the National Parks in the UK – notice how large the parks are. There are also Areas of Outstanding Natural Beauty (AONBs), and these are also protected against development. There are many of these; Figure 2.4 shows the main areas.

Some organisations, such as the National Trust, own vast areas of countryside and coastline in order to protect them from building and over-commercialisation. They encourage visitors so that everyone may enjoy the beautiful scenery.

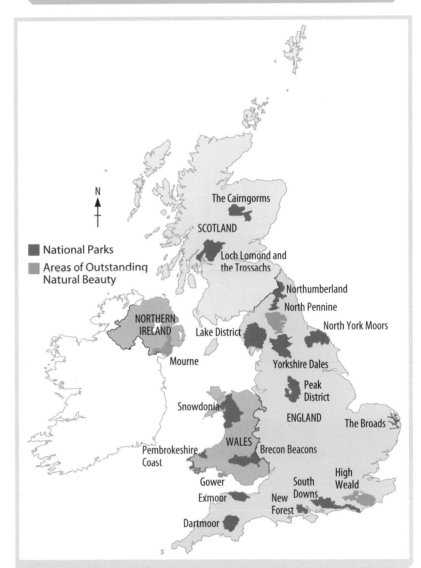

Figure 2.4 The National Parks and main AONBs of the UK.

Activity 2.2   Countryside area map work

Using a blank map:

- add the National Parks that you have visited or would like to visit (you could also find out what activities are carried out there)
- add at least two Areas of Outstanding Natural Beauty, possibly within reach of your local area (you might need to research these online)

Cultural and historical destinations

The UK is culturally rich and has thousands of years of history. This makes it very attractive as a destination, particularly for overseas visitors.

Some destinations are so popular that they attract millions of visitors each year to see their architecture (e.g. Glasgow, Bath), shipping heritage (e.g. Portsmouth, Belfast), links with past civilisations (e.g. York, Stonehenge) or their rich cultural history (e.g. Straford-upon-Avon, Liverpool, Londonderry). We call these '**honeypots**'. The capital cities are also great historical centres, rich in both ancient and contemporary **culture**.

Why do you think the Roman Baths in Bath are such a good tourist destination?

Activity 2.3 — Culture and history map work

Using a blank map:

- locate at least two local historical/cultural centres
- add the 'honeypots' of Bath, York, Oxford, London and Edinburgh
- add at least two destinations that you would like to visit yourself
- add a 'key' explaining what the main attractions are at each destination.

UK gateway airports and UK seaports

Introduction

If you are going to advise passengers properly, you will need to know how they can get to and from destinations. Tourists may arrive in the UK by air, sea or even tunnel. You will need to be familiar with direct ways for tourists to access the UK or the '**gateways**' that tourists can use. Look at Liverpool on a map and consider the points of access.

Key term

Gateway – where passengers can access a country or area. Belfast is a gateway or portal into Northern Ireland because passengers passing through here can travel on to other areas of the country easily.

UK airports

Many people travel to their UK destination by air – some from overseas, others from other parts of the UK. London Gatwick airport has over 34 million passengers a year alone (Source: gatwickairport.com), and many visitors' first experience of the UK is at the airport.

There is a network of routes connecting UK cities and main European and worldwide routes. London, in particular, is a 'hub', where passengers can transfer to many other destinations. Internal UK flight times vary but tend to be quite short. Flights from Paris and Brussels take slightly longer. However, travellers should always take into account the time it takes to travel to and from the airport and the time it takes to check-in for their flight.

Thinking about this, what do you think are the advantages and disadvantages of travelling by air within the UK?

All airports have a three-letter identification code – you can see these on luggage labels and tickets. If a city has only one airport, the code is usually the same as the city, e.g. EDI = Edinburgh airport. However, some cities have more than one airport, so each one has its own code, e.g. for London; LHR = Heathrow, STN = Stansted. Look at Figure 2.5 and note how the whole of the UK is accessible by air. Three-letter codes can be found at the World Airport Codes website. To access the website for this, visit Pearson hotlinks. You can access this by going to www.pearsonhotlinks.co.uk and searching for this title.

Figure 2.5 Main airports in the UK.

Activity 2.4   Airport research

- On the internet look at three UK airlines e.g. British Airways. Find route maps for each and print them out. Display these in your classroom or keep them in your file for future reference.
- Locate at least six gateway airports in the UK on a blank map, and add their three-letter codes.

? Did you know ?

The international language of air transportation is English.

▶ UK passenger seaports

The UK is home to some of the busiest ports in Europe. Many people arrive in the UK by sea from mainland Europe and Ireland. Dover alone has around 14 million passengers a year through its port (Source: Port of Dover). As well as bringing visitors into the UK, ferries also take passengers from the UK to various destinations in Europe and Ireland. See Figure 2.6 for a map of the main seaports and routes.

Take it further ↗

Obtain ferry timetables or look on the internet.

- Find out the time it takes to travel from the UK to Spain.
- Discover the time it takes to travel from Wales to Ireland.
- Compare the facilities available on the ferries.

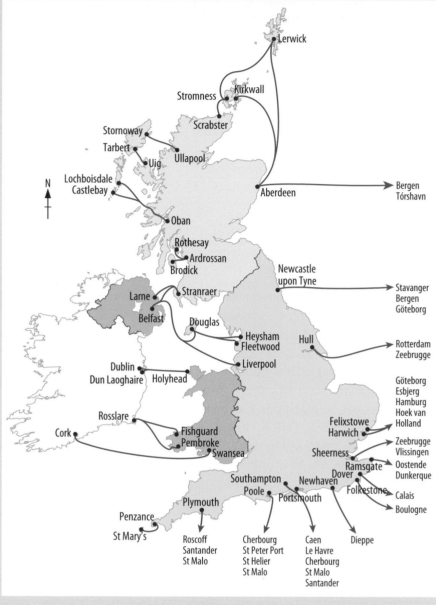

Figure 2.6 Main seaports and sea routes in the UK.

What sort of facilities do ferries provide that keep passengers happy during the crossing?

Many people enjoy the ferry as part of the holiday experience. Modern ferries are comfortable and have many facilities to entertain passengers during the crossing.

Just checking ✓

How much can you remember about the location of destinations and gateways? Without looking at a map, add the following to a blank map:

1 the countries and capital cities of the UK

2 three seaside resorts

3 one National Park

4 two cultural/historical destinations

5 two airports and their three-letter codes

6 two ports

How did you do? Check your maps using this book or an atlas/online map.

▶ Road and rail travel

Introduction

Tourists can travel around the UK by train, coach, car or bike. You will need to be able to advise them on the UK road and rail networks. Large cities, such as London, act as 'hubs' where roads and railways radiate from them. Look at a map of London and see how many stations there are.

▶ Road

Of course, many people travel by road within the UK to get to their destination – listen to any road reports on an August Bank Holiday weekend and you will hear about the traffic jams as everyone leaves at the same time.

The major roads in the UK are the motorways. The main North/South routes are the M1 and the M6, and the East/West route is the M62. The M5 also connects the West Country with the west coast manufacturing areas.

Coaches and buses also use the road network to transport passengers throughout the UK. Coach companies, such as National Express and Stagecoach, take people longer distances and have to be booked in advance. Coaches may also be part of a pre-booked 'package' holiday that includes hotels. Journey times may be quite long by coach, for instance the journey time from London to York is about six hours and Manchester to Plymouth around nine hours. Both journeys would be quicker by car.

Figure 2.7 The motorway systems and main A roads in the UK.

Activity 2.5   Road routes

Using the knowledge you have gained so far, draw a sketch map of two ways to travel between London and Manchester. Add the approximate travel times. You may need to use the internet and/or a road map.

Activity 2.6   Rail/air travel

You need to advise a passenger about travelling from Edinburgh to London. Draw up a table advising them of the time it will take and the route they should travel if they were to go by:

- rail
- air.

Make sure you explain which transport company is involved and the name of the arrival/departure point.

▶ Rail

The rail system covers much of the UK and joins most of the major cities in a grid pattern. Rail lines radiate out of London like spokes from a wheel and each direction has its own terminus, for example trains leave London Kings Cross for the Eastern cities of York and Edinburgh. Western counties are served by Paddington station. Many other cities have stations which are also 'hubs' for rail lines, such as Birmingham New Street or Manchester Piccadilly.

Each area has its own rail company, such as East Coast mainline or South West mainline. ScotRail operates in Scotland and Northern Ireland Railways operates in Northern Ireland.

The Eurostar passenger line from London St Pancras International runs direct to Paris (in under 2.5 hours) and to Brussels (under 2 hours), connecting to many other European cities. This uses the Channel Tunnel from just outside Folkestone to just outside Calais. The coach- and car-carrying train company Eurotunnel, which uses the same rail line, takes about 35 minutes to travel under the channel. For many it is still a special feeling to get on a train in England and arrive in mainland Europe, particularly as the line is so fast.

Assessment activity 2.1

2A.P1 | 2A.P2 | 2A.P3 | 2A.M1

You are on a work experience placement for a travel company that specialises in holidays in the UK. They are updating their website and have asked you to help them with this.

- There is a 'Let us inspire you' section of the website presenting holiday ideas for customers. The company would like to add a map to this section showing the locations of different tourist destinations. They have asked you to develop this. Your map should show four destinations for each category: capital cities, seaside resorts, countryside areas and cultural and/or historical destinations.

- They would like to add a new page to the website giving customers advice on how to get around the UK. This will feature maps showing suggested travel routes. Draw, or label, four maps of the UK that show six airports (including their three-letter codes), four seaports, three motorways and three railway lines. Show possible journeys customers could take using each one. Include journeys from the seaports to the Republic of Ireland and Europe.

- For customers who have very little time, the website offers suggested travel itineraries. The company would like to refresh these with new ideas. Develop detailed plans for three different journeys in the UK: one by road, one by rail and one by air.

Tips

- Customers will find it easier to read your maps if you use different colours or symbols. For example, you could mark all the capital cities in one colour and all the seaside resorts in another. Alternatively, you could use a picture of a beach umbrella for seaside destinations and a picture of a tree for countryside destinations. Look at maps in holiday guides or on the internet to see how these have been designed and try to make your maps customer friendly.

- For the second task, you could either produce one map that shows everything or, if you prefer, you could produce one map to show travel routes by air, one map to show travel routes by rail, etc.

▶ Appeal of UK destinations

Introduction

What makes people go to a particular destination? What is it that 'pulls' them towards one place rather than another? In this section we will look at the factors that affect the appeal of a destination. With a partner, consider a UK destination you would like to see – what is it that makes you want to visit?

▶ Visitor attractions

The UK has a wide range of visitor attractions – there is something to appeal to everyone from historical sites, such as Stonehenge, or heritage buildings, such as Edinburgh Castle, to theme parks like Alton Towers. The most visited fee-paying attraction in 2012 was the Tower of London, which receives nearly 2.5 million visits a year. Westminster Abbey in London received around 2 million visits and Chester Zoo nearly 1.5 million (Source: Association of Leading Visitor Attractions (ALVA)).

Both the National Trust and English Heritage are organisations that look after important buildings and historic sites. Entry is free to members, and both organisations (and their equivalent in Scotland) try to balance conservation with encouraging visitors.

Table 2.1 – A range of attractions.

Types of attractions	Examples
National Trust attractions	Historic houses, e.g. Tatton Park, Cheshire
English Heritage attractions	National monuments, sites and houses, e.g. Hadrian's Wall, Northumberland
Theme Parks	Flamingo Land, Yorkshire; Alton Towers, Staffordshire
Wildlife Parks/Zoos	Edinburgh Zoo, Longleat Safari Park
Museums	Science Museum, London; National Railway Museum, York

Case study

Warwick Castle is part of the UK based Merlin Entertainments group, UK and Europe's largest visitor attractions operator. Merlin also owns LEGOLAND Windsor, theme parks Alton Towers and Thorpe Park, Madame Tussauds and the London Eye. Warwick sets out to be much more than a castle, with shows, battles and live entertainment on offer, currently including shows based on the popular Horrible Histories children's books. As well as the river, towers and ramparts, there are several special areas like the Kingmaker, Princess Tower and an 'interactive experience' based on the television series *Merlin* in the Dragon Tower. Warwick Castle also offers special Halloween and Christmas experiences as well as working models and live guides in costume. There are special deals for school parties and groups.

(Source: www.warwick-castle.com)

Answer the following questions:

1 Where is Warwick? What large conurbation (an extended urban area) is nearby? What transport links are there?

2 Why do you think the castle puts on special events such as celebrating Halloween in October?

3 How does the castle encourage groups to visit?

Even with the UK's changeable weather, hiking and other outdoor activities attract people all year round. What other outdoor activities can you do in th UK?

▶ Natural features

These are geographical features such as:

- mountains, e.g. the Grampians, Scotland
- beaches/coasts, e.g. Pembrokeshire Coast, Wales
- lakes, e.g. Lough Neagh, Northern Ireland
- rivers, e.g. the River Severn, England.

Many of the most visited areas are National Parks, such as Snowdonia in Wales where visitors can do outdoor activities such as walking, climbing or cycling. Lakes such as Loch Ness in Scotland are famous for their beauty (and their 'monster') and for water-based activities such as sailing and fishing. There are long-distance paths around the coasts of the UK, such as the South West Coastal Path, which passes through the Jurassic coast, where many people search for pre-historic fossils.

Activity 2.7	Activities in natural features

Locate three natural features locally. What kinds of activities are carried out there? Make a poster advertising them for your age group.

▶ Accommodation

Link

You can read more about accommodation in *Unit 1: The UK Travel and Tourism Sector*.

This is usually divided into 'serviced' and 'unserviced'. Serviced accommodation includes staff to clean and tidy your room, supply meals and help with booking theatre or other tickets. Unserviced includes self-catering flats and apartments, camping, caravanning and some chalet parks. Some facilities such as Center Parcs provide a choice of either.

Activity 2.8	Accommodation thought shower

In groups, think of as many types of holiday accommodation as you can. Try to include unusual ones such as houseboats or yurts. Display the results. Think about the advantages and disadvantages of each. Look at Table 2.2. Did you miss any? Can you add more to the table?

There is a lot of choice – how can visitors choose what is right for them?

▶ Facilities

Some visitors like to make sure that there are plenty of facilities to keep them occupied at their destination. This is particularly important in bad weather. These may include sport and leisure facilities, such as the SnowDome at Tamworth, or the legacy of the Olympic Park in London. Large leisure facilities which include climbing walls or leisure pools are also popular, particularly with families.

Purpose-built facilities such as the Metrocentre in Gateshead or Westfield in Stratford, London are popular shopping destinations and many of these 'malls' also include cinemas and restaurants to encourage visitors to stay for longer. People also visit major cities to sample international cuisine at famous restaurants. Bradford in Yorkshire is known for its 'curry trail' and has won a tourism award for this.

Table 2.2 – There are advantages and disadvantages to all types of accommodation.

Type of accommodation	Advantages	Disadvantages
Self-catering	Often cheaper, flexible, can cook what you like. Cooking facilities provided.	Someone has to cook and clear up.
Catered hotels and guesthouses	Meals provided, can be part of the experience.	Meal times may be restricted, can be expensive.
Bed and breakfast	Provides mix of catered and flexibility. Homely atmosphere. Often used for short stays.	Can be variable in quality and facilities.
Holiday parks	Can provide mixture of self-catering and catered. Often has sports and entertainment (particularly for children) included.	Can be bustling and crowded.
Boats	Moving around, novelty value.	Can be hard work at locks. Dangerous for young children.
Camping and caravans	Open air feel. Often many facilities. Good value for money.	May be noisy under canvas. Bad weather may limit enjoyment.

Activity 2.9 | Imagine a day trip

Imagine you have been given £50 to spend on a day out. Where would you go? What facilities would you want to find – would you want to go shopping, participate in sporting activities, or see a film? Put together your 'perfect day' and share it with your fellow learners.

Think about your local shopping centre – what kind of facilities would you find there to ensure customers stay as long as possible?

▶ Arts and entertainment

Many towns have theatres offering a variety of community entertainment. Scarborough's theatre is known for opening the popular comedies of Alan Ayckbourn. London's West End theatres and the Royal Opera House are known internationally and attract top-class stars.

Art galleries, such as Tate Liverpool and Tate St Ives, receive local and international visitors. They can arrange group visits and have special programmes for schools. Many galleries have exhibitions that are on for a limited period – the Leonardo da Vinci exhibition at the National Gallery in London sold out almost immediately and was immensely popular.

The summer is a season of festivals and events throughout the UK. The Edinburgh Festival has many different events, including music, theatre and comedy. There is also a thriving 'alternative' festival with exciting emerging acts.

There are also many other music festivals, such as Reading and Glastonbury. Often local areas will have smaller versions of these events which attract mostly domestic visitors.

Activity 2.10	Local events

Research local arts and entertainment facilities. Find out if there are any festivals in your area and produce a 'flyer' advertising some of these.

Why are festivals like Reading and Leeds a good opportunity for the local area?

▶ Sightseeing

Having enticed visitors to a destination, they need to be able to see all that is on offer. Many towns and cities will provide free or good value guided walking tours. There is usually a qualified guide who walks around the town, stopping in various places to tell a local story. There are also ghost tours, such as the Original Ghost Tour of York, where guides in flowing capes try to frighten their audience with blood-curdling tales linked to local incidents. Tours can also be taken by bus (sometimes open-topped) which often have a guide or headphone system giving a commentary on what is being seen. This is a good way to understand the layout of an unfamiliar place.

Towns that are built on rivers, such as Canterbury or Glasgow, often have sightseeing boats, which can cruise through the centre of a city without being held up by traffic. These will probably also have a guide or commentary.

Resorts such as Southend have a land-train, which looks like a train but runs on wheels along the promenade and local streets. This is ideal for the elderly or children unable to walk very far.

▶ Transport links

Of course, equally important is being able to get to the destination in the first place. We have already looked at the transport infrastructure of the UK, and you must always remember that these millions of visitors need to reach their destination as easily as possible. Visitors to cities and larger towns will also need to be able to visit attractions and facilities within the city or town. Visitors are often encouraged to travel on public transport and many attractions provide a bus from the local train station. Some attractions, such as the Farne Islands, have sea links for tourists to visit them.

Link

Read about the rail, road, air and sea links for these destinations in *Topics A2* and *A3*.

Activity 2.11 What appeals?

Choose a destination that you would like to visit for the weekend. Make a table showing each of the factors that affect the appeal of the destination, and give an example for each. In a third column explain why this would appeal to you.

Factors	Example	Why this appeals?

TOPIC B2

▶ Types of visitors

Introduction

There are many different types of visitor. Each of them will have different reasons for choosing the UK as their holiday destination and will be looking for a different experience. Think of a relative and choose an ideal destination for them – what sort of things will they want to do? Would you want to do the same?

Link

You can find out more in *Unit 6: The Travel and Tourism Customer Experience*.

As we have seen, one visitor's ideal destination may be totally wrong for another person. Table 2.3 shows some of the main types of visitor and outlines their different needs. You may be able to think of other types of visitor.

Table 2.3 – There are many different visitor types with varying needs.

Visitor types	Characteristics	Needs
Families with young children	Parents will want to keep children happy and occupied, while also trying to relax themselves. Older children often want independent activities in a safe environment.	Activities on site, safe beaches/play areas, baby changing facilities, children's menu, childcare service
Families with older children/teens		Kids' clubs, activities, sports, interactive entertainment, children's menu
Young adults	Often like to have plenty of opportunity to socialise, experience different activities and sightsee	Sports facilities, activities, bars, clubs, cafes, restaurants
Older people	Often like to have plenty of opportunity to experience different activities and sightsee	Museums, art galleries, entertainment, cafes, restaurants, easy access to facilities
Groups (possibly on a coach)	Often share a common interest, or are looking to benefit from a guided tour rather than finding their own way around a new place	Group discounts, catering facilities for large groups
School/educational groups	Usually visiting key attractions with a link to the curriculum	Education officer, activities, group discounts, catering facilities for large groups
Incoming visitors from other cultures	Usually looking for something different from the things they have at home. Particularly interested in UK history and heritage. May need help or a guided tour.	Cultural understanding, access to specific food, flexibility
Non-English speaking visitors		Leaflets in different languages, guides who can speak different languages
Domestic visitors	Residents in the UK who are taking a holiday in another part of the UK	Good transport links, booking information, catering facilities
Visitors with specific needs	All characteristics that are listed above although these visitors might require additional facilities to improve their experience	Access for physical needs, tactile exhibits and leaflets, induction loops, easy-read leaflets

Activity 2.12   Questionnaire

Find out what your friends and family want in a destination.

Choose **two** groups from Table 2.3 and **two** friends or family members of different ages.

Ask them if they have visited/would like to visit somewhere in the UK and find out what destination would appeal to them and why.

WorkSpace

▷ Sean McGuire

UK Information Assistant

I work at a major airport and am responsible for:

- giving information about onward journeys to destinations
- advising on accommodation
- providing leaflets/brochures/timetables
- giving information on visitor attractions
- welcoming incoming visitors of all cultures.

I love the fact that you never know what people are going to ask and each day is different. I get a real buzz from being able to help people and it's very interesting meeting people from all over the world. They are usually very grateful for the help I can give them, and there is real skill in understanding what they need, especially if there are language difficulties.

People often arrive after a long flight feeling very disorientated and the sight of a friendly welcoming face is a great start to their visit. I know quite a lot about other areas of the UK and can suggest different places that they might like to see.

You need to be able to talk to all kinds of people, and to have a smile even if you have had a long day. You also need to know a lot about destinations in the UK and the best ways to travel between them.

Think about it

1   Think about the maps you have studied in the first topic. You need to have an idea of the relative positions of main destinations and gateways, but you also need to know how to obtain information quickly and accurately. Consider the best ways of doing this.

2   Are you a warm and friendly person? Do you enjoy helping a range of people? What other skills do you think would be helpful in this role?

▶ Increasing appeal

Introduction

Those running visitor attractions or tourist boards need to make sure they attract both new visitors and repeat business. There are many ways to increase appeal – it is important to consider the markets a destination appeals to and how to provide for visitors' needs. Think of a local tourist destination and consider what you would do to improve its appeal for young people.

▶ Improving facilities

With easy access to the sun of the Mediterranean and low-cost flights to many cities, many UK destinations have to compete to attract visitors year after year. The financial crisis has also had an impact – visitors will be thinking more carefully when making decisions about where to spend their holiday. Many seaside resorts have tried to increase their appeal by providing indoor attractions for times when there is bad weather, such as softplay areas for small children, indoor swimming parks and free children's activities.

Museums have tried to increase their appeal by providing interactive displays and guides dressed in character, who will talk to visitors as though they live in a different age, such as at the Ironbridge Gorge museum. Children benefit by being able to take part in the experience.

Parks such as Center Parcs, Hoseasons and Pontins provide accommodation at a reasonable price, and include many facilities such as swimming pools (sub-tropical at Center Parcs) and other activities. More sporting and leisure activities are available at extra cost so that no one need be bored whatever the weather. Butlin's at Bognor Regis have upgraded their chalet accommodation by building three new hotels, one of which has been designed like a ship's bow to make the best of the sea views.

Theme parks will often upgrade their rides so that each white-knuckle ride is more frightening than the last. These can appeal to young adults and older children. Special themed sessions such as 'Fright Nights' at Halloween also encourage visitors even when it is cold. Other parks may include zoos or rides aimed at much younger children, such as Paulton's Park near Southampton. Look for anything advertised as 'new' or 'improved'.

Providing activities for younger children encourages whole families to visit attractions. What other activities do you think young children would enjoy?

Case study

Blackpool has been a seaside resort for nearly 150 years. Its beach is long and sandy, but it has also invested in upgrading the famous Blackpool Tower. The Blackpool Pleasure Beach regularly improves their rides, including an enormous roller coaster. The resort has for some time been famous for the Illuminations, which bring thousands of lights to the promenade in October.

This means that visitors still come to Blackpool in the autumn as well as the summer period. It is important to extend the season for as long as possible, and to encourage groups to use their facilities and conference centres.

Answer the following questions:

1 How do you think the type of visitor going to Blackpool has changed over the last 150 years?

2 What activities does Blackpool Pleasure Beach provide to encourage visitors year-round?

3 What groups can you find that use Blackpool's facilities and conference centres? (Hint: It's a nice change from Downing Street!)

▷ Appealing to specific groups

Visitors from other countries may not speak English well. An attraction can make itself more welcoming by providing translations in a number of languages, and maps with symbols or colours to help visitors. Staff who can speak at least a few words in another language will also encourage repeat visitors.

People with specific needs can also be encouraged to visit. As a result of the Equality Act 2010 attractions must make reasonable adjustments, but the most successful places do more than that. York Minster provides a tactile model, so that people with sight impairments can feel the layout of the building with their hands. Many theme parks will allow people with wheelchairs or other physical disabilities to have a reduced entry price, together with a carer, and to skip queues to enter rides. Some rides can be slowed down to allow access. Audio guides in attractions often have a 'loop' system to allow people who are hard of hearing to hear commentaries.

Discussion point

In groups, choose a local destination, attraction or other feature and consider how it could be improved to appeal to a group or groups of visitors. Write your suggestions on a flip chart and display them. Explain the reasons for your choice to the other groups.

Assessment activity 2.2   2B.P4 | 2B.M2 | 2B.D1

A tourist board in the UK is looking at ways they can increase the appeal of their area as a tourist destination. They have set up a competition to see who can come up with the best ideas. You have decided to enter.

In preparation for this, you decide to look at UK tourist destinations and think about why they appeal to tourists. Look at one town or city destination, one seaside resort and one countryside area. Think about how each destination might appeal to two different types of visitor.

You are now ready to think about your entry for the competition. Focus on the tourist board's destination and make a strong argument about what would increase its appeal to different types of visitors.

Tips

- When deciding on the types of visitors to focus on, you may find it helps to consider types of visitors you are familiar with. Perhaps consider how destinations might appeal to different members of your family.
- Consider all elements that might make a destination attractive, including visitor attractions, natural features, accommodation, facilities, arts and entertainment, sightseeing and transport links.
- Try to give evidence/reasons as to why your ideas might be successful. For example, has another destination taken similar steps with positive results? Say why your recommendations give visitors more reason to visit.

▶ Sources of information

Introduction

You must make sure you use a range of information sources to find out about UK destinations. Destinations are keen to market themselves, so there are many sources available in different media, both online and paper-based. Look at a local destination and see how much you can find out about it in 10 minutes using a variety of sources.

▶ Paper-based sources

Many people like to use paper-based resources because they find these easier to refer to and compare. The main disadvantage is that these may become out-of-date quite quickly.

What kind of information would you find in a guide book?

Guide books such as the *Rough Guide* or the *Lonely Planet* often have a great deal of in-depth unbiased information but further details may be difficult to find.

Local councils and attractions produce free information guides and leaflets for distribution to visitors. Tourist Information Centres often have both local and national information available in bulk supplies.

Holiday brochures can be obtained from travel agents – there may be coach tours or weekend break brochures available, such as brochures for Wallace Arnold or Superbreak.

A good travel atlas is ideal for map work, such as that produced by Columbia Press, and has much more information than just maps. A road atlas, such as those produced by the AA, can also be useful.

▶ Online resources

Online sources tend to be more up-to-date.

Some guide books are available online, although there is a charge. Most leaflets and council brochures are also available online, but if you are using a search engine, make sure that the site you choose has the name of the attraction in the title and that it is a UK site. Many websites provide comprehensive and updated information. If you are looking at a particular town or city, use the council site (.gov or visitwinchester.co.uk for example) rather than a commercial site, as this should give you more comprehensive information. VisitBritain is the official tourist website for those visiting the UK.

If tourists have a leaflet or advert, they may also be able to download more information from a 'QR' square barcode on a smartphone. Smartphones may also have 'apps' available, which can give tourist information.

Bibliography

There are different ways of writing these, but in general, if using a website, state the whole address, together with the date it was accessed, e.g. www.visitbritain.org, accessed 23/9/12.

If using a leaflet, then the title, publisher and date should be given, e.g. City Walk, A Tour of King Alfred's, Winchester, Winchester City Council, printed Oct 2011. A book should have the author's name, year of publication, title and publisher.

Whatever way you write your bibliography, make sure you make notes of resources you have used as you go along as it can take a long time to reassemble all your sources of information once you have finished your work.

Activity 2.13	Online Belfast

A large attraction opened in Belfast in 2012, called the Titanic, based on the shipwreck. Research Belfast tourist attractions online, looking at as many sites as you can. Which sites include the Titanic attraction? Write a list of those that have been updated to include it.

TOPIC C2

UK holiday planning

Introduction

You now know about different destinations and how visitors can access them. You also need to know how to plan holidays for different visitors and how to present this information to them in a clear format, usually known as an itinerary. Look at holiday offers in newspapers or magazines and note what information is included and how it is presented.

Visitor types and needs

Earlier in the unit you considered the different types of visitor who choose destinations in the UK. You also thought about what they might need on holiday and why they might choose certain destinations. You are now ready to plan holidays that will suit these visitors in the same way that tour operators and travel agents plan holidays – be creative and think of the range of experiences available.

Link

See *Topic B2* for more about types of visitors.

Planning

Visitors tend to choose their holiday very carefully. They may think of the following.

- **The preferred date/time of year.** People with school-age children may want to go away in the school holidays. Others may prefer to avoid them, particularly as these times tend to be the most expensive. Consider whether warm or fine weather is a requirement.

If a visitor wanted to go on a surfing holiday what do you think their motivation would be?

- **Travel requirements.** Are the visitors coming from another country via a 'gateway'? How will they travel? Private or public transport? You will need to think of the ease of travel and the time taken to reach their destination. Elderly people may not want to drive, small children may not be able to go long distances – think carefully about what each group might need.

- **Accommodation.** Think about all the different types of accommodation. Will the visitors need a room on a lower floor with a wide door for a wheelchair? Do they need the flexibility of self-catering or the comfort of fully serviced?

- **Motivation.** Why is your visitor travelling? Do they want a fast-paced cultural experience or a relaxing time by the sea? Would they prefer sailing in the Highlands or walking on a coastal path?

- **Features.** What is it about the destination that draws them in? Remember your questionnaire, how do people choose where to go? Are they looking for natural features, culture, facilities?

- **Budget.** Are the visitors on a restricted budget? What sort of destinations and facilities might they choose? Is this a luxury trip?

Activity 2.14   Planning for visitor types

In groups, plan a holiday in the UK for:

- a group of older people living in Manchester wanting an off-season holiday touring historical towns and cities for a week
- a group of students flying from France and wanting to visit a city with art and entertainment for the weekend.

Make sure you address all the bullet points above and give reasons for your choice.

▶ Itinerary

There are many ways to lay out an **itinerary**, and you could be inventive with logos and illustrations. However, there are certain elements that must be included:

1 Date and time of travel.

2 Mode of travel.

3 Departure and destination locations.

4 Type of accommodation.

5 Board basis.

6 Features included.

An example of a basic itinerary is shown in Figure 2.8, but you might like to experiment with the layout.

Key term

Itinerary – this is the schedule of events throughout the holiday. It needs to have all the information laid out clearly for easy reference. Make sure you can spell this word as it is different from the way it sounds.

Itinerary for School Group visiting Bath October 14th/15th	
14th October	
0900	Depart Tillings School car park
	All learners to bring suitable clothing for cold/wet weather and packed lunch
	Travel by private coach
1100	Comfort stop at Gloucester diner. Drinks available
1230	Arrive Bath drop-off point, city centre
	Walk to Roman Baths (5 minutes)
1245	Picnic lunch in education room
1315	Visit to Roman Baths, guided by education officer.
1500	Walk to Costume Museum (15 minutes)
1515	Visit to Costume Museum – activity sheet
1630	Walk to Hotel Bath Spa, 15 minutes 3* hotel, Pountney Square, Bath
	Accommodation provided in 3-bedded rooms
1800	Evening meal (included) followed by activities
15th October	
0800	Breakfast (included), picnic lunch provided by hotel
0900	Depart by coach to National Trust property, Dyrham Park
1015	Private guided tour of house and garden
1200	Picnic and drinks available in tea shop
1300	Depart Dyrham Park for Tillings school
1530	Arrive Tillings car park

Figure 2.8 An example itinerary.

Remember to use all of the knowledge you have gained from this unit to make your decisions when setting out a suitable itinerary for your customer(s).

Assessment activity 2.3   English   Maths   2C.P5 | 2C.M3 | 2C.D2

You are working as an assistant for a travel agent. They are very busy and you have been asked to help them by dealing with customer queries. The following customers have asked you to plan a UK holiday for them.

Customer A: A retired woman of 65-years-old from Canada who is visiting the UK for the first time. She is keen to explore London but would also like to visit some cultural/historical sites outside of the capital city. She would prefer each journey to take no more than three hours, and does not wish to drive.

Customer B: A 20-year-old student on a gap year. She is keen to learn how to surf and is also interested in trying other outdoor pursuits. She has a tight budget.

It will take time to plan these holidays in detail. To make the most out of your research think about the ways these holiday plans could be adapted if a similar brief came from a different type of customer. For example, customer B might be a family of four rather than a 20-year-old student. How would you modify the holiday plan to suit them?

Tips

- You should produce detailed holiday plans including dates and times of travel, methods of travel and types of accommodation.
- Remember to reference the website addresses, holiday brochures and/or guide books you use to support your work.

Introduction

Have you ever thought about why people travel, how they choose where to go on holiday, and how they decide which form of transport to take? What are the trends and issues, and how are these changing? We know that factors like climate change will no doubt have an impact on the type of holiday product on offer in the future.

In this unit you will explore how the UK travel and tourism industry has been shaped in relation to key developments, lifestyle changes and trends. You will also consider the variety of issues that have impacted on the development of the UK travel and tourism sector. Exploring these developments and issues will help you to gain a much broader understanding of the dynamic nature of the UK travel and tourism sector.

Assessment: This unit will be assessed through a series of assignments set by your teacher/tutor.

Learning aims

In this unit you will:

A explore the developments that have helped shape the UK travel and tourism sector

B understand how lifestyle changes and trends have influenced the development of the UK travel and tourism sector

C investigate the issues that have impacted on the development of the UK travel and tourism sector.

I found it really interesting to learn about how the travel and tourism industry has changed over the last few years. I think the internet has really improved choice for the customer, but it makes me sad to think that many smaller, independent, travel agents are closing down because they just don't get the volume of business that they used to.

Maisy, *15-year-old Travel and Tourism student*

The Development of Travel and Tourism in the UK

3

BTEC
Assessment Zone

This table shows what you must do in order to achieve a **Pass**, **Merit** or **Distinction** grade, and where you can find activities in this book to help you.

Assessment and grading criteria

Level 1	Level 2 Pass	Level 2 Merit	Level 2 Distinction
Learning aim A: Explore the developments that have helped shape the UK travel and tourism sector			
1A.1 Outline four key developments that have helped shape the UK travel and tourism sector.	**2A.P1** Describe key developments that have helped shape the UK travel and tourism sector. **See Assessment activity 3.1, page 82**	**2A.M1** Explain key developments that have helped shaped the UK travel and tourism sector. **See Assessment activity 3.1, page 82**	**2A.D1** Evaluate key developments that have helped shape the UK travel and tourism sector. **See Assessment activity 3.1, page 82**
1A.2 Outline four developments in transportation that have helped shape the UK travel and tourism sector.	**2A.P2** Describe four developments in transportation that have helped shape the UK travel and tourism sector. **See Assessment activity 3.1, page 82**		
1A.3 Outline four developments in legislation that have helped shape the UK travel and tourism sector.	**2A.P3** Describe the developments in legislation that have helped shape the UK travel and tourism sector. **See Assessment activity 3.1, page 82**		
Learning aim B: Understand how lifestyle changes and trends have influenced the development of the UK travel and tourism sector			
1B.4 Describe, with support, two lifestyle changes that have influenced the UK travel and tourism sector.	**2B.P4** Describe four lifestyle changes that have influenced the UK travel and tourism sector. **See Assessment activity 3.2, page 90**	**2B.M2** Explain four lifestyle changes that have influenced the UK travel and tourism sector. **See Assessment activity 3.2, page 90**	**2B.D2** Analyse key lifestyle changes and trends that have influenced the UK travel and tourism sector. **See Assessment activity 3.2, page 90**
1B.5 Describe, with support, two trends that have influenced the UK travel and tourism sector.	**2B.P5** Describe four trends that have influenced the UK travel and tourism sector. **See Assessment activity 3.2, page 90**	**2B.M3** Explain four trends that have influenced the UK travel and tourism sector. **See Assessment activity 3.2, page 90**	
Learning aim C: Investigate the issues that have impacted on the development of the UK travel and tourism sector			
1C.6 Outline how two selected issues have impacted on the development of the UK travel and tourism sector.	**2C.P6** Describe how four selected issues have impacted on the development of the UK travel and tourism sector. **See Assessment activity 3.3, page 95**	**2C.M4** Explain how four selected issues have impacted on the development of the UK travel and tourism sector. **See Assessment activity 3.3, page 95**	**2C.D3** Evaluate how selected issues have impacted on the development of the UK travel and tourism sector. **See Assessment activity 3.3, page 95**

How you will be assessed

This unit will be assessed by a series of assignments set by your teacher/tutor. You will research the developments that have helped to shape the UK travel and tourism sector and then consider the influence of lifestyle changes and trends. You will also need to demonstrate your understanding of the various issues that have impacted on the development of the travel and tourism sector.

Your evidence required for this unit will be generated on an ongoing basis. Any evidence that you produce will be stored in a portfolio, together with any observation records or witness statements. You should include any notes that you make while researching key information.

Your assessment could be in the form of:

- a report using ICT
- a multimedia presentation using ICT
- a wall display using charts and images
- a booklet including detailed written information
- a travel journal including feature articles.

Remember

As you progress through this unit, keep a record of all of the sources that you use to collect information. These sources might include books, journals, travel magazines, atlases and websites.

▶ Key developments in travel and tourism

Introduction

Development is about change or improvement that takes place over time. The development of the travel and tourism sector in the UK has been driven by a range of factors: the ingenuity and ambition of individuals, innovations in technology and the ever-changing demands of consumers. Can you think of five examples of developments that you know have taken place within the travel and tourism sector?

Take it further

Cox and Kings are still in existence as an independent tour company operating from the UK, India, USA and Japan. Research the type of holidays that are available from Cox and Kings using the internet. Compare these holidays with those available from Thomas Cook.

▶ Early development of package holidays and notable people

Cox and Kings are widely recognised as the world's first 'modern' travel company, founded in 1758. Initially the company provided a range of services to the military, including arranging the payment of wages and the purchase of uniform and clothing. The company also arranged travel to the Indian subcontinent. Throughout the ages, other travel companies started to form.

Figure 3.1 What do you think experiencing the 'Grand Circular Tour' would have been like?

Thomas Cook

In 1841, Thomas Cook – often considered to be 'the father of tourism' – founded his travel company. A religious man, Cook believed that many of the problems experienced by working class people at the time, such as excessive drinking, could be improved through the introduction of mass excursions using the 'great powers of railways and locomotives'. His company coordinated the travel for 165,000 people to attend the Great Exhibition at the Crystal Palace in London in 1851, and in 1855 it started to organise excursions to Europe that became known as the 'Grand Circular Tour'. Those who joined the tour – usually the very wealthy – were able to visit many famous cities and landmarks, including Brussels, Cologne, the Rhine, Heidelberg, Baden-Baden, Strasbourg and Paris, returning to London via Le Havre or Dieppe.

Activity 3.1   Visiting the Great Exhibition

The Great Exhibition of 1851 is recognised as one of the first major 'honeypot' events in history that drew people to London from all over the UK and even abroad. What sort of transport problems do you think Thomas Cook was faced with in 1851? How might these compare with the transport issues associated with the Olympics that took place in London in 2012?

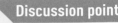

Billy Butlin

In 1937, Billy Butlin opened his first holiday camp in Skegness. An entrepreneur, Butlin saw the huge potential of introducing purpose-built sites that provided consumers with an all-encompassing holiday experience. Targeted towards the working class, Butlin promoted his holidays as affordable, adopting the slogan 'A week's holiday for a week's pay'. The development of Butlin's holiday camps coincided with the passing of the Holidays with Pay Act in 1938, which enabled workers to take a holiday with pay for the first time. After the Second World War the popularity of his camps boomed, accommodating around 5,000 people.

Discussion point

During the Second World War many returning soldiers experienced visiting foreign soil for the first time. Do you think this had any impact on demand for foreign travel?

Research the resorts that were available in the late 1800s and think about where you would have liked to visit.

Did you know?

In 1972 Butlin's experienced a peak in visitor numbers with over one million bookings. Why do you think Butlin's was still popular in the 1970s when relatively inexpensive package tours to Mediterranean resorts were available?

When holiday entitlement was introduced in the 1870s, the number of people taking holidays increased. Many seaside coastal resorts developed around the UK, such as Blackpool, Southport, Scarborough and Skegness, and spa towns, such as Matlock Bath and Builth Wells.

Vladamir Raitz

In 1945, after the Second World War, there was much interest in travelling abroad; many returning soldiers had experienced foreign soil for the first time and some had even travelled by aeroplane. By 1950, using the name Horizon Holidays, Vladamir Raitz had chartered a flight to Corsica. In accordance with the principle of '**economy of scale**' Raitz chartered the whole aircraft as opposed to booking a selection of seats on a scheduled air service. Raitz was able to fill every seat; this meant that he was able to reduce the **unit cost** of his air transport and pass on the savings to his customers. Although in his first year of operating only 300 passengers used his service, within a few years his business was profitable.

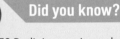

Key terms

Economy of scale – the increase in efficiency of production as the volume of goods or services being produced increases.

Unit cost – the cost to an organisation of producing and selling one unit of a particular product, such as a seat on an airline.

A few tourists discover a suitable area or destination, commonly a beach resort.

↓

Local businesses develop or adapt existing facilities for the growing number of tourists.

↓

The government funds improvements to meet the demands of the growing numbers of tourists.

↓

Mass tourism develops, relying on large-scale production and sale of affordable holiday packages/options.

Figure 3.2 Why do some destinations want to encourage mass tourism?

▶ Growth of mass market and specialist holidays

Since the mid 1990s the internet has given customers the opportunity to customise their holiday experience by providing easy access to information about activities, destinations, prices and availability. At the same time the deregulation of European airspace triggered the development of the low-cost airline. This enabled the consumer to create a dynamic, flexible package holiday. Lower airfares meant that consumers were no longer restricted to taking traditional one- or two-week holidays; weekend breaks to cities across Europe such as Prague, Rome and Berlin have increased in popularity.

Other developments in transport technology have also facilitated the growth of the European city break. The Seacat ferry is capable of reaching Dublin from Holyhead in less than two hours, while the Eurostar is able to reach Paris, Lille and Brussels in less than two hours from London.

▶ Overseas package holidays and how they have changed

Inspired by Vladamir Raitz's use of chartered flights as part of holiday packages, other tour operators began to offer similar products. By the early 1960s package holidays to Mediterranean destinations were becoming more commonplace. These were predominantly to the Spanish coastline and Balearic islands; however Italy, Greece and a number of smaller islands such as Malta and Corsica welcomed 'mass market' holidaymakers. Passed in 1969, the Development of Tourism Act coordinated and gave a voice to the different organisations operating in the UK travel and tourism sector.

Take it further

Can you think of any disadvantages relating to the growth of mass market tourism? Research the negative impact of mass market tourism on the environment and the people that live in host resorts.

Case study

The Costa del Sol, translated as 'coast of the sun', is a coastal region in the south of Spain. The Costa del Sol is located between the less well known Costa de la Luz and Costa Tropical. The Costa del Sol includes the city of Malaga and the resort towns of Marbella, Torrox and Fuengirola. Before the development of mass tourism most of the population lived in small fishing villages that were dotted along the coastline. The area was initially developed for tourism in the 1950s and has since grown to become one of the most popular Mediterranean destinations for foreign tourists.

1 What made the Costa del Sol so suitable for visitors from the UK?

2 What have been the main benefits of tourism for the Costa del Sol?

3 Do you think that the Costa del Sol will remain a popular destination for tourists in the future?

Key terms

Bespoke – means custom made or tailored to a buyer's needs and demands.

Long-haul travel – typically refers to destinations that take six hours or longer to reach by air.

Such overseas package holidays were considered by some to focus on low price rather than quality. Demand increased from more wealthy customers for a more '**bespoke**' experience. At the same time developments in technology allowed aircraft to fly further distances in shorter times. This enabled the development of **long-haul** tourism to exotic destinations such as the Caribbean.

▶ Different types of holidays

How have changing customer needs impacted on the different types of holiday that are now available?

All-inclusive

All-inclusive holidays offer the holidaymaker flights, accommodation and services and products, such as the inclusion of food and drink within the selected resort, for a set price. These holidays are popular because they enable the consumer to budget for the holiday, knowing that they will not have to spend too much money at the selected resort. However, all-inclusive holidays are not always beneficial for the host community. There is little motivation for the tourist to leave the resort and experience the local culture, so local businesses do not really benefit.

Long-haul

Long-haul destinations are at least a six-hour flight away from the UK. Some of the most popular long-haul destinations are located in North and South America, Australasia and the Caribbean, as well as many islands in Pacific and Indian Oceans.

All of the major tour operators offer long-haul travel provision; however, some long-haul travel is coordinated by specialist tour operators benefiting from extensive knowledge of tourism opportunities in certain parts of the world. Due to its expense, long-haul travel is often associated with special events such as weddings and honeymoons.

Cruising

The 1950s saw a shift in operations from liner voyages to enormous, purpose-built cruise ships. Initially, one of the main problems was that many of the smaller seaports within areas such as the Mediterranean could not accommodate the huge cruise ships, so cruises were limited to a number of larger ports. However, in the 1980s and 1990s developments in marine technology combined with changing demand from consumers facilitated the construction of smaller, more streamlined cruise ships. Today, the most popular cruise areas for UK tourists are the Mediterranean, Scandinavia and the Caribbean.

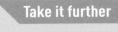

Take it further

Research the types of short city breaks that are now available for customers from the UK. Classify them as:

- UK
- continental Europe
- worldwide.

Travel Agents

Multiples

The term '**multiple**' refers to a travel agency that has more than 50 branches. The majority of travel agents are part of a multiple chain. Well-known examples of multiples include Thomas Cook and TUI.

A '**miniple**' is a travel agent that has between five and fifty branches. Those with fewer than five branches are known as 'independents'. Most multiples, miniples and independents operate on the high street and/or online.

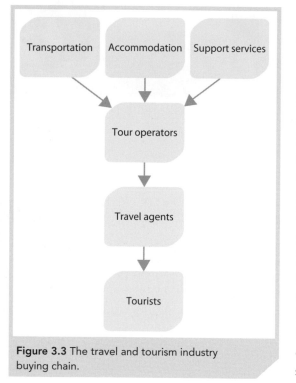

Figure 3.3 The travel and tourism industry buying chain.

Products and services

Travel agents offer a number of products and services for different types of customer, including leisure tourists and business tourists. Figure 3.3 highlights that traditionally travel agents acted as a link between the customer and the tour operator. Although this is still the case, most travel agents also offer flights, rail, ferry and coach bookings independent of tour operators. Travel agents offer an important service to customers who might need advice about the suitability of destinations and potential travel in relation to their needs. They also provide a range of other services such as travel insurance, advice about immunisation and booking airport parking.

One function that a high street travel agent provides that an internet-based travel agent could not is ancillary services that involve physical products such as currency exchange. Also travel agents display physical copies of tour operator's brochures. For some customers who do not have internet access, this is the only way for them to find out about holiday products. However, producing physical copies of brochures is extremely inefficient, equating to a cost of around £20 for every holiday sold. Electronic brochures available online provide a more cost-effective alternative to printed copies; furthermore they can be amended to reflect changes in costs and the products and services available.

Tour operators

Tour operators organise different components of a holiday which include the 'principles' of transport, accommodation, transfers and activities. Traditionally tour operators sold their holiday products via high street travel agents; however, it is more profitable for them to sell directly to the customer using direct advertising in magazines, call-centres and the internet. Television-based Teletext was also an important outlet for tour operators to advertise their products until it ceased operation in 2010; however the actual organisation Teletext still exists online.

Mergers between tour operators along the chain of distribution

The chain of distribution represents how holiday principals are 'packaged' by the tour operator and distributed to the customer. Along the chain of distribution, larger tour operators seek to merge with other tour operators to increase market share.

This is known as 'horizontal integration'. Along with increasing market share for tour operators, horizontal integration can also increase profitability.

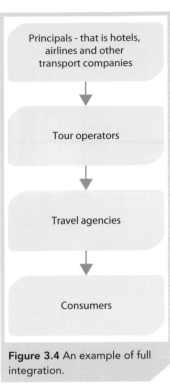

Principals - that is hotels, airlines and other transport companies

↓

Tour operators

↓

Travel agencies

↓

Consumers

Figure 3.4 An example of full integration.

Case study

A recent example of horizontal integration occurred when Thomas Cook, the Co-operative Group and the Midlands Co-operative agreed a merger in 2011, operating under the Thomas Cook brand. Thomas Cook estimated that the merger would save the company around £35 million a year.

1 What are the benefits of horizontal integration for Thomas Cook?

2 What might the negatives of Thomas Cook's horizontal integration be for the wider travel and tourism sector?

Some larger tour operators also seek to merge with, or take over, organisations operating at different levels along the chain of distribution. This is known as vertical integration. Vertical integration can be backwards (upstream), or forwards (downstream). Vertical integration allows tour operators to control all aspects of the holiday, save costs and pass on savings to the customer. A recent example of vertical integration is when in 2009 TUI AG began to operate TUI Cruises through a merger with Royal Caribbean cruises.

▷ Decline and rebranding of coastal resorts

In the 19th century it was perceived that bathing in saltwater promoted health and well-being; towards the end of the century the middle and working classes became more prosperous. Increases in disposable income for the middle and working classes, combined with more leisure time and development of railway transportation, helped to facilitate the growth of the British seaside resort.

Decline

Resorts such as Blackpool boomed between the 1870s and 1950s. However, after the 1950s and 1960s many British seaside resorts began to experience decline. After the Second World War disposable income increased, as did paid annual leave. As the middle and working classes again became more prosperous, their demand for a different type of holiday experience was met by the introduction of foreign package tours. Resorts such as Blackpool could not offer the same experience as a foreign package tour, not least because of the unreliability of the weather in the UK. Resorts such as Blackpool did attract some private investment into upgrading facilities during the 1960s and 1970s but this was not enough to halt the decline. Blackpool had lost much of its family holiday appeal compared to foreign resorts and came to rely on day visitors and the stag/hen party business, which contributed to the negative image of the town.

Rebranding

However, compared to other UK resorts Blackpool did have some unique historical attractions such as the Blackpool Tower and illuminations, which first began in 1879. Linked to this, research by English Heritage shows that many people consider British seaside resorts have nostalgic appeal and historical character. Resorts have tried to capitalise on this resurgence in appeal by attempting rebranding activities,

Take it further

Locate promotional material for at least two different British seaside resorts. Look carefully at how each destination is promoted. Compare the different appeal of each destination.

Can you find any other examples of a UK seaside resort rebranding itself?

including the production of glossy promotional materials. Southport, located along the Lancashire coast, has recently invested heavily in literature that promotes the resort as a 'cosmopolitan hub' offering historical attractions, vibrant nightlife, upmarket bars and restaurants and a range of natural features.

▶ Technological developments

Computer reservation systems

Before the introduction of computer reservation systems (CRS) in the 1960s, flight bookings were organised manually using office wall charts. This method was usually fairly accurate, but not completely secure; damage to a chart could lead to booking details being lost.

CRS provided up-to-date and reliable information about available flights and most appropriate routes. The system also meant that more complex bookings requiring more than one flight could operate effectively. Other bookings such as other forms of transport and accommodation could be made using CRS.

The internet

Take it further

Pick a place in the UK to visit for a weekend and use a site such as TripAdvisor to plan your trip in detail.

The internet has revolutionised many aspects of our lives, not least how we access travel and tourism-related products and services. Without having to leave their home, customers now have instant access to information about travel, accommodation, activities, prices and availability. Using the internet to access travel and tourism orientated products and services allows customers to save money and customise the holiday experience. Mass internet use in the 1990s coincided with the deregulation of European airspace and the creation of the low-cost airline.

Dynamic packaging

Dynamic packaging is when the customer organises their own travel, accommodation and holiday activities without the use of a third party travel agent. This allows customers greater control to design a holiday that meets their needs and also save money by booking the different elements of the holiday directly from the supplier rather than from a travel agent. Like other retail chains, many high street travel agents have struggled to compete with internet services and have closed down. In 2013, Thomas Cook announced that they were to close 195 high street travel agents in the UK.

Just checking

1 What was the Grand Circular Tour?
2 Why did many British seaside resorts suffer decline during the mid to late 20th century?
3 What is the difference between horizontal and vertical integration?
4 Why do some customers prefer to use the internet over high street travel agents to book products and services?

TOPIC A2

Developments in transportation

Introduction

Transport enables people to access different places; without developments in transportation the UK travel and tourism sector would not exist. What are the key developments in rail, sea, air and road transportation that have enabled the UK travel and tourism sector to grow into the dynamic, ever changing industry that we see today?

Rail transportation

Thanks to a plentiful, cheap supply of coal, rail travel became more affordable from around 1840 onwards. Excursion trains facilitated the mass movement of people to popular destinations and events; Thomas Cook organised for around 165,000 people to attend the Great Exhibition of 1851 at the Crystal Palace in London. Rail networks provided an important link between popular destinations and urban centres. One-off events like the Great Exhibition of 1851 aside, seaside resorts were undoubtedly the most popular types of destination, for example in the 1890s Blackpool could accommodate up to 250,000 visitors at a time by railway; three million annually. In response to demand from holidaymakers, seaside resorts began to develop attractions such as piers, theatres, peep shows and amusement arcades.

The UK rail network was privatised in the mid 1990s in an attempt to make the rail sector more competitive and profitable and also to improve service efficiency for customers. Now Network Rail owns and operates Britain's rail infrastructure. Network Rail's main customers are from the private sector, known as Train Operating Companies (TOCs); they include Virgin Trains, Arriva and ScotRail.

Modern rail provides a faster alternative to car travel. Virgin Trains operate a high speed service from Manchester Piccadilly to London Euston in around two hours. According to the RAC route planner, the same journey by car would take over four hours. In January 2012 the government announced that a high speed rail network known as HS2 would be introduced in 2026 to connect Birmingham to London. At an estimated cost of £33 billion, the scheme is controversial; wildlife groups have warned that the development could cause damage to at least 160 important wildlife sites.

Pendolino

The first Pendolino tilting train was introduced in the UK by Virgin in 2002, at a cost of f11 million. Pendolino trains are capable of reaching London in around four and a half hours from Glasgow. The trains reach speeds of up to 135 mph on some sections of railway. Pendolino trains have a special tilting mechanism that enables them to travel at higher speeds around corners providing a more comfortable experience for customers.

Eurostar

In 1987 the governments of Britain and France agreed to build an underground rail tunnel to connect the two countries. After many delays

? Did you know?

The government-led process of awarding contracts for rail operations to TOCs made the headlines in August 2012 when the contract for operating the West Coast Main Line was awarded to First Group rather than the existing service provider, Virgin Trains.

It was later discovered that mistakes had been made during the consideration of the bids, and Virgin Trains were temporarily reinstated to operate the West Coast Main Line.

How has Eurostar changed the way we travel to continental Europe?

the Channel Tunnel was finally opened in May 1994. The rail service that currently works the Channel Tunnel route is Eurostar. Eurostar first began operating a cross-channel service in November 1994 between Waterloo International station in London to Gare du Nord in Paris and Brussels-South railway station in Brussels. In September 2007, a high speed Eurostar service broke a crossing speed record when it reached London St Pancras from Paris Gare du Nord in 2 hours 3 minutes and 39 seconds.

▶ Sea transportation

Superferries

Stena Line has recently invested £375 million in two state of the art superferries. The Stena Hollandica was launched in May 2010 and the Stena Britannica was launched in October 2010. Both ferries were introduced to meet increased demand on the Harwich – Hook of Holland route in the North Sea. The new superferries offer 30 per cent more capacity with 5.5 km of vehicle deck space, including spaces for 230 cars, 300 freight vehicles and 1,376 beds in 538 cabins.

Case study

The Costa Concordia entered service in July 2006. Built in Italy, the ship measured just over 290 metres long and cost £372 million to build. On the night of 13th January 2012 the Costa Concordia partially sank after colliding with a reef off the coast of Isola del Giglio. The ship's captain, Francesco Schettino, had attempted a 'close sail' past the island, rather than following the predetermined electronic route. After the ship was grounded, Captain Schettino was accused of abandoning ship and leaving the 3,206 passengers and 1,023 crew and personnel to fend for themselves. In total, 32 people died in the disaster.

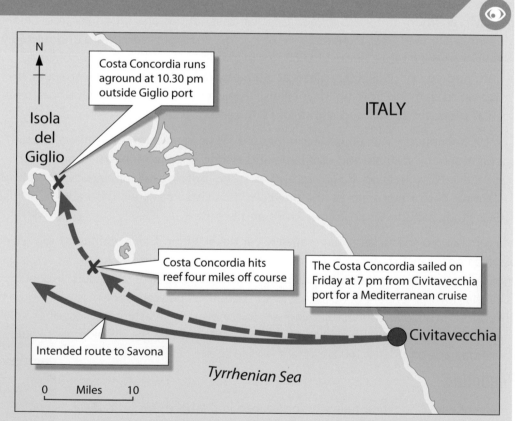

Costa Concordia runs aground at 10.30 pm outside Giglio port

ITALY

Isola del Giglio

Costa Concordia hits reef four miles off course

The Costa Concordia sailed on Friday at 7 pm from Civitavecchia port for a Mediterranean cruise

Intended route to Savona

Civitavecchia

Tyrrhenian Sea

0   Miles   10

1 Why do you think the captain deviated from the set route?

2 What do you think the impact of this incident was for Costa Cruises, the operator of the Costa Concordia?

Cruise ship developments

Reflecting the growing demand from consumers for cruise holidays; there have been nine or more purpose-built cruise ships, all at least 100,000 tonnes, introduced since 2001. The Queen Mary 2 (QM2) was introduced by Cunard in 2004. Operating as both an ocean liner and cruise ship, the QM2 is capable of speeds up to 28.5 knots, with a carrying capacity for over 2,500 passengers and 1,250 crew. The largest passenger ship between 2004 and 2006, the QM2 was surpassed for size and carrying capacity by Royal Caribbean International's Freedom class liners in 2006. In 2009 and 2010 Royal Caribbean introduced the Oasis class vessel which is currently the largest cruise liner in operation.

This continual growth within the sector highlights that many different market segments demand cruise package tours. Early cruises in the 1950s were relatively long and expensive and seen as the preserve of the upper and middle classes. However, today many tour operators offer shorter cruises that are much more affordable, for example in 2012 Thomas Cook offered a two-night December cruise to the Mediterranean for £240 per person. Other tour operators offer family friendly cruises, for example Disney offer a number of cruises around the Caribbean.

P&O Cruises

Formed in 1837 as the Peninsular Steam Navigation Company, P&O Cruises is one of the most well known brands in cruise operations. P&O offer cruises to 90 different countries which are marketed as offering a 'cosmopolitan British' experience with the backdrop of a foreign destination. They currently operate seven cruise ships with a total passenger capacity of 14,970 and a 5 per cent market share of the global cruise industry. The most recent vessel, the MV Adonia, officially entered service in May 2011. At 30,000 tonnes the MV Adonia is the smallest of the seven ships operated by P&O Cruises.

▶ Air transportation

Aircraft technology

Introduced in 1936, the American-built Douglas DC-3 operated as a military aircraft for the USA during the Second World War and also provided commercial flights transporting customers internally within the country. Becoming the first aircraft to make a profit operating commercial flights, the Douglas DC-3 was also used by Vladamir Raitz for his first UK foreign package tour to Corsica. In relation to these achievements, the Douglas DC-3 is considered to be one of the most important commercial aircraft in the history of aviation.

Currently the largest commercial airliner in operation is the Airbus A380. Entering the commercial market in 2007, the Airbus A380 has four engines, twin aisles, a double deck and a maximum carrying capacity of 853 seats in an all-economy service.

Looking beyond growing carrying capacity, recent technological developments allow aircraft to fly further, faster and with improved fuel efficiency. This is particularly important as airline profits are closely linked to ever fluctuating oil prices. In the UK travel and tourism sector demand for commercial flights has increased over the past ten years.

Link

See *Unit 2: UK Travel and Tourism Destinations* for information about air and sea gateways, and the UK transport system.

Figure 3.5 Why has demand for regional airports increased in the UK?

Growth of low-cost airlines

After the deregulation of European airspace in the 1990s, a number of entrepreneurs, such as the Ryan family, founders of Ryanair, and Sir Stelios Haji-Ioannou, founder of easyJet, saw the potential of offering low-cost flights as an alternative to 'full service' airlines. Predominantly offering short-haul European flights, low-cost airlines offer the consumer the opportunity to purchase the flight directly from the airline often via the internet. As a travel agent is not involved in the transaction, the airline is able to retain a greater share of the profit and pass savings on to the customer. However, the 'hidden' charges associated with low-cost airlines have been well documented in recent years, as most low-cost airlines:

- charge the customer extra for food, drink, and in-flight entertainment
- operate extra charges to reserve seats
- charge for any baggage which goes in the aircraft hold.

Growth of airports

The development of the low-cost airline sector has facilitated the growth of regional airports for commercial flights. Regional airports are generally located within or close to cities and larger towns, such as Leeds, Exeter, Newquay, Bristol and Blackpool.

Activity 3.2 Comparing developments in aircraft technology

A major rival to Douglas was Boeing. In 1954 the Boeing 707 was introduced although it did not enter the commercial market until 1959. With a higher carrying capacity than its main rivals (the Douglas DC-8 and de Havilland Comet) the Boeing 707 became the market leader. Realising that one key to profitability in commercial aviation was carrying capacity, Boeing introduced a new larger airline in 1960 – the Boeing 727. In 1970 the Boeing 747 double decker 'jumbo jet' began commercial operations. With room for 450 passengers, the Boeing 747

held the record for passenger carrying capacity for 37 years.

1 How might rivalries, such as that between Douglas de Havilland and Boeing, benefit customers?

2 Research the fortunes of these three organisations. Which has been the most successful? Why do you think this is?

3 What do you think future developments in aircraft technology will look like?

Low-cost airlines tend to offer more flights from smaller regional airports to keep operating costs to a minimum. Another advantage of this is that consumers no longer rely on a few, larger airports; regional airports are often less busy and offer a more personalised service than bigger airports. In terms of growth, regional airports have expanded at a faster rate than larger airports over the last few years. The issues surrounding the proposed expansion of Heathrow are well documented within the media. Already the largest airport in the UK, proposals for further expansion of Heathrow have been met with objection from a range of stakeholders including local residents, environmental campaign groups and MPs. Alternative proposals to the expansion of Heathrow include the development of a new airport in the River Thames estuary.

Link

Find out more about Heathrow's expansion in *Unit 1: The UK Travel and Tourism Sector*.

▶ Road transportation

Low-cost intercity

Low-cost intercity bus travel offers a cheaper alternative to rail travel between towns and cities in the UK. The market leader in low-cost intercity bus companies is Megabus. Megabus launched operations in the UK in 2003 and currently serves more than two million passengers a year. Easybus, also launched in 2003, is another low-cost intercity bus service that specialises in travel between London destinations and Luton, Gatwick and Stansted airports.

Luxury coaches

A number of organisations within the UK travel and tourism sector offer luxury coach travel services. National Express, Shearings and Archers Direct are amongst the larger providers of luxury coach travel, operating routes both within the UK and to continental Europe. Smaller, specialist firms such as The Kings Ferry offer bespoke luxury coaches for hire, that include aircraft-style seating, air conditioning, tinted windows, kitchen/refrigerator, DVD players and filter coffee machines. They also offer helicopters and limousines.

Why do you think the maintenance of public transport systems is so important to a city's reputation as a tourist destination?

Congestion charging and road tolls

The London Congestion charge became operational within the Congestion Charge Zone (CCZ) in February 2003. The congestion charges were introduced as a traffic management strategy aimed at reducing congestion in London city centre and improving environmental conditions, particularly air quality. Almost half of the revenue generated via congestion charge is spent on operating and enforcing the charge system. However, all remaining revenue, by law, is spent on maintaining and developing London's public transport infrastructure.

The M6 toll road opened in 2003, connecting M6 junction 4 at the NEC Birmingham to M6 junction 11A at Wolverhampton with 27 miles of motorway. The idea behind the toll road was to alleviate congestion on the M6 around the Birmingham area. This busiest section of the M6 was designed to carry 72,000 cars a day; before the introduction of the toll road, it was carrying up to 180,000 cars a day.

Europcar

Europcar is a global leader in car hire with over 3,300 car hire stations throughout Europe, Africa, the Middle East, Latin America and Asia Pacific. Europcar provides a range of different types of vehicles for rental including standard cars, luxury cars, minivans and trucks. Europcar also offers airport services whereby the customer can collect their hire vehicle directly from the airport.

Hertz

The original company was founded in Chicago, USA by Walter L. Jacobs in 1918. In 1923 Jacobs sold his company to John D. Hertz who renamed the company 'Hertz Drive-Ur-Self System'. Today, Hertz offers a range of vehicle rental services including Hertz Rent a Car, Hertz local edition, Hertz Car Sales and Hertz Truck and Van Rental. They also offer a 'green collection' of environmentally friendly vehicles such as the Toyota Prius and they also operate a 'car sharing' rental scheme, where people are able to rent cars by the hour as and when they need access to a car. The idea behind car sharing is that it cuts down on the number of people that actually need to own a car.

Just checking

1 What is a Pendolino?
2 Who are the biggest operators in the cruise sector?
3 Why have regional airports grown in demand?
4 What are the main benefits of having congestion charges and toll roads?

▶ Developments in legislation

Introduction

Legislation impacts upon our daily lives. Although legislation is sometimes perceived to constrain our freedoms, without it we would be open to exploitation. Can you think of three examples of how legislation has improved people's lives both in the past and the present?

▶ Working Time Regulations

The 2003 Working Time Regulations legislate for workers within the European Union to be entitled to a minimum number of days' holiday each year, paid breaks from work and rest of at least 11 hours within any 24-hour period. Also the maximum working week should be no more than 48 hours in seven days, although in the UK it is possible for people to opt out of this regulation and to work for more hours. As excessive working time can cause stress, depression and illness, the main aims of the 2003 Working Time Regulations are to ensure the health and safety of workers and improve general working conditions for those employed within the European Union.

Package Travel, Package Holidays and Package Tours Regulations

These regulations were created in 1992 in response to an EU directive to standardise consumer rights when booking package holidays and related products. The regulation improved the rights of consumers by legislating against tour operators:

- providing misleading descriptions of products and services
- making changes to agreed prices.

The regulations also gave the consumer the right to cancel the holiday and protected them in the event of the failure of the travel company.

To ensure the financial protection of consumers, the regulations stipulate that all travel agents and tour operators selling package holidays must purchase security bonds. This is an essential condition of membership for the Association of British Travel Agents (ABTA) and the Air Travel Organisers' Licencing (ATOL).

Equality Act

The Equality Act of 2010 provides overarching anti-discrimination legislation applicable within the UK. Although previous acts of parliament covered the key areas of equal pay, sex discrimination and race relations, the Equality Act of 2010 now provides definitive legislation that all people are treated equally. Specifically this act requires equal treatment in access to employment and public and private services, regardless of age, disability, gender, marriage or civil partnership status, race, religion or belief, sex and sexual orientation. The act also legislates for employers and service providers to make their premises accessible to people with disabilities. Also pregnant women are afforded certain rights and protections.

Activity 3.3 — Negotiating employment rights

By law employers have to comply with the requirements of legislation that is applicable to their organisation. However, the government has suggested that organisations should be allowed to negotiate with employees to exchange certain employment rights for shares in the company in which they work.

1 What might the benefits of such a scheme be for organisations?
2 What might the benefits of such a scheme be for employees?
3 What might the problems of implementing legislation be for smaller organisations?

Data Protection Act

The Data Protection Act was introduced in 1998 to protect the personal data of living people residing within the UK. In practice the act has been difficult to implement because of its complexity and the need to balance the protection of data with factors such as national security. In relation to the UK travel and tourism sector, organisations have to ask permission from individuals before sharing information for marketing and sales purposes.

Aviation regulations

The Civil Aviation Authority (CAA) is an independent regulator with responsibility for the UK aviation sector. The CAA monitors that travel organisers sell holidays and flights that are 'fit for purpose'. The CAA also regulates the Air Travel Organisers' Licencing (ATOL) which is required by all tour operators that include flights as part of a package holiday. As part of the ATOL agreement the CAA require that organisations purchase a security bond. If a firm collapses, like XL in 2008, the CAA will use the bond to fund arrangements for the customers to finish their holiday, or where appropriate offer a refund.

Assessment activity 3.1

You have been asked by a local travel organisation to produce a presentation which evaluates and explores the developments that have helped to shape the UK travel and tourism sector. To lead to your conclusion you will divide your presentation into three sections.

- A section focusing on developments such as early package holidays and tours, mass market and specialist holidays, different types of holidays, travel agents and tour operators, decline and rebranding of coastal resorts and technological developments.

- A section showing that you understand how developments in rail, sea, air and road transportation have helped to shape the UK travel and tourism sector. Consider the importance of transport in relation to holiday provision.

- A section exploring how developments in UK and international legislation have affected the UK travel and tourism sector.

Tips

- For each section, discuss the positive and negative aspects of each development, including how and why they have helped to shape the sector and consider any further improvements or developments that you think could be made within the UK travel and tourism sector.

- Include a conclusion in which you consider the overall effect of developments within the sector and offer your own opinion about which developments you feel have had the biggest impact and why.

Learning aim B   **TOPIC**   **B1**

▶ Lifestyle changes

Introduction

Lifestyles are very different now compared to a century ago. Developments in working-time directed legislation and domestic technology mean that people are enjoying more leisure time than ever before. Can you think of three reasons why lifestyle changes have influenced the development of the UK travel and tourism sector?

▶ Increase in paid holidays

Did you know?

The initial week long holiday experienced by workers in Victorian mills and factories only came about because operations were shut down for a week in the summer to allow for essential maintenance work to be carried out; however, these holidays were almost always without pay. Why do think these mill and factory owners did not usually give holiday pay?

Prior to 1871, the majority of the working class population experienced almost no leisure time away from work. Most people experienced a six-day working week with Sundays off. However, as a holy day, it was expected that people visit church at least twice on a Sunday. Some more benevolent employers allowed their workers extra holy days off, such as Easter and possibly Christmas; however, there was no legislation to enforce this as consistent practice. Due to pressure from Victorian lobbyists Parliament introduced:

- the Bank Holiday Act in 1871
- the Holiday Extension Act in 1975.

As a result of this early legislation, the formalisation of organised holidays was beginning to occur. In the 1880s holiday clubs known as 'going off' clubs were formed in many Lancashire towns. Employers were beginning to recognise the value of allocating leisure time. In 1889 millworkers in Darwin and Oldham enjoyed a full week's holiday.

However, it was not until the 1938 Holidays with Pay Act that it became a legal obligation for organisations to allocate a minimum amount of time for employees to enjoy paid holidays. The onset of the Second World War in 1939 initially negated any benefits to be experienced by the masses as a result of this act.

After the Second World War, the UK travel and tourism sector experienced rapid growth at a far quicker rate than ever before. Initially, UK resorts experienced the most rapid growth; however, by the end of the 1960s the demand for foreign package tours was increasing. Further legislation such as the 1993 Working Time Directive has helped to ensure that today most UK employees receive at least four weeks' paid holiday a year.

Research where workers involved in saving schemes will have gone for their holidays.

▶ Flexible working patterns

Legislation introduced in 2006, the Work and Families Act, gives parents of children under 16, or disabled children under 18, the right to request flexible working arrangements. Furthermore, from April 2007 the right for maternity pay was extended from six months to nine months, with fathers gaining the right to request up to 26 weeks' additional paternity pay.

▶ More disposable income

It is a common misconception that all working class mine and mill workers employed in the 19th century were poorly paid. For example in the Lancashire cotton industry, wages were relatively high. As it was common for families with older children to all be in employment, they could pool their wages together and save for holidays via saving and mutual insurance schemes. In Oldham one such mutual saving scheme enabled a 'going off' club to enjoy a full week's holiday in the summer.

Since the Second World War there has been a steady increase in the amount of disposable income that people have to spend. However, it was reported by the Centre for Economics and Business research that families in 2011 were more than £3,000 a year worse off than in 2007, before the global economic recession started. This is as a result of a number of factors; wages in the public sector have been frozen since 2010, the cost of household essentials such as bread and milk have increased, petrol prices continue to increase and inflation is currently higher than the 2010 government target of 2 per cent. One main impact of this reduction in disposable income is that people have less money to spend on pursuing their leisure interests and going on holiday.

▶ Increased leisure time

As you are aware, various acts and directives have paved the way for people to enjoy more leisure time especially at weekends. However, developments in areas such as domestic technology have also been important. Labour-saving devices such as washing machines were introduced commercially in the 1930s, dishwashers with electric elements were introduced in the early 1940s and vacuum cleaners were popular in middle class homes towards the end of the 1940s.

▮▶ Increased second-home ownership

Second-home ownership is a controversial issue; it can push up house prices in areas popular with tourists, for example Castleton in the Peak District. This in turn can 'price' local people out of the housing market and lead to feelings of resentment towards second-home owners. Furthermore as second-home owners may only inhabit their second homes during holidays and possibly at weekends, local services such as pubs and shops may suffer from low volumes of business, particularly during the off-season when there are fewer day visitors.

Similar in principle to second-home ownership in terms of permanence, static caravan sites provide a more affordable alternative. Unlike second-home ownership, static caravan sites have little impact on local house prices; furthermore council tax charges ensure that caravan owners contribute to the local economy. Depending on residency arrangements, static caravan sites generally tend to operate on a seasonal basis. For example, Point Lynas Caravan Park in Anglesey operates from March through to December.

A luxury second home in the Cotswolds, an Area of Outstanding Natural Beauty (AONB). How does second-home ownership impact upon such areas?

▮▶ Use of technology to plan and arrange bookings

As you will be aware, internet access has revolutionised the way people access holiday products and services. Mass usage of the internet via personal computers (PCs) developed during the mid-to-late 1990s. Initially PCs held a monopoly on the way people accessed the internet; however, more recent technological developments have further broadened the way in which people access the internet. Media devices such as mobile telephones and tablet computers now provide people with instant, remote access to the internet. Previously, people could only access the internet from home or specialist facilities such as libraries and internet cafes. However, the development of 3G networks and universal broadband, for example via BT Openzone, means that more and more people have instant access to the internet to plan and arrange bookings. Many travel organisations, such as Thomas Cook, have introduced 'apps' which can be downloaded and used by the customer to find out specific information about the products and services that they offer and to make purchases.

Just checking

1 Why was the introduction of the Bank Holiday Act in 1871 significant for the UK travel and tourism sector?

2 Why do people spend less money on pursuing leisure interests and holidays during times of recession?

3 Can you explain three problems associated with second-home ownership?

4 Why might the way we access the internet today be described as 'dynamic' compared to the mid-to-late 1990s?

TOPIC B2

▮▶ Trends

Introduction

Consumer expectations of holiday products and services are ever changing and influenced by a multitude of external factors. To gain a competitive edge, the most successful organisations are dynamic and able to adapt their own products and services to meet the demands of consumers. Can you think of three impacts of organisations not being able to match their products and services to the demands of consumers?

▮▶ Niche market holidays

Sports tourism

Sports tourism generally involves the participation in sporting activities or the spectatorship of sporting events. The UK saw a huge influx of sports tourists in the summer of 2012 to watch the Olympic Games in London.

Case study

It had been predicted that an influx of tourists visiting Britain to watch the Olympics would boost tourism-related spending by £16.5 million. However, wary of the pressure on public transport systems, widespread publicity campaigns warned people of travelling to central London. As a result many shop and restaurant owners reported a drop in trade. Furthermore, the Office for National statistics reported that only 3.18 million trips were made to the UK in July 2012, compared to 3.36 visits in 2011.

1 Explain the reasons some people might have had for not travelling to central London during the 2012 Olympics.

2 Compare the positive and negative aspects of Olympic related tourism for;

a) London

b) Britain as a whole.

3 'The London Olympics will soon be forgotten; there will be no lasting legacy for tourism.' Discuss to what extent you agree or disagree with this statement.

How did the London Olympics impact upon visitor numbers to Britain in summer 2012?

Many tour operators offer specific sports tourism services; for example Thomas Cook Sport specialises in offering package tours to sporting events such as Champions League football.

There are five specific areas of sports tourism:

- **sports tourism attractions,** for example Old Trafford in Manchester
- **sports tourism resorts,** for example Carden Park near Wrexham, Wales
- **sporting tours,** for example the Australian cricket team tour of the UK
- **event-based sports tourism,** for example the 2012 London Olympics
- **adventure sport tourism,** for example pot-holing in the Peak District.

Safaris, adventure tourism and trekking

More active and adventurous forms of tourism such as safaris, adventure tourism and trekking have increased in popularity over recent years, particularly with certain market segments. As disposable income has generally been rising over recent years, particular groups, such as adult couples without children, have had more money to spend on these types of holidays.

Conservation tourism

Conservation tourism is about careful and planned tourism in fragile and precious areas that maintains the natural environment for future generations. One such area, the Galapagos Islands, was awarded protected status as the world's first United Nations Educational, Scientific and Cultural Organization (UNESCO) World Heritage Site in 1979. Tourists are allowed to visit under strict guidelines that are designed to protect and enhance the natural beauty of the Galapagos Islands. They arrive by small boats that stop at designated points around the islands. The boats are owned by local islanders, as is the accommodation; this ensures that the income generated from tourism stays within the local economy. Also for each visit the Galapagos Conservation Trust receives £25 towards protecting the local environment. Intentionally, the cost of touring the Galapagos Islands is expensive, as this helps to keep tourist numbers to a minimum, while maximising the amount of revenue generated for the local economy.

Pre-wedding holidays

There are many different types of pre-wedding holidays, including the bride and groom-to-be holidaying together in order to relax in anticipation of the wedding event or holidaying apart at destinations such as spa resorts. Increasingly popular are pre-wedding holidays that involve the families and friends staying in accommodation together for a period of time before the wedding event. Venues such as Pickwell Manor in Devon provide accommodation for large pre-wedding parties.

Cultural and heritage tourism

The Victorian-age industrial themes represented in the critically acclaimed London 2012 opening ceremony have focused attention on the many cultural and heritage attractions within the UK. Organisations such as the National Trust, English Heritage, Historic Scotland and the National Museum of Wales, specialise in operating and maintaining sites of cultural and heritage interest.

Case study

An operational coal mine between 1860 and 1980, Big Pit Colliery in Blaenavon, Torfaen, South Wales was opened to visitors from 1983, assisted with funding from the National Museum of Wales Amgueddfa Cymru – received in 2001 when Big Pit became part of the museum. The site offers interactive exhibitions and tours that highlight the experiences of Welsh coal miners between the industrial revolution and mid-to-late 20th century. The plight of younger mine workers is highlighted within the tours and pre-booked workshops exist where children are encouraged to

actively participate, by taking on similar job roles to enable them to empathise with the experience of working in a coal mine.

In 2000 the whole Blaenavon industrial landscape achieved recognition as a World Heritage Site; currently Big Pit Colliery is the most popular single attraction within the accredited area. Discussing the popularity of the Blaenavon industrial landscape, tourist Huw Rees commented 'the industrial landscape around the Blaenavon area is fascinating. My ancestors are originally from the area, so I decided to bring my family so that they could see what life would have been like working in a coal mine. The children loved visiting the Big Pit Colliery, although they found some aspects of it really frightening.'

1 Why are cultural and heritage attractions in the UK popular with tourists, especially since summer 2012?

2 Why do you think it is important to ensure that attractions include activities that are suitable for children?

3 Why is it important to share our industrial story with younger generations and people from other countries?

▶ Growth of low-cost airlines and availability of flights to more destinations

Initially low-cost airlines such as easyJet and Ryanair operated flights to major European cities. Seeing a market for offering 'no-frills' air travel, other airlines such as British Airways, Virgin and Monarch began to offer low-cost flights. Low-cost or 'light' fare flights now operate to long-haul destinations. For example in October 2012 Air France was offering return flights from London Heathrow to destinations such as Rio de Janeiro from £500, Hong Kong from £541 and Johannesburg from £552.

Although, the more well known low-cost flight operators are fully ATOL protected, it emerged in 2012 that some organisations have been operating low-cost return flights without full ATOL protection. One of the consequences of this for the customer is that if the organisation collapsed the customer would have no means of transport and no entitlement to alternative flights, refunds or compensation for costs incurred.

▶ Purpose-built resorts and themed destinations

Center Parcs

A purpose-built resort, the first UK Center Parc was opened in 1987 at Sherwood Forest in Nottingham. Center Parcs UK, a sister company of Center Parcs Europe, operate three further resorts in the UK at Elveden Forest in Suffolk, Longleat Forest in Wiltshire and Whinfell Forest in Cumbria.

The popularity of Center Parcs as an active destination that offers a range of outdoor pursuits and sports-based activities highlights the changing tastes of the UK consumer for a more active and adventurous holiday experience.

Disneyland Paris

Disneyland Paris, originally known as Disneyland resort was opened in Paris, France in April 1992 as only the second resort to operate outside of the USA. The resort includes two theme parks, seven hotels, and a retail and entertainment complex. In 2009 the resort received 15,405,000 visitors, making it the most visited themed attraction in Europe.

Case study

Part of Merlin Entertainments' portfolio, the Alton Towers Resort opened as a theme park in April 1980 and it is now the UK's No 1 theme park with some of the best rides in the world as well as two hotels – the Alton Towers Hotel and Splash Landings; an indoor waterpark, spa and conference centre. While Merlin does not release visitor numbers for individual attractions (they welcomed 55 million visitors worldwide in 2012), the Alton Towers Resort is one of their primary attractions and one of the top five attractions in the UK, with several million visitors every year. A report from industry research body TEA believes the Alton Towers Resort to be the most visited themed attraction in the UK and the ninth most visited themed attraction in Europe with 3 million visitors each year on year (Source Themed Entertainment Association and AECOM). The addition of hotels and other secondary attractions also underlines Merlin's strategy to spread visitor numbers across the year by developing each of its theme parks into short break destinations, reflecting changing holiday trends, and encouraging visitors to enjoy everything on offer by staying two to three days. The Alton Towers Resort is increasingly becoming one of the most popular family break destinations in the UK.

1 What is the appeal of Alton towers as a visitor attraction?

2 What are the benefits of Alton Towers incorporating hotels and a water park into its business operations?

3 Alton Towers is owned by Merlin Entertainments. Can you find out what other UK visitor attractions are owned by Merlin Entertainments?

WorkSpace

▷ Jessica Shaw

Tour Manager for AdventuringUK

I work as a tour manager for AdventuringUK. I am responsible for:

- developing domestic package holidays to a wide range of UK 'adventure' destinations
- designing exciting, flexible tour packages that meet the needs of our customers
- exploring and researching new destination opportunities
- communicating itinerary instructions to customers
- responding to queries and dealing with problems that may arise during a tour.

I find my job really rewarding and exciting. I love the research part of my job; one of my main roles is visiting different places in the UK and finding suitable destinations. It's great being able to accompany the holidaymakers on the trip; it means that I am there to help if anyone has any problems, but I also get to join in with the fun activities too!

AdventuringUK is a small tour operator that was established about 15 years ago in response to the demand for more active, adventurous holidays. When they first began operations, AdventuringUK employed four staff. I've been working here for five years and I have seen the business grow; we now employ 18 staff. Customers are really positive about their experiences; they often tell me that they would much prefer to be doing something active and exciting on a holiday rather than just lounging around in the sun.

To work in this industry you need to be highly motivated and flexible. When you are working away from home on a tour, you are effectively on call for 24 hours a day so you need to have good stamina! You also need to be friendly and good with people. Most of the customers are great, but when you do get the occasional customer moaning you have to be able to deal with them in a calm and considerate manner.

Think about it

1   Why do you think that demand for adventure holidays has increased over the last few years?

2   Can you think of any other types of holiday that have grown in demand over the last few years?

3   What would be the main demands of working such flexible shift patterns?

▶ Seaside resorts

Decline of traditional seaside resorts

The popularity of resorts or destinations is often dictated by changes in tastes and whether a resort is seen as 'in fashion'. A number of factors have influenced the fate of British seaside resorts, not least the emergence of relatively cheap foreign tours that were established in the 1950s and really took off in popularity towards the end of the 1960s. These circumstances triggered the decline in popularity of many seaside resorts such as Bognor Regis, Morecambe and Southport. Such resorts were publicised as unfashionable because of unreliable weather, outdated attractions, and because they appealed to an unfashionable clientele including 'undesirables' and older holidaymakers who enjoyed the nostalgic appeal of the traditional British seaside resort.

Regeneration

In recent years destinations that have experienced the most significant regeneration have tapped into the consumer needs and demands of a young, vibrant user group. Newquay in Cornwall has experienced regeneration as a result of its appeal as a watersports destination, and is particularly popular with surfers. A current trend in the UK travel and tourism sector is the growth of adventure destinations that support outdoor pursuits; this trend is reflected in the current popularity of Newquay. Brighton is another interesting example of a destination that has experienced regeneration.

> **Did you know?** ❓
>
> Unlike northern resorts like Blackpool that grew in response to demand from industrial workers from the 1850s onwards, Brighton had visits from the social elite and middle classes from the 1780s onwards due to its close proximity to London. Today Brighton appeals to many wealthy visitors from London. Brighton is well known as a tolerant destination, drawing on the cosmopolitan appeal of its many pubs, restaurants and bars.

Assessment activity 3.2   2B.P4 | 2B.P5 | 2B.M2 | 2B.M3 | 2B.D2

A new tour operator is trying to plan the holidays they will offer their customers and how they will offer them. They ask you to explore how changing lifestyles and trends have influenced the development of the travel and tourism sector in the UK. Your report should be split into two main parts.

- **Lifestyle:** explore how changes in working arrangements, including holidays and pay, have affected the way people take holidays. You should also consider the influence of other factors such as second-home ownership, the economy and how we use technology to organise holidays. In all, you will need to cover four lifestyle changes.

- **Trends:** show that you understand how trends have influenced the UK travel and tourism sector.

These trends include a growing demand for niche market holidays, low-cost airlines and the way other operators are offering 'light' fair flights, the availability of different types of holiday destination, and the decline and regeneration of seaside resorts. Again, you need to make sure that you cover four trends in your work.

In your work you need to show that you understand that there is a link between lifestyle changes and trends, for example how our use of computer technologies has influenced demand for niche market holidays. Also discuss how and why lifestyle changes and trends have had such a strong influence on the UK travel and tourism sector. In all you need to explore at least three linked developments.

Tips

- Use information from travel articles, data and statistics to support your ideas.
- Keep a note of all of the sources of information you have used and include a list of these with your finished work.

▶ Issues

Introduction

In an ever-changing unpredictable world, many issues, both national and international, potentially impact upon the UK travel and tourism sector. Widespread flight and holiday cancellations to North America in 2012 as a result of Hurricane Sandy highlights the susceptibility of the UK travel and tourism to external events. Can you think of three issues that have occurred over the last five years that have had an impact upon the UK travel and tourism sector?

▶ Economic issues

Collapse of airlines

Changing consumer demand as a result of the economic recession in Europe has contributed to the collapse of a number of European airlines in 2012, including Hungarian airline Malev and Spain's fourth largest airline Spanair.

Collapse of tour operators

Tour operators have also been affected by the economic recession; in September 2008 XL, the UK's third largest tour operator at the time, collapsed.

Case study

FlyGlobespan, a major UK-based airline, ceased trading in December 2009. After the collapse, around 4,500 UK passengers were left stranded, mostly in Spain, Portugal and Cyprus. The Civil Aviation Authority (CAA) took on responsibility as part of a bonding agreement to ensure that customers were repatriated safely without incurring extra costs.

1 Why do you think a number of European airlines have experienced difficulties?

2 Why do you think other European airlines such as Ryanair are trading successfully?

3 How would you feel if you were left stranded abroad because of the collapse of an airline?

More recently, in August 2011, Holidays 4 UK collapsed. The company specialised in travel from the UK to Turkey. The collapse affected approximately 12,800 holidaymakers in Turkey at the time and a further 20,000 holidaymakers who had made future bookings. The difficulties experienced by the company were blamed on the results of the economic downturn faced by the travel industry as a whole in 2010 and 2011. Again, the CAA took on responsibility to ensure that customers were repatriated as quickly as possible.

Oil/fuel prices

In summer 2011 the International Air Transport Association (IATA) cut its profit forecast to $4 billion for the whole airline industry as a direct result of rising oil prices. In 2010 the airline industry made a profit of $18 billion, partly because oil prices had fallen dramatically from over $125 a barrel in summer 2008 to around $40 in early 2009 because of the global economic recession. However, a global recovery from mid-2009 onwards, combined with disruptions in supply from countries with significant oil reserves, such as Libya in early 2011, contributed to a steady rise in oil prices peaking at about $120 a barrel in spring 2011. These figures highlight the volatility in the price of oil and the impact that the price of oil has on the profitability of airline operations. Aside from passing on increases in costs to the customer, airlines are constantly looking to make flights more economical and cost effective. Boeing have recently adapted their 737 aircraft to allow for more seating; therefore increasing the carrying capacity of the airline while using the same amount of fuel.

Fluctuating currency rates

Greece and other European countries like Ireland, Portugal, Italy and Spain accumulated significant debts to fuel spending on growth projects after the introduction of the Euro in 1999. However, many financial experts felt these debts were unsustainable; the Eurozone currency crisis was triggered in May 2010 as a result of fears that Greece would imminently default on its debt to banks located across Europe. In order to restore confidence in the Euro currency, several bail-out packages for countries have since been arranged and the European Central Bank has now committed unlimited funds to backing the Euro currency. As a result of this uncertainty the Euro currency has fluctuated quite wildly in value since 2010.

Furthermore, the issue of currency fluctuations causes huge challenges for tour operators when setting the prices of holidays. Tour operators usually pay the costs of accommodation, transport and transfer costs in the host resort's currency. Therefore they have to 'price in' currency fluctuations when deciding on what to charge for a particular holiday product. Fluctuations in **currency exchange rates** can make the holiday more or less profitable for the tour operator.

> ### Key term
>
> **Currency exchange rate** – also known as foreign exchange rate, is the rate at which one currency can be exchanged for another.

▶ Environmental issues

Climate change

Climate change is a controversial issue for the UK travel and tourism sector. It is well documented in the media that the carbon footprint left by airlines has contributed to global warming. Many destinations around the world that are visited by UK holidaymakers are located in low-lying coastal areas. It is predicted that if global warming continues, the polar ice caps will melt and consequently sea levels will rise, potentially submerging low-lying coastal destinations.

Natural disasters

Tourism infrastructure is extremely susceptible to natural disasters. In 2010 an ash cloud created by a volcanic eruption in Iceland plunged the European and global airline sector into chaos when flights were cancelled as a safety precaution. It was initially feared that any aircraft coming into contact with the ash cloud could potentially suffer from engine failure as the ash particles would melt when ingested into the engine causing the engine to stall. In UK airports holidaymakers were left unable to take their flights and UK holidaymakers abroad were left stranded. In total around 1,000 flights were cancelled, 10 million people were stranded and the cost to airlines was estimated at £1.7 billion. Some of the major airlines such as British Airways and Ryanair challenged the safety precautions as being a major overreaction. British Airways operated a test flight into 'red zone' high density ash over Scotland and northern England for 45 minutes at different altitudes and reported no problems at all.

▶ Political issues

Civil unrest

In December 2010, a Tunisian street vendor Mohamed Bouazizi set himself on fire in protest to the way he was treated by Tunisian government representatives. This act

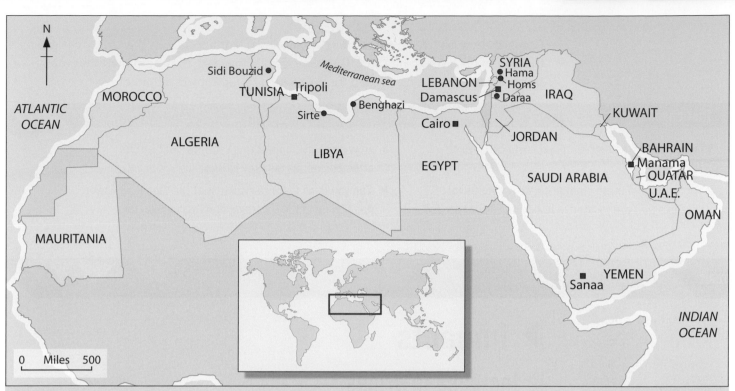

Figure 3.6 A map showing the key countries and cities involved in the 'Arab Spring' uprisings. How did these impact on travel and tourism across North Africa and the Middle East?

triggered a series of uprisings across North Africa and the Middle East; events collectively known as the 'Arab Spring'. The uprisings helped to force leadership change in Tunisia, Egypt, Libya and Yemen. These events have had significant impacts on travel and tourism.

War on terrorism

Although the war on terrorism began after the 9/11 attacks in 2001 with a particular focus on eradicating al-Qaeda, there have been many incidents of the terrorist group plotting and carrying out attacks on western tourists. In November 2012, the Foreign & Commonwealth Office raised the terror threat level in Egypt from 'general' to 'high' in response to a foiled al-Qaeda plan to attack holidaymakers from Europe, including the UK.

▶ Social issues

Recession and unemployment

The rise in UK unemployment triggered by the global economic recession that began in 2007 highlights the sensitivity of the employment market to economic conditions. In October 2012 the UK unemployment rate stood at 2.5 million; significantly 1 million of these unemployed are classified as **NEET**. The social implications for these young people include family tensions, loss of housing, loss of confidence and self-esteem and increased likelihood of turning to crime. Significantly for the UK travel and tourism sector, in July 2012 leading tour and public bus operators including National Express, Stagecoach, First Group and Go-Ahead pledged to support NEETs by offering free or heavily discounted travel.

Demographics

The UK is increasingly becoming an **ageing population**. Certain regions of the UK such as East Devon already have a population **demographic** that is skewed towards more elderly residents. The spending power of the elderly consumer, known as the **grey pound**, is significant for the UK travel and tourism sector.

 Key terms

NEET – refers to young people not in employment, education or training.

Ageing population – when the average age within a population rises.

Demographic – a particular sector of the population.

Grey pound – refers to the economic spending power of pensioners.

Research by Age UK estimates that the money spent annually in the UK by people over the age of 65 is set to hit the £100 billion mark. However, they comment that many opportunities are being missed for businesses to tap into this market.

Just checking

1 What problems do rising fuel costs cause for airlines?

2 Why might climate change cause problems for resorts that are located in low-lying coastal areas?

3 How does civil unrest impact upon tourism to affected countries? Why is this?

4 Can you think of three effects that the global recession has had upon the UK travel and tourism sector?

▶ Impacts

▶ Increase in prices

Frequently, factors outside of the control of travel organisations can significantly impact upon the pricing of products and services. Fluctuating oil prices mean that airlines frequently have to adjust the prices of flights to reflect the price of oil. In February 2011, it was reported that airlines had already increased their air fares four times since the start of the year, compared to only three rises in the whole of 2010.

▶ Withdrawal of destinations

Holiday destinations are withdrawn from sale for a number of reasons. Of paramount importance for tour operators is the safety of holidaymakers. In 2011, as a result of civil unrest, tours to North African and Middle Eastern destinations including Tunisia and Egypt were temporarily withdrawn after the Foreign & Commonwealth Office advised that people refrain from visiting places where their safety could not be guaranteed. There were reports of sporadic attacks on tourists who remained in places like Tunisia. In one incident, a group of Swedish tourists in Tunisia were reportedly dragged from their taxi by a crowd of people, beaten and robbed of their possessions.

Another reason why a destination or resort may be withdrawn from sale is because of lack of demand. Between 1936 and 1966 nine Butlin's holiday camps were built at locations throughout the UK. During the 1980s and 1990s six of the nine camps were closed, with only those at Bognor Regis, Minehead and Skegness remaining open. Since then, some of the camps have reopened under different ownership, for example the Butlin's camp at Ayr was reopened in 1998 as a Haven Park.

▶ Repatriation of customers

Repatriation means to return to your original country. Recently, there have been a number of instances of the repatriation of customers by travel companies and the CAA for reasons of war, political unrest,

What are the main reasons why travel is disrupted? What are the impacts of disruption to travel for tourists?

pandemic outbreaks or economic reasons, including the collapse of tour operators and airlines.

▶ Disruption to travel

Disruption to travel can occur for many reasons including accidents, terror alerts, traffic congestion, strike action and natural events. In October 2012 Hurricane Sandy struck the Eastern seaboard of the USA, and as a result most flights between Saturday 27th October and Friday 2nd November were cancelled.

▶ Growth/decline in sales of travel and tourism products or services

Tourism makes an important contribution to the UK economy. The World Travel and Tourism Council is predicting the travel and tourism industry will expand its total contribution to UK gross domestic product (GDP) by 1.7 per cent in 2013, compared with overall growth of 0.6 per cent predicted for the wider economy (Source: WTTC and BBC). Sales of travel and tourism-related direct and indirect products and services are expected to contribute over £100 billion to the economy and generate 2.3 million jobs; 1 in 13 of all jobs in the UK (Source: WTTC).

However, from within the sector there are some sharp contrasts to this picture of growth. In January 2012 it emerged that Thomas Cook had seen a 33 per cent reduction in summer holiday bookings, reflecting the sales issues surrounding those organisations that had a large high street presence; consumers are becoming more and more inclined to purchase products and services online via the internet. Furthermore, in November of 2011 Thomas Cook requested funds of £100 million from the banks in order to secure the organisation from financial collapse. This impacted on sales because customers were fearful that the collapse of the organisation would lead to the cancellation of holiday products that had been paid for. Positively, in August 2012 Thomas Cook reported a surge in late bookings, as a result of the terrible weather conditions experienced n the UK throughout the summer months of 2012.

Did you know?

After Hurricane Sandy, in 2012, some insurance companies from the UK refused to refund travellers for cancelled flights, citing that the Foreign & Commonwealth Office (FCO) had not warned against travelling so any claims made were not eligible for a refund. What sort of publicity do you think this issue generated for the travel insurance sector?

Assessment activity 3.3

2C.P6 | 2C.M4 | 2C.D3

A new tour operator would also like to know about the current issues that are affecting the UK travel and tourism sector and their impacts and have asked you to produce another report. Your report should focus on one issue each of the following types.

- **Economic issues** e.g. the collapse of airlines, tour operators, fluctuating fuel prices and currency rates.

- **Environmental issues** e.g. climate change and natural disasters.

- **Political issues** e.g. civil unrest and the war on terrorism.

- **Social issues** e.g. recession, unemployment and demographics, such as the ageing population.

Tips

- For each issue that you explore, you must make clear links to the impacts on the UK travel and tourism sector, such as effects on prices, withdrawal of destinations, repatriation of customers, disruption of travel and the effects on sales of products and services.
- You should discuss how travel and tourism organisations are responding to the issues that you explore.
- Remember to reference the articles, data and statistics that you use to support your work.

Introduction

Who would have thought that we would ever be able to use the internet to view Earth from space and that within seconds we could zoom in to see street level scenes in Rome, Rio or virtually anywhere else that takes our fancy? Television programmes add another dimension, bringing the excitement of Las Vegas and the wonder of African safaris into our homes. We live in an age where international travel has become a possibility, even an expectation, for many people. Travel companies woo us with tempting offers for holidays around the world showing us that there is a whole wide world out there, just waiting for us to explore.

In this unit you will locate and investigate destinations around the world, learning about their features and their appeal to different types of visitors. You will plan routes and holidays to further develop your knowledge of international travel and tourism destinations.

Assessment: This unit will be assessed through a series of assignments set by your teacher/tutor.

Learning aims

In this unit you will:

A know the major international travel and tourism destinations and gateways

B investigate the appeal of international travel and tourism destinations to different types of visitor

C be able to plan international travel to meet the needs of visitors.

> I enjoy watching travel programmes on TV. One of my favourites was *Africa*. Seeing the landscapes, and the antics of all those animals, has really fired me up to go on an African safari sometime. That's definitely top of my list for the future.
>
> Christina, *16-year-old Travel and Tourism student*

International Travel and Tourism Destinations

4

BTEC Assessment Zone

This table shows you what you must do in order to achieve a **Pass**, **Merit** or **Distinction** grade, and where you can find activities in this book to help you.

Assessment and grading criteria			
Level 1	Level 2 Pass	Level 2 Merit	Level 2 Distinction
Learning aim A: Know the major international travel and tourism destinations and gateways			
1A.1 Locate three major gateways, from at least two different continents, with support.	**2A.P1** Locate six major gateways, from at least two different continents. **See Assessment activity 4.1, page 112**	**2A.M1** Explain four typical routes of air travel in relation to European and worldwide tourism. **See Assessment activity 4.1, page 112**	
1A.2 Locate one of each type of European and worldwide destination, with support.	**2A.P2** Locate two of each type of European and worldwide destination. **See Assessment activity 4.1, page 112**		
Learning aim B: Investigate the appeal of international travel and tourism destinations to different types of visitor			
1B.3 Outline three features that contribute to the appeal of one European and one worldwide destination, for one visitor type, with support.	**2B.P3** Describe three features that contribute to the appeal of one European and one worldwide destination, for two different visitor types. **See Assessment activity 4.2, page 118**	**2B.M2** Explain how the features contribute to the appeal of one European and one worldwide destination, for two different visitor types. **See Assessment activity 4.2, page 118**	**2B.D1** Compare and contrast the contribution of different features to the appeal of one European and one worldwide destination, for two different customer types. **See Assessment activity 4.2, page 118**
Learning aim C: Be able to plan international travel to meet the needs of visitors			
1C.4 English Maths Plan holidays to one European and one worldwide destination, producing an itinerary for each, with support.	**2C.P4** English Maths Plan holidays to one European and one worldwide destination, for different visitor types, producing an itinerary for each. **See Assessment activity 4.3, page 123**	**2C.M3** English Maths Plan holidays to one European and one worldwide destination, for different visitor types, producing an itinerary for each and justifying choices made. **See Assessment activity 4.3, page 123**	**2C.D2** English Maths Analyse ways in which the two planned holidays could be adapted to meet the needs of different types of visitors. **See Assessment activity 4.3, page 123**

English Opportunity to practise English skills

Maths Opportunity to practise mathematical skills

How you will be assessed

This unit will be assessed by a series of assignments set by your teacher/tutor. You will be expected to show your knowledge of locations, travel routes and destinations around the world, and to be able to explain the appeal of destinations for different types of visitors. The tasks will be based on scenarios involving working in a travel and tourism setting. For example, you might be asked to imagine you are working for a tour operator and have been asked to research suitable destinations for holidays. Or you could take on the role of a trainee travel consultant planning international travel to meet the needs of different types of customers.

Your assessment could be in the form of:

- informative materials such as travel guides
- brochures or multimedia presentations
- practical tasks such as map work and role plays.

▶ International destinations

Introduction

Imagine you are going to book a once in a lifetime holiday to Australia. Would you be confident booking with a travel consultant who showed little knowledge of travel geography? You would probably expect travel agency staff to have a good awareness of significant destinations. Can you think of other jobs where this knowledge would also be important?

In the following section we will look at the appeal of different parts of the world to tourists.

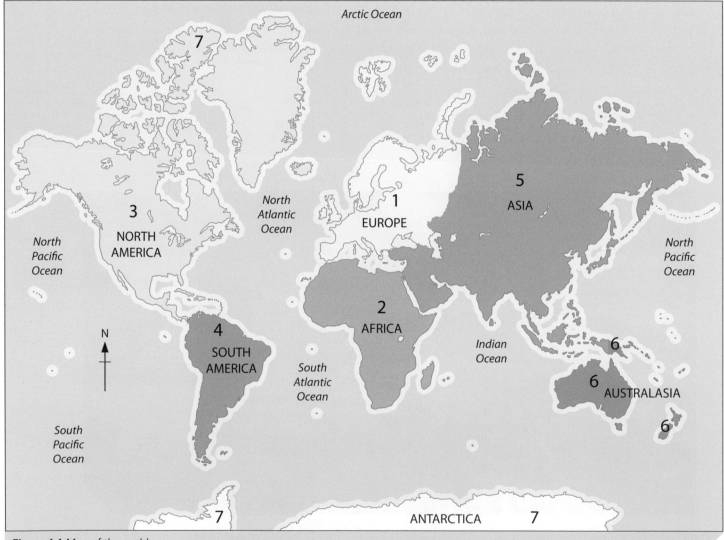

Figure 4.1 Map of the world.

Activity 4.1   Researching the EU and the Eurozone

Using a map of Europe highlight all of the countries that are members of the EU and those that are part of the Eurozone. Are you surprised by the results in any way? Are there many European countries that don't fall into either of these groups?

1 Europe

Europe is a diverse continent and its countries are popular with holidaymakers from the UK. The Mediterranean climate attracts tourists to countries like Spain and Turkey for summer and winter sun. Alpine and Scandinavian countries like Austria and Norway offer excellent opportunities for winter sports. Culture is high on the list for tourists visiting ancient sites in Italy and Greece. Many UK residents now have permanent or second homes in Europe, taking advantage of the varied attractions, culture and climate.

Like the UK, many European countries are members of the European Union, and some are also part of the Eurozone where the Euro is the official currency.

2 Africa

In Africa, the second largest continent, ancient Egypt contrasts with bustling Morocco, laid-back Gambia and South Africa's cosmopolitan cities. Inland, the Sahara desert offers adventure, while the safari experience is the main pull to countries like Kenya and Botswana. Africa's east coast and the island beaches of the Indian Ocean are a magnet for honeymooners.

3 North America

Located wholly in the northern hemisphere, North America is dominated by Canada and the USA. Mexico, the Caribbean islands and the countries of Central America add to its rich culture and variety. Cities like New York and Washington DC have wide appeal, as do the natural wonders of the Grand Canyon and Niagara Falls. Florida adds the fun, Las Vegas the glamour, and the Caribbean a chance to relax.

4 South America

Brazil is probably the best known of the South American countries. It's topical too, with Rio de Janeiro hosting the 2016 Olympics. The continent is home to the world's largest rainforest and the longest river, the Amazon. Trekking the Inca Trail to Peru's Machu Picchu is a 'must do' experience on many South American itineraries.

5 Asia

Asia is the world's largest continent, dominated in size by Russia, but incorporating diverse landscapes and cultures including Thailand, India, China and Vietnam. The Far East attracts many gap year travellers en route to Australia, while the Middle East brings sharp contrasts with the spectacular developed attractions of Dubai.

6 Australasia

Located in the southern hemisphere, Australasia's main countries are Australia and New Zealand, both popular **VFR** destinations. Sometimes known as Oceania, it also includes surrounding Pacific islands. Australia has exciting cities like Sydney and natural attractions like the Great Barrier Reef and Uluru (Ayers Rock). New Zealand's natural beauty was captured on film in *The Lord of the Rings*.

7 Arctic and Antarctic

Cruise expeditions into the icy wilderness of the polar regions of the Arctic and Antarctic have opened up opportunities for visitors to witness spectacular glacial scenery, wildlife and culture.

Regions

Destinations are often defined as 'European' and those beyond Europe as 'Worldwide'. You may also find them categorised as short, medium and long haul. This corresponds to their flight time from the UK, with short-haul flights up to three hours from the UK, medium-haul between three and six hours, and long-haul over six hours.

Key term

VFR – a term used for people who travel to destinations to visit their friends and relatives.

Take it further

Find out about the World Wildlife Fund's (WWF) Global Arctic Programme to protect the fragile polar environments. You can research this on the WWF's website which you can access by going to www.pearsonhotlinks. co.uk and searching for this title.

▶ Major gateways

Introduction

How can you travel to Paris? Is it easier to fly, drive or take the train? These are the kinds of questions you will ask yourself whenever you plan a trip. Why is accessibility so important to destinations? How much will a destination's popularity be affected if it is difficult and expensive to get to?

▶ Airports

A gateway airport is one that serves as an entry point for international flights. If you fly from the UK to an overseas airport your arrival airport will be the gateway airport. Sometimes you will have to transfer to another flight or use another means of transport for your onward journey. Most international airports have good transport links to the city centres.

Some destinations like Paris have several gateway airports. Some of the **low-cost airlines** like Ryanair choose to use smaller, less conveniently located airports because they have lower charges and this helps them to keep their costs down. Transfers to the city centre or resort can take longer and be less frequent than from major airports. This may be acceptable to a traveller who is on a budget and has time to spare, but a business person working to a tight schedule would probably prefer the most convenient option, regardless of price.

Key terms

Low-cost airlines – sometimes called no frills or budget airlines, they offer cheaper flights, but charge extra for meals, hold luggage, allocated seats, etc.

IATA – the International Air Transport Association. The three-letter codes they give to airports are used in civil aviation. Civil aviation covers non-military flights.

Are low-cost airlines always the cheapest travel option?

Airports are distinguished by **IATA** three-letter codes. These are used throughout the travel industry. AMS for Amsterdam is easy to remember. However others, like AGP for Malaga in Spain, are not so memorable. Codes are essential for consistency around the world, and also to distinguish between different airports in the same city.

In time, depending on where you work in the travel industry, some of these codes will become familiar to you. You need to check codes and locations carefully. If you don't, you could book a customer for the wrong airport. Imagine a customer's surprise if you booked them a flight to San Jose in California (SJC) instead of San Jose in Costa Rica (SJO), over 3,000 miles away.

▶ Train terminals

The opening of the Channel Tunnel in 1994 changed the way that you could travel to Europe. Vehicle-carrying trains took motorists and their cars through the tunnel between Folkestone in Kent and Calais, France. Passenger trains through the Channel Tunnel did not start until 2003 when Waterloo International Station was opened as the London terminal for Eurostar. In 2007 the beautifully restored St Pancras International Station replaced Waterloo as London's Eurostar terminal.

On the French side Eurostar terminates at the Gare du Nord in Paris. From here rail passengers transfer to other stations in Paris to continue their journey by train in France and to other European countries.

Although air travel has replaced rail for many journeys, train terminals around the world are often restored architectural treasures, built during the great age of steam trains in the 19th century.

Take it further

Find the airports that serve Paris, their three-letter codes and transfer options into central Paris. Can you find a flight from the UK to each of the airports? Which would be the most convenient from where you live?

What are the advantages of travelling by train compared to travelling by aeroplane?

Case study

Sirkeci Station in Istanbul is where travellers on the luxury Orient Express used to end their journey from Paris and embark on their travels to 'the Orient'. The Orient Express was like a luxury hotel on wheels. The journey from Paris to Istanbul (or Constantinople as it was known at that time) took several days and its guests (including royalty) enjoyed superb food and service and plush sleeping compartments.

Although the Orient Express has long since stopped its journeys to Istanbul, Sirkeci Station is still Istanbul's terminal for rail travel from Europe.

1 Research the route of the original Orient Express and plot it on a map. Which countries did it travel through?

2 How long would it take to fly from the UK to Istanbul? What is Istanbul airport's three-letter code?

▶ Seaports

There are many car ferry services operating between the UK and continental Europe. Channel ports have developed their facilities to cater for the superferries that now operate on many European routes. These ports offer quick and efficient embarkation and disembarkation of vehicles so that motorists can be on their way quickly. Brittany and P&O Ferries are well known ferry operators offering regular daily crossings to ports like Calais, Caen and St Malo in France, Zeebrugge in Belgium and Bilbao in Spain.

Cruise holidays have seen a phenomenal increase in passengers in recent years. According to the Passenger Shipping Association's 2012 Cruise Review, one in every eight package holidays booked was a cruise, and 40 per cent of passengers were first-time cruisers. The Mediterranean, Norway and the Atlantic Islands were among the most popular destinations for the UK market. Many UK cruise passengers choose to travel from UK ports, with Southampton being the most popular.

One of the busiest cruise ports in the world is the port of Miami. It has seven terminals and handles nearly 4 million cruise passengers each year. Its close location to Miami airport makes it convenient for British holidaymakers taking a Caribbean fly cruise with popular cruise lines like Carnival and Disney.

Cruise ports have had to develop their facilities to cope with the increasing size of cruise ships. Royal Caribbean's Allure of the Seas has 16 decks making it longer than the Eiffel Tower is tall, which makes it similar in length to three and a half football pitches.

Discussion point

What are the pros and cons of starting a cruise from a UK port rather than taking a fly cruise, where you fly to the first overseas port?

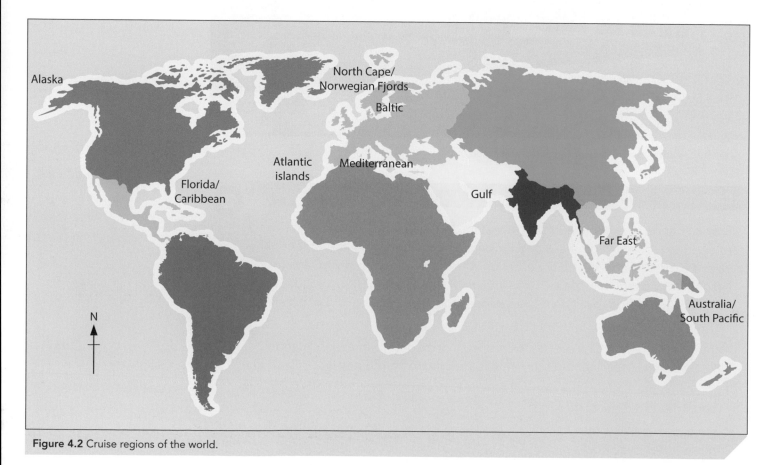

Figure 4.2 Cruise regions of the world.

Types of destinations

Introduction

Ask a dozen people for their ideal destination and you would probably receive a dozen different answers. Fortunately, there are destinations across the world to meet our every need and to tempt us to expand our horizons.

If money was no object, what would be your perfect destination? How does that compare with your friends and family?

▶ European destinations

Summer sun

Since the first air package holidays to the sun in the 1950s, summer sun holidays to the Mediterranean have become an annual event for millions of British tourists. Small fishing villages like Benidorm have developed into huge resorts with all kinds of accommodation, restaurants, beach facilities and entertainment for a summer sun break.

Major tour operators, including Thomas Cook and Thomson, have weighty summer sun brochures, featuring European holidays from Portugal's Atlantic Coast, all the way across the Mediterranean to the eastern-most countries of Greece, Cyprus and Turkey. There are summer sun destinations to suit all kinds of visitors: family friendly resorts in Menorca and Portugal's Algarve, elegant, sophisticated resorts in the South of France, and party destinations like Ibiza, Faliraki and Ayia Napa, favoured by the 18 to 30s market.

Winter sun

Changing lifestyles and working patterns mean that most people are no longer tied to just taking one holiday in the summer. The climate in the southern Mediterranean and Canary Islands is very appealing during our gloomy winter months. Budget airlines have also made it easier to take a short winter break in the sun with flights to the Canaries featuring in all their winter schedules.

Winter sun holidays are particularly popular with retired visitors who enjoy the warm, but not excessively hot, temperatures and the less busy resorts. Specialist tour operators like Saga Holidays offer a wide range of short and long stay winter sun holidays for the over 50s, many with excursions included and all-inclusive options to provide exceptional value for money.

Research winter sun destinations and find out which are the most popular.

Winter sports

Downhill skiing is still the main winter sport in Alpine and Scandinavian resorts. Snowboarding and cross-country skiing are growing in popularity and many visitors enjoy sleigh rides, skating and curling too.

Austria, Switzerland, France and Italy have Alpine resorts for all levels and interests, with ski schools and nursery slopes for beginners and black runs for accomplished skiers. Many have a lively **après ski** scene. There are many specialist winter sport tour operators catering for all budgets and offering a wide choice of travel options by air, coach, rail and self-drive. Did you know Eurostar has a ski train direct from London to the French Alps for access to the top resorts of Courchevel, Meribel and Les Arcs?

If you are looking for something different, Finland has excellent snow conditions for snowmobiles, dog sledding and ice fishing. In December a visit to Lapland to see Father Christmas can be a magical treat.

Which European winter sports resorts offer the longest seasons?

Countryside areas

When the snow has melted, the alpine regions make great active holiday destinations with mountain biking, paragliding and even summer tobogganing down the mountains. Austria's Tyrol and Switzerland's Bernese Oberland are popular with British holidaymakers.

Picturesque lakes offer scenic locations for either a relaxing holiday or water sports. Italy's Lake Maggiore and Lake Como appeal to tourists and the rich and famous, with many exclusive homes along their shores.

In contrast you may have heard of Germany's Black Forest, so called because its densely packed trees look black, which is home to the famous cake of the same name.

City breaks

Most European capital cities are tourist destinations, and they attract business visitors too. Paris' Eiffel Tower and Rome's Coliseum are well known, and they combine with other attractions, excellent restaurants, shopping, museums, art galleries and good access to make them top destinations for visitors from the UK.

Other cities often have special features and sights that make them attractive for short breaks. For example, you might be attracted by the canals of Venice and Amsterdam, or Pisa's Leaning Tower. Sometimes cities host events that encourage visitors at certain times of the year, like Munich's Oktoberfest and the Christmas markets hosted by many cities, especially in Germany and Austria.

City breaks tend to be shorter, between two and four nights, and visitors often have quite specific motivations, for example to celebrate an anniversary, or a hen or stag weekend. The cities of Riga in Latvia and Prague in the Czech Republic have made something of a name for themselves as party destinations for hens and stags.

> **? Did you know?**
>
> Thomas Cook's 2012 Top Ten City destinations in the world included nine European cities: Rome, Paris, Prague, Dublin, Venice, Barcelona, Reykjavik, Amsterdam and Madrid. Can you guess which worldwide city was also in their Top Ten? (Hint - the Big Apple.)

Activity 4.2	Escaping to an European city

Imagine you have been asked to put forward proposals for a residential study visit to a European city. Carry out a poll to find out which city would be the most popular and why.

Cruise areas

Europe has popular, contrasting cruise areas and different types of cruises appealing to different interests, lifestyles and budgets.

- **UK** – traditional leisurely cruises around Britain calling at the most northerly ports of the Shetlands and Orkneys
- **Norway and the North Cape** – scenic cruises of the Norwegian fjords and beyond with opportunities to witness the **Northern Lights** and **Land of the Midnight Sun**
- **Baltic** – calling at the historic ports of St Petersburg, Helsinki and Stockholm
- **River cruises** – passing romantic Rhineland castles, or the Danube cities of Vienna and Budapest
- **Eastern Mediterranean** – luxury or informal friendly cruises of the Greek islands, Cyprus and Turkey
- **Western Mediterranean** – popular summer cruises with varied itineraries including the Balearics, French Riviera, Sicily and Malta
- **Atlantic Islands** – popular winter sun cruises to the Canary Islands and Madeira.

> **Key terms**
>
> **Northern Lights** – spectacular natural light show in the night sky in North Norway. Check out some images on the internet.
>
> **Land of the Midnight Sun** – towards the Arctic Circle, where the mid-summer sun never sets.

▶ Worldwide destinations

City breaks

Many worldwide cities feature in films, so even if you haven't been lucky enough to visit them, you may have a good idea of what cities like New York and Las Vegas have to offer. Despite their distance from the UK, cities like these have become popular short break destinations for shopping, entertainment, sightseeing and special occasions.

Case study

Luxury at the Burj Al Arab – would the presence of iconic buildings make you more likely to visit a destination?

Dubai set itself ambitious development targets to become a world class tourist destination. And it has certainly succeeded. Although development was hit by worldwide recession in recent years, Dubai welcomed nearly 9 million visitors in 2012. It is home to the world's first seven star hotel, the Burj Al Arab built in the iconic shape of a sail. At 828 metres and with 162 floors, the Burj Khalifa was the world's tallest building when it was completed in 2010.

Dubai has much to offer the visitor. Where else could you spend one day on an Arabian desert safari and the next skiing and snowboarding at SkiDubai, the first ski resort in the Middle East? You can enjoy relaxing on beautiful beaches or having fun at the Wild Wadi Water Park. Add to that the biggest shopping malls in the world, the contrasting traditional souks, year round sunshine and Persian Gulf location – it's little wonder that Dubai has seen its popularity increase.

Abu Dhabi, Dubai's fellow United Arab Emirate and near neighbour, is now developing as a destination. Blessed with the same natural attractions and climate, it too has ambitious plans to compete for tourists and business travellers.

Research both destinations.

1 Where could you stay?

2 What could you do?

3 Which one would you rather visit?

Beach resorts

With the exception of the polar regions, each continent has some fabulous beach destinations whether you are looking for an exclusive or laid-back holiday.

- North America has fine sand beaches on Florida's Gulf Coast where you can swim with dolphins. Across the country on the Pacific Coast are California's famous Malibu and Venice Beaches and some excellent surfing beaches too.

- In South America Brazil's Copacabana Beach attracts millions of revellers to its New Year's Eve celebrations.

- On Africa's east coast the beautiful Indian Ocean beaches of Kenya are a welcome retreat after an exciting safari break. Friendly Gambia on the west coast is a popular beach destination.

- Gap year visitors travel in their thousands to the informal beach resorts of Thailand, Malaysia and India. There are luxury resorts too for special occasions and wellbeing holidays.

- Australia has long stretches of unspoilt beaches in North Queensland, while South Queensland is home to the 40-mile plus fun-filled Gold Coast, including Surfers Paradise. Many VFR visitors enjoy the winter sunshine, and a festive break visiting family could mean celebrating Christmas on the beach.

Islands

Their distance from the UK make idyllic islands like those of the Maldives and Seychelles an expensive option for a sunshine holiday. However, they have become popular for weddings and honeymoons and many have excellent diving opportunities too.

Caribbean islands like Jamaica, Barbados and the Dominican Republic are closer and more accessible for the UK market, attracting a family market as well as couples.

Much more distant from the UK, the Hawaiian islands are famed for their friendly welcome – *Aloha!* They are part of the state of Hawaii, America's most distant state, thousands of miles from the Pacific coast of the USA.

Not all islands are famous for their beaches and hotel-based holidays. The Galapagos Islands, 600 miles off the Pacific coast of Ecuador, are famous for their wildlife and they have featured in many TV documentaries. Here you can find giant tortoises, iguanas and many creatures that do not exist anywhere else on earth.

Famous for a different kind of wildlife, the island of Borneo in South East Asia is the third largest in the world and mostly covered by rainforest. Environmentally sensitive holidays, treks in the jungle and visits to orang-utan sanctuaries offer the visitor a totally different experience.

Take it further

Use Google Earth to locate some of the destinations on this page. Use holiday brochures to find out about the kinds of holidays they offer. Think about the types of visitors they would attract.

Winter sports

Worldwide winter sports destinations open up opportunities for British visitors to experience superb snow conditions outside Europe. Benefiting from a longer snow season than many European resorts, Canada's famous winter sports centres like Whistler compete with Aspen and Vail over the border in Colorado, USA.

Keen skiers and snowboarders can head east to Nagano in Japan or go in search of 'summer' skiing in the southern hemisphere mountains of Chile and New Zealand.

The Winter Olympics are held every four years in destinations around the world. The most recent, and next two, Winter Olympics hosts are:

- 2010 Vancouver, Canada
- 2014 Sochi, Russia
- 2018 Pyeongchang, South Korea.

UNESCO world heritage sites

Key term

UNESCO – the United Nations Educational Scientific and Cultural Organisation. This is an international organisation and one of its roles is to recognise outstanding natural and cultural sites. There are over 900 UNESCO world heritage sites.

The Great Wall of China and the Taj Mahal are much photographed world heritage sites, featuring prominently in country tourism promotions. **UNESCO** world heritage sites like these attract thousands of visitors every day and there is a danger that so many tourists will damage these heritage sites.

Machu Picchu in Peru has had to limit daily visitors to 3,000 in order to manage the sheer volume of visitors and protect its ancient ruins. Many gap year visitors are drawn to South America and a trek along the Inca Trail to Machu Picchu is an almost compulsory experience.

Research how you might travel the Inca Trail to Machu Picchu. What kind of people would the different types of trips appeal to?

Activity 4.3

How good is your knowledge of worldwide travel destinations? Test yourself using one of the many interactive quizzes available online, for example the geography quiz on the Lizard Point Consulting website. To access the website for this, visit Pearson hotlinks. You can access this by going to www.pearsonhotlinks.co.uk and searching for this title.

▶ International Travel Routes

Introduction

Give yourself 48 hours – how far could you travel? Could you get to the other side of the world and back? For some people travelling by the fastest means is a priority, while others would prefer to have a **stopover** and see something along the way. Which would you prefer?

Key terms

Stopover – when you break up a long journey and take a short break en route, for example stopping over in Dubai en route to Australia.

Indirect flight – when you have to change to a different aircraft to complete your journey.

Advances in air transport have opened up travel routes to destinations around the globe. Even the most distant destinations from the UK can be reached by air in little more than a day.

Airline websites have made it a fairly straightforward process to plan international travel. If you are looking for European flights the widest choice of flights are with the low-cost airlines. Examples of these are easyJet, Ryanair and Jet2.

Alternatively many countries have 'national' airlines. Some are state owned but others are privately owned. In Europe these include British Airways, Lufthansa (Germany), TAP (Portugal), SAS (Scandinavia) and Air France.

Sometimes it is not possible to find a direct flight to a destination and you may have to use an **indirect flight**.

For example, if you wanted to fly from Manchester (MAN) to Oslo (OSL) with SAS, you will most likely find that this is an indirect flight via Stockholm (ARN) in Sweden.

Most low-cost flights from the UK are to European destinations. If you are searching for flights outside Europe you may find the most direct flights using the 'national' airlines. Some examples of worldwide 'national' airlines include Emirates (United Arab Emirates), QANTAS (Australia), Cathay Pacific (Hong Kong) and Singapore Airlines.

Activity 4.4

A businessman wants to travel from London to Sydney on 8th October and spend at least two days in Dubai. Use the Emirates website to find suitable flights. To access the website for this, visit Pearson hotlinks. You can access this by going to www.pearsonhotlinks. co.uk and searching for this title.

Access the Emirates website to make a booking

↓

Choose multiple destination option

↓

Enter destinations and dates

↓

Select your flights

EXAMPLE:

| Flight EK022 | Tues 8 Oct 2013 | depart LGW 10:00 | arrive DXB 20:00 | Journey time 7 hours |
| Flight EK412 | Fri 11 Oct 2013 | depart DXB 10:15 | arrive SYD Sat 12 Oct 07:00 | Journey time 13 hours 45 minutes. |

Whenever you see flight departure and arrival times on an airline website they are always 'local' times using the 24-hour clock. This means that they have taken into account any time changes when you travel across different time zones.

Link

Find out more about time zones and the 24-hour clock in *Unit 5: Factors Affecting Worldwide Travel and Tourism.*

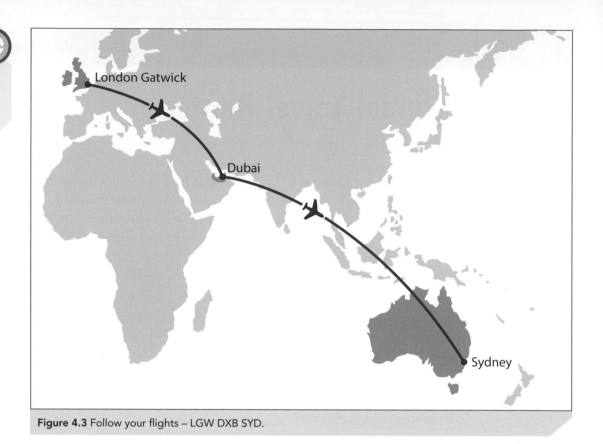

Figure 4.3 Follow your flights – LGW DXB SYD.

Assessment activity 4.1   2A.P1 | 2A.P2 | 2A.M1

As part of your initial training as a travel consultant you have to work through the company's training manual. One of the aims of the manual is to train you to use different websites, brochures, atlases, etc. Your supervisor will be checking to see that you have completed the tasks accurately and completely and explained air travel routes to customers.

You need to show that you can correctly locate gateways and different types of destinations in Europe and worldwide, and plan air travel to selected destinations.

You have been given a blank map of **Europe** to add the locations for two summer sun destinations, two winter sun destinations, two winter sports destinations, two countryside areas, two city breaks, two cruise areas and two channel tunnel or Eurostar terminals in mainland Europe.

Next, using blank **worldwide** maps, add the locations for two beach resorts, two city breaks, two islands, two

winter sports resorts, two UNESCO world heritage sites, two gateway airports and their three-letter codes, and two ferry and/or cruise ports.

Having satisfied your supervisor that you can accurately locate destinations, you have been asked to find and explain flights for four customers. They all want to travel during the first few days in September.

- Customer A would to fly from Birmingham to Madeira.
- Customer B would like to fly from Edinburgh to Dubrovnik.
- Customer C would like to fly from Newcastle to Las Vegas.
- Customer D would like to fly from Manchester to Abu Dhabi.

Find suitable flights, create travel plans and meet your supervisor to explain the journeys you have selected.

Tips

- Show the breadth of your knowledge by using a range of countries for your European map work, and varied continents and countries for your worldwide and gateway map work.
- Be prepared to explain the air travel routes you have found by showing them on a map and then explaining the routes to your supervisor. Remember to use the correct three-letter codes.

▶ Features of international travel and tourism destinations

Introduction

The different features of destinations help to define the types of visitors they will appeal to. If you like the outdoor life then natural features might appeal, whereas if you like to party the nightlife will be top of your list when choosing a destination. What do you look for in a destination?

▶ Natural features

For many visitors travelling overseas enables them to experience natural landscapes and features that are completely different from those at home.

- Climate is one of the main features that determines where we might travel. Sunshine is usually top of the list. Figure 4.4 shows how Tenerife's climate makes it a popular all-year round sunshine holiday destination. At the other extreme, climate is important for skiers who will choose mountainous destinations with the best chance of guaranteed snow.

- Mountains are a key feature for climbing and hiking holidays. The Rockies and Grand Canyon are spectacular to visit in summer or winter. In Asia you can choose to climb Mount Everest for the ultimate challenge.

- North America's Great Lakes are beautiful and have water sports too. Visitors may be attracted to world famous waterfalls – Niagara Falls are spectacular. In South America, the Amazon and its rainforest offer real adventure.

- Beaches have huge appeal. Menorca's flat sandy beaches will appeal to families with small children, whereas Australia's Bondi Beach will attract surfers. Scuba diving is popular in the Caribbean and other exotic destinations.

- The deserts of Arabia and Sahara can offer a different kind of adventure: camel treks, nomadic camps and jeep desert safaris.

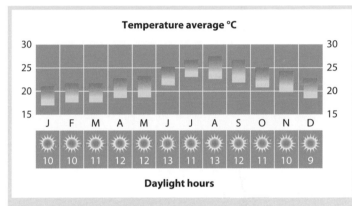

Temperature average °C

	J	F	M	A	M	J	J	A	S	O	N	D
Daylight hours	10	10	11	12	12	13	11	13	12	11	10	9

Figure 4.4 Tenerife – an all-year sunshine destination.

Links

Finding out about the effects of Iceland's Eyjafjallajökull volcano eruption in 2010 will support *Unit 5: Factors Affecting Worldwide Travel and Tourism*.

Case study

Iceland has little in the way of big towns and cities outside its capital, Reykjavik, so it is the natural features that attract the majority of its visitors. It is known as the 'Land of Ice and Fire' in recognition of the huge glaciers and ice masses that exist alongside fiery volcanoes. Beneath the ice there are bubbling hot springs that burst into life with geysers jetting boiling water metres into the air. You can bathe in naturally warm waters even when the air above is below freezing, but be prepared for the smell. The natural sulphur is not pleasant at all.

1 Look at some package holidays to Iceland. Who would they appeal to?

2 Can you find any other examples of destinations that rely on natural features to attract visitors?

Local attractions

Local attractions will help you to decide if a destination is the right one for you.

Some visitors will plan a holiday based around **historical sites**. A cruise along the Nile will include the pyramids of Egypt and an insight into ancient Egypt. You can learn about the ancient Mayan civilisation if you visit Mexico.

Heritage sites include UNESCO sites and others that may be protected. Kakadu National Park in Australia has caves with aboriginal paintings going back thousands of years.

Religious sites include places of pilgrimage like Lourdes in France and Mecca in Saudi Arabia. Many Roman Catholics visit the Vatican City in Rome at least once in their lifetime. In Thailand, Buddhist temples are beautiful ornate buildings, much visited by tourists.

Why does Florida's Walt Disney World Resort have such wide appeal? Do Disney resorts in other countries have the same appeal?

Theme parks are popular for all ages. Some, like Walt Disney World Resort and Universal Studios in Orlando, Florida, are destinations in their own right. Others, like Port Aventura in Spain, are usually a day trip as part of a longer beach holiday. Most popular summer sun beach destinations have water parks nearby for day trips too.

Visiting **museums and art galleries** might not be your idea of a holiday, but the Louvre in Paris and the Guggenheim in New York are a must for art lovers. Quite different, Graceland, the home of Elvis Presley, in Memphis, Tennessee, would attract Elvis fans.

Some attractions are **iconic structures or buildings**. No visit to New York would be complete without seeing the Statue of Liberty or the Empire State Building, and the same goes for Sydney's Opera House, Harbour Bridge and Paris' Eiffel Tower.

Large scale events like the Olympics or the World Cup will bring millions of visitors to a destination. While not as grand as Rio's celebrations, 'Karnival' is celebrated in many European countries in February each year.

Accommodation

A good range of accommodation to meet all budgets and expectations can draw a wide range of visitors to a destination.

- Hotels can range from seven star luxury to simple one star. In Scandinavia you can stay in hotels made of ice, while Las Vegas' Venetian Hotel has canals inside, complete with gondolas.

- Campsites are used extensively in Europe, particularly by specialist tour operators like Keycamp. Their customers can choose from luxury tents to top of the range mobile homes, and tree houses too.

- Apartments are excellent for people who prefer to cater for themselves or sample local cuisine. They offer a more flexible kind of holiday, popular with families and young people on Mediterranean holidays.

- Villas offer more privacy than apartments and often have their own private pools. Villas are a popular choice in Florida and also in many sunshine destinations in Europe.
- Hostels are used all over the world by gap year travellers where they can be as cheap as a few pounds a night in the Far East and South America.

▶ Facilities and services

Local transport

Local transport can add to an attraction including New York's yellow cabs, Venice's gondolas, San Francisco's cable cars and Switzerland's scenic trains, like the Glacier Express.

Shops

Shopping is a great attraction if the exchange rates are in your favour. Buying local souvenirs will remind you of your travels. In Africa tourists are encouraged to support local communities. Local markets offer local crafts. At the other end of the spectrum are glittering Middle Eastern shopping malls and world famous stores like New York's Bloomingdale's and Macy's.

Nightlife

New York's Broadway is a must for seeing the best shows, while Paris is home to the famous Moulin Rouge and the Can Can. Las Vegas has the wow factor with its out of this world shows, casinos and nightclubs.

Venice's gondolas are iconic – so iconic that Las Vegas has recreated Venice in a hotel. Do you think this can ever replace visiting the real thing?

Sport and leisure

Sport can attract both participants and spectators. Golf holidays are popular in Portugal's Algarve and Florida. The Grand Prix has a loyal following wherever it is staged, as do football and cricket. Wellbeing holidays are growing in popularity and many luxury worldwide destinations offer spa holidays, with yoga, treatments and relaxation.

Eating out

The gastronomic regions of Italy and France will attract 'foodies', but many visitors enjoy sharing simpler local food and drink. In Marrakech there are huge outdoor kitchens set up every evening where tourists mix with locals to eat traditional Moroccan food.

Sightseeing

Most cities now have hop-on hop-off city sightseeing tours. These are a great way for tourists to get around and learn about a destination.

Weddings

Many couples now choose to travel overseas for their wedding. There are many different types of wedding to choose from, ranging from relaxed weddings on the beach in the Seychelles to an Elvis themed wedding in Las Vegas.

Activity 4.5	Tying the knot overseas

Carry out some research into getting married overseas. Which are the most popular destinations?

Cultural features

Culture can include traditions, music, dance, art, festivals and religion. Celebrations for Chinese New Year in Hong Kong manage to incorporate most of these. In Rio de Janeiro the annual Carnival is a spectacular event with fantastic parades, music and dancing.

It is important that you do not cause offence when you travel overseas, so knowing about local and religious customs is very useful. This is known as travel etiquette.

English is widely spoken around the world, but the locals always appreciate visitors making an effort to learn some local phrases, if only 'hello' 'please', 'thank you' and 'goodbye'.

Activity 4.6   Local phrases

Find out how to say 'hello', 'please', 'thank you' and 'goodbye' in one country in each continent.

Why is it important that you learn about the culture you are visiting before you travel?

Special interest tourism

The rise in special interest tour operators has been dramatic. There are many different types of special interest tourism in countries all around the world, including:

- winter sports, including downhill or cross-country skiing and snowboarding, with instruction or without
- water sports; for example, sailing, canoeing and scuba diving, with instruction or without
- walking, cycling and other outdoor pursuits
- sport as a spectator or participant; for example, tennis and football coaching, travelling to watch a Grand Prix or the Olympics

- developing skills; for example, painting, photography, cookery, learning a language
- volunteer tourism – giving up your time on holiday to help others or the environment
- health tourism; for example, travelling abroad for a facelift or dental work, yoga, a wellbeing or spiritual retreat
- culture; for example, travelling for festivals, music, theatre trips, art exhibitions
- adventure tourism; for example, trekking, mountaineering, wild water rafting
- dark tourism; for example, visiting battlefields or areas of man-made disasters
- religious tourism; for example, visiting a holy shrine or making a pilgrimage to Lourdes.

> **Take it further**
>
> Use the internet to find examples of special interest tour operators and different countries where you can participate in specific special interest holidays. Who would these holidays appeal to?

TOPIC   B2

Types of visitor

Introduction

To be successful, travel and tourism organisations have to meet and exceed customer expectations. In order to do this they must know their customers and their needs. Think about young people, families, retirees and school groups. How do their needs differ? How can different organisations meet and exceed their needs?

Families

A family with very young children will have completely different needs and expectations, compared to a family with teenagers. These needs can influence travel arrangements, accommodation and the selection of the destination to meet their ages and interests. Families may have budget considerations too. Some families will enjoy active sports and may be interested in family cycling, skiing or sailing holidays. Others may prefer a relaxing hotel with a children's club in a family friendly resort.

Activity 4.7   Promoting Paphos

Imagine you have been asked to promote Paphos in Cyprus as a family destination. Work in pairs to produce posters; one highlighting features that would appeal to families with pre-school children, and the other aimed at families with teenage children. Compare your posters and discuss the similarities and differences.

Groups

Groups come in all shapes and sizes. Some of their needs will be the same, for example they will want to travel together. However, due to their differing motivations, a trip to the same destination could be quite different for different types of groups. The accommodation and what they choose to see and do could vary considerably.

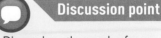

> **Discussion point**
>
> Discuss how the needs of a group of art students on a residential study trip will differ from those of a hen or stag group.

Different ages

The youth market has groups with different motivations. Young people celebrating the end of exams are likely to head for the party islands of Ibiza, Crete or Zante for a one- or two-week break in the sun. In contrast, gap year travellers will often be more independent 'backpacking' through Asia or South America. They will have different expectations in terms of what they see and do, their choice of accommodation and transport, and their budget.

At the older end of the market some over 50s may be adventure travellers making the most of their retirement years by undertaking world travel, going on safari, volunteering and trekking. Some retired people have good pensions and can afford luxury holidays with very high standards, but others may have more modest budgets. Coach tours and cruises appeal to some over 50s who would like everything arranged for them.

Customers with special needs

Some customers may have specific needs and you must take them into consideration if you are planning holidays for them. You will need to choose a destination carefully if they have mobility issues. Hilly destinations or those with poor local transport may not be suitable. Special arrangements may have to be made to cater for customers who are sight or hearing impaired.

Assessment activity 4.2   2B.P3 | 2B.M2 | 2B.D1

You and your travel agency colleagues are taking it in turn to brief one another on how destinations appeal to visitors in different ways. Your investigations will focus on features of one European and one worldwide destination.

Give a presentation to show how the different features of two destinations contribute to their appeal for at least two different types of visitors.

Be prepared to compare and contrast the ways that at least three different features appeal to the different visitors.

Tips

- Choose different types of destinations, for example a European summer sun destination and a worldwide city break.
- Choose at least two visitor types for one destination and two different visitor types for the other.
- Include images to help show the appeal of different features.
- Features include natural features, local attractions, a range of accommodation, facilities, special interests and traditions/culture.
- Remember to look at the destinations' appeal through the eyes of your selected visitors. Consider why certain aspects might appeal more to one visitor type than the other.

WorkSpace

▷ Anna Plews

Travel Consultant

I work for an independent retail travel agent. Along with my colleagues I am responsible for:

- helping customers to find holidays to meet their needs
- providing information about different destinations
- selling holidays
- planning travel and preparing itineraries.

I love the variety of my job. No two days are the same. One minute I can be selling holidays to Majorca, and the next to Mexico. Customers trust me to give them good, accurate advice. I enjoy researching destinations as it's important to find holidays that meet customer needs.

Many of our customers rely on us to make all their travel plans, finding out about transport options as well as where to stay and what to do. Not all customers are going on holiday; some are business travellers too. It's important that I get everything right so that they don't end up missing a flight.

Sometimes I have the opportunity to travel to different destinations on a 'fam' trip. These are organised by tourist boards and tour operators to 'familiarise' us with destinations we might be selling. They're great fun, but can be hard work too because we pack a lot into a short trip. I have travelled to three different continents and have loved finding out at firsthand what different destinations have to offer. I hope I achieve my ambition to travel to each continent before I reach 30.

Think about it

1 How will the knowledge gained so far in this unit help to prepare you for a role like Anna's?

2 How can you continue to develop your knowledge of travel and destinations around the world?

3 What other jobs in travel and tourism would benefit from having staff with a good knowledge of international travel and tourism destinations?

▶ Plan international travel

Introduction

If you are planning a trip, which resource do you turn to first? Do you check out review sites to see what other people think, or view images on websites? Maybe you prefer to flick through holiday brochures or talk to a travel agent to see what's on offer? Planning has never been so easy with all the resources available.

▶ Sources of information

There are many different sources of information available when you are planning international travel.

Websites

Discussion point

What are the advantages and disadvantages of using websites as a source of travel information?

These are by far the most popular way of finding out about travel to destinations, where you can stay and what you can do when you get there. Transport operators, for example airlines, ferry, bus and train operators, use websites to display their most up-to-date timetables, take bookings and provide information about their products and services. Hotels and other different types of accommodation providers use websites to promote their facilities to an international audience and take online bookings. Tourist Boards have excellent websites to promote their destinations at a national and regional level, while many attractions and other types of travel and tourism providers also have an online presence. Advances in technology mean that websites can be accessed via smartphones so you can research from almost anywhere.

Guidebooks

These are used by many people when they are visiting a destination for the first time. Pocket-sized guidebooks are particularly useful as they can be taken on holiday and they contain maps and information about the main sights, attractions and facilities. Well-known brands include Berlitz, Eye Witness and Fodor.

Atlases

These are a more traditional way of locating destinations around the world. However, advances in technology have opened up opportunities to locate and view destinations via online atlases and programmes, switching from space to street level in moments.

Holiday brochures

These are provided by tour operators to promote their holidays. They are costly to produce. Most customers collect holiday brochures from travel agencies. They contain detailed information and photographs about the holidays to encourage the customer to buy. Some holiday brochures are now available as 'e-brochures' on tour operators' websites. You can view Kuoni Holidays' brochures online, and watch video clips of destinations and accommodation.

Tourist information centres

These can be found in many airports and city centres. Tourists can visit them for information on the local area, book accommodation and to pick up leaflets about local attractions. Most tourist boards now have their own websites, and prospective visitors can use them to find out about a destination before they travel, from the comfort of their own home.

Tourist leaflets

These are produced by most attractions and can be picked up from tourist offices and hotels. Often they will include a discount voucher to encourage tourists to pick up a leaflet and pay them a visit.

▶ Types of visitors, their needs and characteristics

When planning itineraries and international travel you have to find out exactly what your customers are looking for. Even if they are travelling to the same destination, two sets of customers are likely to have very different needs and your holiday recommendations should be tailored to meet their needs.

You have already looked at different types of visitors and have started to consider their differing needs. When it comes to holiday planning, the focus changes depending on the very specific needs of the customer.

Activity 4.8	Ensuring mobility abroad

Consider the needs of two customers with mobility problems wanting an overseas sunshine holiday:

1 an older person, travelling alone, using walking aids, but able to cope with walking short distances and short flights of stairs unaided

2 a young adult, wheelchair-dependent and unable to walk unaided; travelling with a group of young able-bodied friends.

How do their characteristics differ?

What are their needs in terms of transport, assistance, accommodation and choice of resort?

▶ Holiday planning

When trying to find holidays for customers, you will have to question them to establish exactly what the customer is looking for.

If you manage to find a holiday that meets or exceeds a customer's needs there is a good chance that they will want to use your services again. On the other hand if you plan a holiday that is not well-suited to the customer they will probably complain and you may lose their future custom. The things you need to consider when planning holidays for others are covered in Table 4.1.

Links

Unit 6: The Travel and Tourism Customer Experience will help you to understand further how you can meet the needs of different types of customers.

Table 4.1 – Planning considerations

Planning consideration	What you need to know from your customers
Visitor requirements	How many people are travelling?
	Are there any children?
	Do they have preferred dates or times of the year?
	What is their preferred duration?
Travel requirements	Do they have a preference for travelling by air, train, cruise or any other method or combination?
	If flying, would they like to travel from their local airport?
	What class of travel do they want?
Accommodation requirements	What type of accommodation are they looking for, for example hotel, apartment, villa?
	What standard of accommodation?
	Do they want half board, full board, all-inclusive, bed and breakfast or room only?
Motivation	What is the main purpose of the holiday, for example relaxation, special occasion, activity (walking, sailing, etc.), sightseeing, culture?
Features	What are the most important features for them, for example safe beach, family attractions, cultural attractions, nightlife, shopping, good restaurants, good transport?
Budget	Do they have a maximum budget per person or for the group?

Activity 4.9   Role play

Role playing is excellent practice for working in the travel and tourism industry. Work in small groups of three to write 'customer profiles' and then take it in turn to be the travel consultant, customer and observer.

As the travel consultant, question the customer to find out exactly what type of holiday they want. Use the internet and holiday brochures to find a suitable holiday for your customer.

Meet the customer again and go through the holiday with them.

The observer should give feedback, highlighting positive aspects and areas for improvement.

▶ Itinerary

An itinerary is an important document. It is prepared by travel agents or tour operators to record the travel arrangements they have arranged for their customers. A basic travel itinerary will contain information about:

- dates and times of travel (using the 24-hour clock)
- mode of travel, for example air, rail, coach
- departure and destination location
- accommodation and board basis
- specific features.

Some itineraries can be quite lengthy. For example, if a customer is booking a coach tour, the itinerary might contain details of what they will be doing each day of the tour, as well as the travel arrangements for joining the tour. A long round-the-world trip will have a detailed and complex itinerary combining travel details and essential information in **chronological** order for the whole trip. It is very important that itineraries are checked for accuracy as customers rely on them to make sure they arrive at airports in good time and have contact details for accommodation and transport providers.

Key terms

Chronological – means in the correct order, starting with day 1 and working through to the last day of the holiday.

ATOL – is the Air Travel Organisers' Licencing. If an ATOL protected company goes out of business their customers would get their money back or be brought home if they are already on holiday. You can find out more through the Civil Aviation Authority's website, which you can find by visiting Pearson hotlinks. www. pearsonhotlinks.co.uk, and searching for this title.

Itinerary Mr and Mrs Johnson ref CV546 SBEL 0712

Names: Mr Thomas Johnson/Mrs Sandra Johnson

Date of outward travel: 12 July	**Date of return travel:** 19 July
Departure airport: London Gatwick North Terminal	**Departure airport:** Amilcar Cabral Airport , Sal
Times: Check in: 11.50 Depart: 13.50	**Times:** Check in: 16.55 Depart: 18.55
Carrier/flight number: Thomson Airways TOM 782	**Carrier/flight number:** Thomson Airways TOM 783
Booking Reference: V343JKYK	**Booking Reference:** V343JKYK
Arrival airport: Amilcar Cabral Airport, Sal	**Arrival airport:** London Gatwick North Terminal
Arrival time: 17.55	**Arrival time:** 02.35 (on 20 July)

Accommodation: Clubhotel Sal Bellevue, Santa Maria, Sal, Cape Verde 0203 027 3375

Board basis: All-inclusive

Specific features: Sea view room and balcony, air conditioning, 2 swimming pools. Included taxi transfer on arrival/departure.

Santa Maria:
Santa Maria has a beautiful sandy beach with water sport facilities. You will find several restaurants offering local seafood. You can buy local handicrafts from the shops. Your local representative will help you to arrange local excursions. These include fishing trips and boat trips with opportunities for snorkelling.

Please note:
Full passport and visa required.
Electronic ticket – please follow the instructions for online check-in and
print out your boarding passes before travelling to the airport.
Your holiday is **ATOL** protected.

Assessment activity 4.3   Maths   English   2C.P4 | 2C.M3 | 2C.D2

Finding the right holiday to meet customer needs is an essential part of your job as a travel consultant. As part of your training your supervisor has asked you to plan holidays for customers with different needs and motivations. This will involve planning the holidays and producing itineraries.

Plan separate holidays to the same European destination for two visitors with different needs and motivations. You will have to prepare separate itineraries to give to your supervisor and have a meeting with them to justify why you have chosen the specific holidays for each visitor type.

Having satisfied your supervisor that you have a good awareness of what different types of visitors need from a European holiday, you can now expand your research worldwide. Choose another two types of visitors with differing needs and motivations and plan holidays for them to a worldwide destination. You will prepare separate itineraries and meet your supervisor to explain why you have chosen the different holidays for the selected two visitor types.

Discuss how the itineraries could be changed to meet the needs of different types of visitors. This will mean you have to review in detail what the destinations could offer different visitors.

Tips

Don't use the same destinations as those in Assessment activity 4.2.

Choose destinations that would have different appeal features for visitors with different needs and motivations. For example:

- a summer sun European holiday for a family with young children. A summer sun holiday in the same destination for a group of young friends
- a luxury worldwide honeymoon. An adventure trekking holiday in the same destination for an active older couple.

Consider the different needs of your customers:

- dates and times of the year
- travel requirements
- accommodation requirements
- motivation, for example do they want activities, relaxation, culture, is it a special occasion?
- features, for example beaches, attractions, guided trips, local transport, eating out, nightlife, excursions, weather
- budget.

Introduction

Can you imagine what it must have been like centuries ago when setting sail from the UK to explore the world? Britain's famous explorers ventured into dangerous and unknown territory, sailing for months on end to discover the world. Today we can travel much faster and more safely, but there are still many challenges that present themselves to the modern-day traveller.

Knowing how our holiday and travel arrangements can be affected by different factors allows us to be better prepared when making our plans. Some things are outside our control and we can never be fully prepared for the weather and other external factors that can wreak havoc on our travel plans. However, we can consider the effect of journey times, the best times to travel, how to stay healthy and how to stay safe. Armed with this knowledge we can hope that our travel adventures will be memorable for the right reasons.

Assessment: This unit will be assessed through a series of assignments set by your teacher/tutor.

Learning aims

In this unit you will:

A investigate how climate, and worldwide time, can affect the appeal of worldwide destinations

B understand influential factors on worldwide travel and tourism destinations.

> When I've looked at holiday brochures I've never really thought about all the planning that goes on to choose the right destinations, transport us there and keep us safe on holiday. It must be interesting working for a tour operator making all these arrangements, and having to deal with the unexpected.
>
> Ashiq, *15-year-old Travel and Tourism student*

Factors Affecting Worldwide Travel and Tourism

5

BTEC
Assessment Zone

This table shows you what you must do in order to achieve a **Pass**, **Merit** or **Distinction** grade, and where you can find activities in this book to help you.

Assessment criteria

Level 1	Level 2 Pass	Level 2 Merit	Level 2 Distinction
Learning aim A: Investigate how climate, and worldwide time, can affect the appeal of worldwide destinations			
1A.1 Outline two climatic conditions that affect the appeal of destinations, including examples, with support.	**2A.P1** Describe how climatic conditions affect the appeal of two short-haul and two long-haul destinations. **See Assessment activity 5.1, page 132**	**2A.M1** Explain how different climatic conditions can affect the appeal of destinations. **See Assessment activity 5.1, page 132**	**2A.D1** Compare and contrast climatic conditions and seasonal variations that affect the appeal of one short-haul and one long-haul destination. **See Assessment activity 5.1, page 132**
1A.2 Outline seasonal variations that affect the appeal of two short-haul and two long-haul destinations, with support.	**2A.P2** Describe seasonal variations that affect the appeal of two short-haul and two long-haul destinations. **See Assessment activity 5.1, page 132**	**2A.M2** Assess seasonal variations that affect the appeal of destinations. **See Assessment activity 5.1, page 132**	
1A.3 Maths Outline what time zones are, including two examples of calculated worldwide time differences, with support.	**2A.P3** Maths Describe what time zones are, including four examples of calculated worldwide time differences. **See Assessment activity 5.1, page 132**	**2A.M3** Maths Explain how time zones can affect visitors when travelling. **See Assessment activity 5.1, page 132**	
Learning aim B: Understand influential factors on worldwide travel and tourism destinations			
1B.4 Outline the importance of using passports and visas to two travel destinations.	**2B.P4** Describe the importance of, and reasons for, using passports and visas for two travel destinations. **See Assessment activity 5.2, page 138**		
1B.5 Outline health risks and precautions related to four different destinations, with support.	**2B.P5** Describe health risks and precautions related to four different destinations. **See Assessment activity 5.2, page 138**	**2A.M4** Explain health risks and precautions related to four destinations. **See Assessment activity 5.2, page 138**	
1B.6 Outline two emergency situations that have affected different destinations.	**2B.P6** Describe two emergency situations that have affected different destinations, including examples. **See Assessment activity 5.2, page 138**	**2A.M5** Explain the effects that two emergency situations have had on travel, including examples. **See Assessment activity 5.2, page 138**	**2B.D2** Assess the short- and long-term effects that one emergency situation and one health risk have had on travel, including examples of destinations. **See Assessment activity 5.2, page 138**

Maths Opportunity to practise mathematical skills

How you will be assessed

This unit will be assessed by a series of assignments set by your teacher/tutor. You will be expected to show your knowledge of different factors that affect worldwide travel. The tasks will be based on scenarios involving working in a travel and tourism setting. For example, you might be asked to imagine you are working for a tour operator and have been asked to research the best times to travel to different destinations around the world. Or you could take the role of a trainee travel consultant providing information to customers about travel health and safety.

Your assessment could be in the form of:

- informative materials such as travel guides
- presentations
- practical tasks such as calculating time differences.

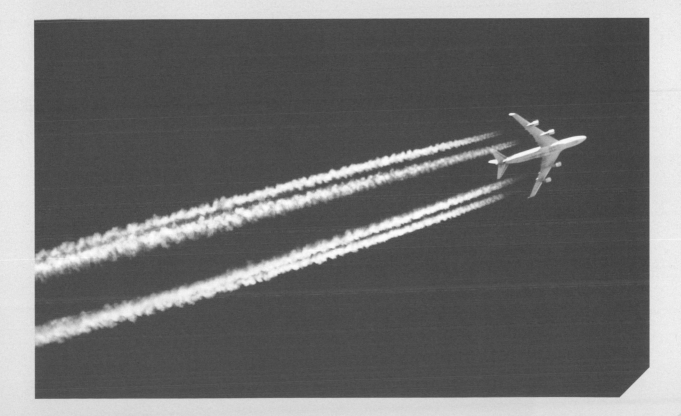

▶ Climatic conditions affecting the appeal of travel and tourism

Introduction

Imagine sitting under a palm tree on a beautiful sandy beach in the Maldives. Sounds idyllic? Well, imagine your disappointment if the sun turns to torrential non-stop rain. Weather is an important feature for many holidays. How can you make sure you choose the right time of year for your holiday?

▶ Climatic conditions

Different climatic conditions around the world influence the appeal of destinations.

- Tropical storms include **hurricanes**, **typhoons** and **cyclones**. They vary in intensity with winds reaching over 150 miles per hour at their most extreme. Usually accompanied by torrential rain, severe tropical storms can wreak terrible devastation on destinations by closing airports, wrecking buildings, cutting off power and communications, and even resulting in loss of life.

- Monsoon winds bring torrential rainfall, often known as the 'rainy season'. The wet and dry seasons cause many problems for travellers. During the dry season scorching temperatures dry out the land, but when monsoon rains fall flooding can occur. Some monsoon rain comes in short, sharp bursts, with brilliant sunshine in between, but when rainfall is prolonged holidays can be spoiled.

- Humidity is the amount of water vapour in the air. Countries with high humidity can be uncomfortable; it's often referred to as a 'sticky' heat. Countries with warm temperatures and low humidity are more pleasant.

- Sunshine is one of the main attractions for many holidaymakers, and package holidays to the sun are the choice of millions of visitors. However, too much sun is dangerous, especially scorching desert sun.

- Guaranteed snow is top of the list for winter sports. However, snow can disrupt travel, closing airports and roads.

- Prevailing winds are those that blow frequently across a particular region. They can bring warmth or cold depending on their origin.

Key terms

Hurricanes – tropical storms in the North Atlantic, Gulf of Mexico and Caribbean.

Typhoons – most common in the north western Pacific Ocean.

Cyclones – mainly in the south western Pacific Ocean.

How important is weather for different types of holidays?

▶ Seasonal variations

When planning a holiday it is worth finding out whether extreme climatic conditions are seasonal, as well as determining the best times to travel for favourable conditions.

Locations and times of the year to avoid

Tropical storms have distinct seasons depending on their location. The main hurricane and typhoon seasons are between June and November with peak months of August and September. The cyclone season is between November and March.

The Caribbean and Florida Coast are popular with British holidaymakers. Some visitors will avoid planning a holiday to high risk destinations like these during the hurricane season, especially if it is for a special occasion like a wedding or honeymoon.

The beautiful islands of the Indian Ocean and Asian countries like India are affected by the monsoon wet season from June to September. Eighty per cent of India's rain is said to fall during the wet season and this can cause floods. Weather-dependent destinations like the Maldives are less appealing during the wet season.

Locations and times of the year with favourable conditions

The Mediterranean has some of the most favourable conditions for British sunshine holidays. Spring and summer can be pleasant with temperatures suited to young families. You must travel further south to the Canary Islands and other countries at a similar **latitude** for year-round sunshine.

Snow is also seasonal. It occurs at high altitude in mountainous regions of Europe and North America in the northern hemisphere during our winter months of November to March. During our summer months you can ski in countries like Chile in the southern hemisphere. European alpine countries and Scandinavia are the most attractive for British holidaymakers because they have excellent access from the UK.

Locations in respect of global aspects

As the name suggests, tropical storms are found in tropical areas, around the Tropic of Cancer in the northern hemisphere and the Tropic of Capricorn in the southern hemisphere.

Countries around the Equator are the hottest, too intense for many holidaymakers, especially families with children. In contrast the polar regions have year-round ice, and conditions are too extreme for all but the more intrepid travellers on polar expeditions.

Do not forget how seasons vary in the northern and southern hemispheres. In Australia you could be sweltering on a beach on Christmas Day and watching the falling autumn leaves in April. These would be appealing times of the year to visit.

> **Key term**
>
> **Latitude** – refers to imaginary horizontal lines running parallel to the Equator.

> **Link**
>
> Find out more about the appeal of worldwide destinations in *Unit 4: International Travel and Tourism Destinations*.

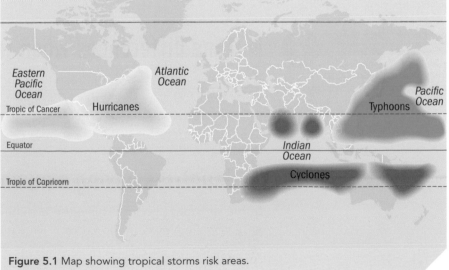

Figure 5.1 Map showing tropical storms risk areas.

▶ The effect of worldwide time

Introduction

Why does a flight take ten hours to get there and only five hours to get back? This is a question you might be asked as a travel agent. Would you be able to explain to customers why one journey appears to last longer than the other?

▶ Time zones

Greenwich in London gives its name to Greenwich Mean Time (GMT). Time zones start from here. In different countries times may be ahead of or behind GMT; this is often referred to as GMT+1, GMT+2 or GMT-1, GMT-2 and so on, to show how many hours they are ahead of or behind UK time.

There are 24 time zones across the world. If you travel overseas you will usually experience a time change. For example, when flight crew announce the local time on landing in Spain it will be one hour ahead of UK time. This is because Spain is in a time zone called Central European Time which is one hour ahead of the UK.

▶ Lines of longitude and the Prime Meridian

Lines of longitude are imaginary lines that run from the North Pole to the South Pole and each one broadly represents a different time zone.

Greenwich is the Prime Meridian at 0° longitude. At the opposite side of the world is the International Date Line, located twelve time zones away from the UK, both east and west. The International Date Line is part way across the Pacific Ocean. As the name suggests the dates differ either side of the line.

The farther away you travel from the UK east or west, the more time zones you will pass through. If you look at the map of time zones in Figure 5.2 you will see that time zones do not follow the lines of longitude exactly because many countries want to keep the same time even if a line of longitude runs through them.

▶ Time differences when travelling east and west

If you travel east from GMT, each time zone you enter is another hour ahead of the UK. When you travel west each time zone is another hour behind UK time. Therefore times in Dubai are ahead of GMT, whereas in the USA they are behind GMT. You can see this is Figure 5.2.

▶ Countries having a number of different time zones

Some very large countries like the USA have a number of different time zones. When it is 12 noon in New York on Eastern Time it will be 9 a.m. in Los Angeles on Pacific Time.

Link

To find out more about time zones, check out the International Date Line and to view an interactive time zone map go to timeanddate.com. To access the website for this, visit Pearson hotlinks. You can access this by going to www.pearsonhotlinks.co.uk and searching for this title.

Did you know?

New Zealanders are already celebrating the New Year by the time you are eating lunch on New Year's Eve.

Activity 5.1 — Time zones

- Can you find a large country that has kept a single time zone?

- What are the advantages and disadvantages of large countries having a single time zone?

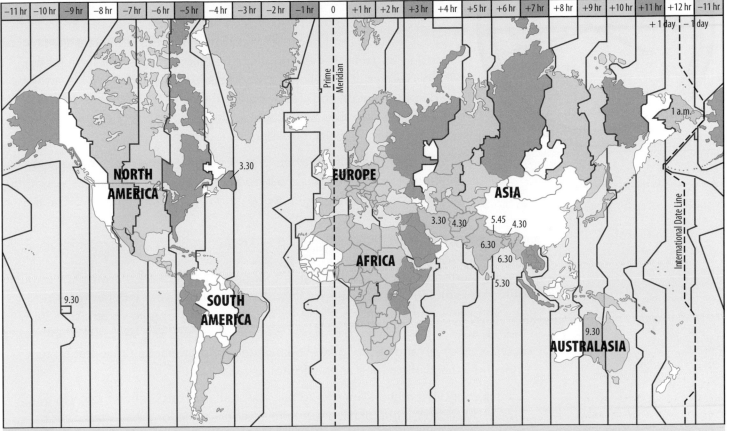

Figure 5.2 Time zones. New York is 5 hours behind GMT and Dubai is 4 hours ahead. Place them on the time line and then count the number of hours between the two to calculate their time difference.

▶ Daylight saving time

Many countries have daylight saving time when they adjust their time by one hour in the spring and summer. In the UK we often refer to pulling our 'clocks forward' by an hour on the last Sunday in March and putting our 'clocks back' on the last Sunday in October. Between these dates we are on British Summer Time (BST), which is one hour ahead of GMT.

▶ Calculating worldwide time

Using a time line can make it easier to calculate the difference in time between different destinations.

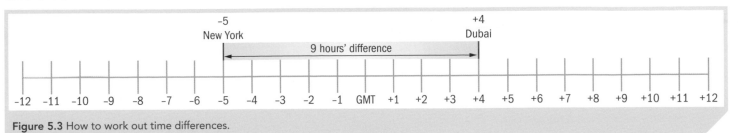

Figure 5.3 How to work out time differences.

Figure 5.4 A 24-hour clock. Why do you think this is used in the travel industry?

You should be aware that the travel industry uses the 24-hour clock as standard business practice. This means that times after 12 noon change to 13:00, 14:00. You can see this in Figure 5.4.

▶ Human health

Travelling long distances across numerous time zones can impact on your health. This is because it takes time for your body to adjust to losing or gaining time. Long-haul travellers often suffer from jet lag. This can result in feeling dizzy and disorientated, being wide awake during the night and sleepy during the day. It can be very difficult for cabin crew on long-haul flights as their body clocks become confused and they find it hard to readjust to local time.

Another health issue when flying long-haul is the risk of deep vein thrombosis (DVT). This is a blood clot caused by inactivity when sitting on a long-distance flight. It is a serious condition that can be fatal.

| Assessment activity 5.1 | Maths | 2A.P1 | 2A.P2 | 2A.P3 | 2A.M1 | 2A.M2 | 2A.M3 | 2A.D1 |

Having started working for a worldwide tour operator there are many things to do before recommending destinations to customers. During your induction period you've been invited to carry out some product briefings for fellow trainees. Your team leader has asked you to research climatic conditions and seasonal variations in two short-haul and two long-haul destinations and prepare a presentation to show how these affect their appeal for tourists.

During your presentation you should talk about all four destinations, but you should then choose one of the short-haul and one of the long-haul destinations and compare and contrast the ways in which the climatic conditions and seasonal variations affect their appeal. You could also look at how the time zone that the destination is located in affects its appeal.

Your team leader now wants to check your understanding of time zones and time differences around the world.

Then describe what time zones are and explain how they can affect visitors. Provide at least four worked examples to show that you can make correct calculations when travelling east, west and across the International Date Line.

Tips

Choose destinations that have been affected by climatic conditions in the last five years. Use real case studies from sources, such as newspaper articles, to help show the effects on the selected destinations.

- When making your presentation, don't forget that climate can have both negative and positive impacts on destinations.
- In your presentation make links to the global aspects such as proximity to the equator, the tropics or differences in the northern and southern hemispheres.
- There are some specific terms to include in your description of time zones, including lines of longitude, Greenwich Mean Time, International Date Line, Daylight Savings Time, and you need to show how time changes as you travel east and west.

▶ How entry/exit requirements affect different destinations

Introduction

Imagine planning a fantastic holiday overseas and then finding out too late that you need a visa. Travel agents will give you visa advice, but if you book independently it is down to you to do your homework, and make sure you get it right. How can you make sure you have the correct documentation?

▶ Reasons for, and importance of, exit/entry requirements

Passports

You have to have a valid passport to travel to any country outside the UK. Some countries insist that your passport must be valid for six months after the return date, so you need to check well in advance to make sure there is time to obtain a new passport if required.

Visas

Visas are special endorsements to your passport, required by some countries, giving permission to enter and leave the country. Visa requirements vary depending on the nature of a trip and have conditions restricting work and length of stay.

Departure taxes

You may be surprised to learn that many countries like Mexico and Australia impose a departure tax when you leave the country. Usually this amount is included in the price of the air ticket, but you should check in advance to avoid any unpleasant surprises at the return airport.

Airport Passenger Duty

Often abbreviated as APD, Airport Passenger Duty is a tax charged to people travelling out of the UK by air. It is added to the flight cost and the amount varies according to the destination airport. It is an unpopular tax and some national newspapers started up petitions against APD.

Take it further

You can find information about entry requirements in the country travel advice sections on the Foreign & Commonwealth Office (FCO) website. To access this website for this, visit Pearson hotlinks. You can access this by going to www.pearsonhotlinks.co.uk and searching for this title.

Discussion point

Why are passports and visas important travel documents?

Case study

Airport Passenger Duty was introduced in 1994, with a £5 rate for UK/EU flights and £10 elsewhere. Since then there have been numerous increases prior to the controversial introduction of four geographical bands in 2009, based on the distance of a country's capital city from London. From April 2013 the APD for a Band D economy flight seat was £94, and £188 for a premium class seat. For a family of four that is a significant additional cost. Some countries have seen tourism numbers from the UK drop considerably as a result of APD and it has been claimed that some airlines have had to withdraw certain routes due to the impact of APD.

1 Can you find examples of destinations or airlines that have been affected by the introduction of APD?

2 Plan a trip to an American city. How much APD will you need to pay?

▶ Effects

Inconvenience to travellers

Having to obtain a visa can be inconvenient and costly. If you are planning a holiday you will need enough time to organise a visa. Some tourist visas can be obtained online and many travel agents offer a visa service. However, business travellers may need to visit a country at short notice and visa requirements for that country might prevent them from doing so. Some visas have to be applied for in person at a country's embassy. These are usually located in London which can add to the inconvenience and cost.

Additional security for destinations and travellers

One of the reasons for countries issuing visas to potential visitors is that it gives them time to carry out security checks on the applicant. In turn this can speed up the arrival process as the immigration officers will have fewer checks to carry out on visitors.

Requirements associated with different destinations

Visa requirements for different countries change constantly, therefore it is essential to check the most up-to-date information before you book your flight. Some countries have other entry requirements, for example relating to money or having a return ticket, so you need to find out about these before you travel.

| Activity 5.2 | Visas |

Choose one country in each continent.
- Find out if visas are required and any other entry requirements.
- How much would visa costs or any other entry requirements influence your decision to visit a country?

Requirements associated with different types of traveller

Countries usually have different entry requirements for different categories of visitor. It is in their interests to have free or reasonably priced visas to encourage tourists and business travellers. Many countries have special visas for students or gap year travellers who might want to work as part of an extended stay.

| Activity 5.3 | Going to Australia |

Most visitors to Australia need an Instant Tourist Visa. These are convenient to obtain online and are relatively cheap. However, they are time and work restricted. If you are a student on a gap year, a Working Holiday Visa would be the one to choose. This is aimed at those aged 18 to 30 who would like to stay and work for up to a year.

Find out what other types of Australian visa are available for different types of visitor.

Decide which would be the best type of visa for the following three people:
- a young doctor who wants to work in Melbourne for a year
- an ambitious thirty-something who is planning to open his own business in Sydney
- a retired couple who plan to move to Brisbane permanently.

▶ How health issues affect travel and tourism

Introduction

Wouldn't it be awful if you came back from your holiday with some tropical disease rather than just your photos and souvenirs? Do you know how to protect your health abroad? It's something we should all be aware of, but too often we just think 'It won't happen to me'. But one day it might.

Key term

A **pandemic** – when an infectious disease spreads through populations across continents, for example the swine flu pandemic in 2009, which affected tourism, especially in Mexico.

▶ Travel health risks

Some diseases are fatal; therefore if you are travelling to a risk area you should take preventative action to protect your health abroad.

Table 5.1 – Diseases to be aware of when travelling abroad.

Disease	How transmitted	Prevention	Main risk areas
Malaria	Bites from infected mosquitoes	Tablets, mosquito repellent, protective clothing and net, vaccination	Africa, India
Human immunodeficiency virus (HIV)	Contaminated needles, unprotected sex	Avoid these	Sub-Saharan countries, e.g. South Africa, Zimbabwe, Mozambique
Pandemics, e.g. swine flu, bird flu	Airborne virus, hand contact, bird droppings	Vaccination	Anywhere
Typhoid	Contaminated food and water	Vaccination	Parts of Africa, Asia, Indian sub-continent, South America
Hepatitis A	Contaminated food and water	Vaccination	Africa, Far East, Central and South America
Hepatitis B	Infected blood, contaminated needles	Vaccination	All over the world
Tetanus	Bacteria, dirty cuts and scratches	Vaccination	Anywhere
Yellow fever	Bites from infected mosquitoes	Vaccination	Tropical Africa and South America
Dengue fever	Bites from infected mosquitoes	Protective clothing and net, mosquito repellent	South East Asia, Pacific Islands, South and Central America, Indian sub-continent, Caribbean, Africa

Pick a country and research the kind of vaccinations you may need to get before you travel.

Discussion point

Why is it important to have travel insurance?

Take it further

Find out about health risks, prevention and treatment for different regions of the world by visiting the National Travel and Health Network Centre website. To access this website, visit Pearson hotlinks at www.pearsonhotlinks.co.uk and search for this title.

▶ Precautions

Vaccinations

Visitors must plan ahead if they are considering travelling to areas of risk. Vaccinations are available to guard against some diseases. Often these have to be administered within specific time frames and sometimes more than one dose is required in order to build up resistance.

Clothing

In malaria risk countries it is advisable to wear loose-fitting, long-sleeved clothes and long trousers in the evenings to guard against mosquito bites. You can buy clothing that has been treated with insect repellent from outdoor sports shops. In regions where the risk is great, you can wear a head net or hat to protect your face.

Medicines

Tablets are used to protect against malaria. Some have to be taken before, during and after a visit to a risk area. Most are available by prescription only. When travelling to less developed countries it is not uncommon to suffer from gastroenteritis and travellers should take medication with them to ease the symptoms.

Equipment

Insect repellent and mosquito nets are the main forms of protection against mosquito bites. Plug-in devices are useful in hotels to release insect repellent into the air. Iodine tablets for disinfecting water and portable water filters are useful when travelling to countries where tap water is not chlorinated or where sanitation is poor.

▶ Emergency situations that affect travel and tourism

Introduction

It could be a frightening experience if you were confined to your hotel room listening to hurricane winds or the sound of rioting out in the streets. You cannot always plan for these situations, but they do affect travellers and impact on the appeal of destinations. How can you find out what is happening around the world?

▶ Emergency situations and their effects

Extreme weather

Taking a holiday to an 'at risk' area like the Caribbean during the hurricane season could mean that you experience an emergency situation at first hand. This is when there is threat to life and major structural damage to buildings. In extreme cases airports close, guests are confined to hotels for their own safety and windows are boarded up. Sometimes visitors are taken away from coastal resorts to places of safety. Communication systems can be affected as well as all local transport. Usually the **FCO** will publish a travel alert. Airlines and tour operators will have to make alternative arrangements to bring people home and deal with those whose holidays have been disrupted.

Terrorist attacks

Terrorist attacks are usually sporadic meaning that they are 'one off', resulting in short-term disruption, fear and reluctance to travel to a destination. Airport security is stepped up if there is an increased threat of terrorist activity, as is security around major tourist attractions, transport and accommodation. The FCO provides essential up-to-date travel advice on its website to advise visitors if it is safe to travel to a destination.

Wars and riots

Tour operators avoid running holidays to countries where there are wars and will withdraw destinations immediately if war breaks out. However, unexpected rioting can occur in and around tourist destinations and tour operators have to assess the risk to their customers. The FCO will publish advice for travel to these areas and tour operators follow this advice, bringing customers home and cancelling holidays if necessary. It can take time for a country to recover from the adverse publicity that rioting brings.

After the storm – how quickly can destinations recover from extreme weather?

Key term

FCO – the Foreign & Commonwealth Office. You should check out their country travel advice at their website before you travel. You can access this by visiting Pearson hotlinks, www.pearsonhotlinks. co.uk, and searching for this title. If you travel to a country against FCO advice your insurance may not be valid.

Case study

Since 2011, Egypt's tourism industry has suffered from adverse publicity generated by several years of rioting and unrest. With its ancient pyramids, Nile cruises, and beautiful Red Sea resorts, the country has been a magnet for tourists. Tourism numbers are said to have reduced by 30% from 2010 to 2011. Ongoing disturbances have continued to affect tourism providers, from pyramid guides to major hotels.

Check the FCO website to find the current travel advice for Egypt.

1 Would you want to travel to Egypt under the current guidance?

2 How does the FCO's guidance affect the kind of insurance you could get for a holiday to Egypt? Research online to find out.

Take it further

Find a recent example of a hurricane or cyclone that has affected a tourist destination in the last five years. What were the long- and short-term effects on the destination? How long did it take the destination to recover?

Figure 5.5 The Pacific Ring of Fire.

Natural disasters

Countries like Japan and New Zealand are in the 'Pacific Ring of Fire', an area of regular earthquakes and volcanic eruptions. Earthquakes deep under the ocean can cause tsunamis, huge tidal waves that gather momentum and can cause damage to buildings and loss of life when they reach land.

Assessment activity 5.2

2B.P4 | 2B.P5 | 2B.P6 | 2B.M4 | 2B.M5 | 2B.D2

After your induction period with a tour operator, you have started work in the customer services department. One of your first projects is to update some of the customer travel documentation.

Using the title 'What you need to know before you go' produce information packs with useful information for travellers.

- In Section 1, describe the importance of, and reasons for, passports and visas with specific reference to two travel destinations.

- In Section 2, provide information about the health risks associated with travel to four destinations, and the precautions people should take before/during their trip. For one of the health risks, assess the short- and long-term effects on travel.

- In Section 3, focus on emergency situations by presenting two case studies. In each case study you should focus on an emergency situation that occurred within the last five years and look at how this affected travel. For one of these examples, you should weigh up the short- and long-term effects.

Tips

- Provide evidence of your research and give examples to add depth to your work.

- When looking at health, choose destinations where health risks are significant and where you can find evidence of their impact.

- Consider how emergency situations could result in disruption to travel, cancelled holidays, reduced visitor numbers, personal safety, repatriation and restricted seasons.

WorkSpace

▶ Michael Abeyie

Airport Passenger Handling Agent

I work for a UK airport handling agent. My main responsibilities are:

- checking in passengers and their luggage
- asking security questions
- issuing boarding passes
- giving information about boarding times and locations.

I love working at the airport. My job is on check-in so I'm one of the first people travellers come into contact with when they start their holidays or business trips.

First impressions are really important so it's service with a smile, even when I've had a five o'clock start. Travellers are often tired and can be difficult to deal with.

Most days run fairly efficiently, but sometimes there is a major incident that can bring the airport to a standstill. This can be anything from severe fog in the UK, a major security alert or even volcanic ash closing down airspace. If the flights can't leave the airport it soon becomes very crowded and we just have to stay professional and keep people informed as soon as we have any information. The airport was closed for days due to the volcanic ash cloud – thousands of travellers had their flights cancelled. It was very frustrating because it was outside our control.

Fortunately, most days are fairly routine. I enjoy meeting people and helping to get their trip off to a good start but you never know what will be next – a forgotten passport, a missed flight or maybe a hurricane whirling across the Atlantic. It's all in a day's work.

Think about it

1. How will this unit help you when planning holidays in the future?
2. What are the benefits of booking your worldwide holiday through a travel agent?
3. What skills and qualities would you need to carry out a job like Michael's?

Introduction

Travel and tourism organisations provide dreams and experiences for their customers. That's really an exciting and enjoyable part to play in their lives. Customers of travel and tourism organisations – whether they are travelling on business, or on holiday, or for other personal reasons – will have needs and expectations when it comes to the services that are provided. Your organisation must ensure its products and services meet, and even exceed, those needs and expectations.

When you are working as part of the industry, you have a powerful part to play in providing customers with service that sparkles. It is the service you and your organisation provide that will make the customer decide whether to buy from you and, importantly, come back to give you more business. There are plenty of competitors out there keen to take your customers from you – don't let them.

In this unit you will explore the definition and aims of customer service and the ways different organisations seek to provide it to different types of customer.

Assessment: The unit will be assessed by a series of assignments and tasks set by your teacher/tutor.

Learning aims

In this unit you will:

A investigate travel and tourism customer service

B explore the needs and expectations of different types of customer in the travel and tourism sector

C understand the importance of customer service to travel and tourism organisations.

This unit helped me understand that customer service doesn't just happen. I discovered that organisations have to really understand their customers to make sure they are providing what they want, in the style that they want it. Their staff must be willing and able to provide excellent customer service.

I enjoyed learning from some real examples of how customer service is delivered. I found it useful to explore how I could provide customer service and it was fun practising it on my own and with my group.

Josh, *17-year-old Travel and Tourism student*

The Travel and Tourism Customer Experience

Assessment Zone

This table shows you what you must do in order to achieve a **Pass**, **Merit**, or **Distinction** grade, and where you can find activities in this book to help you.

Assessment criteria			
Level 1	Level 2 Pass	Level 2 Merit	Level 2 Distinction
Learning aim A: Investigate travel and tourism customer service			
1A.1 Outline the main aims of customer service for travel and tourism organisations.	**2A.P1** Describe the main aims of customer service for three different travel and tourism organisations. **See Assessment activity 6.1, page 148**	**2A.M1** Explain, using relevant examples, the main aims of customer service for two different travel and tourism organisations. **See Assessment activity 6.1, page 148**	**2A.D1** Compare and contrast the main customer service aims for two different travel and tourism organisations. **See Assessment activity 6.1, page 148**
Learning aim B: Explore the needs and expectations of different types of customer in the travel and tourism sector			
1B.2 Identify the needs of one internal and one external customer type.	**2B.P2** Explain the needs of three customer types and how they are met. **See Assessment activity 6.2, page 163**	**2B.M2** Compare, using relevant examples, how two travel and tourism organisations meet and exceed customer expectations. **See Assessment activity 6.2, page 163**	**2B.D2** Evaluate the success of two different travel and tourism organisations in recognising and meeting the needs of their customers. **See Assessment activity 6.2, page 163**
1B.3 Outline how three travel and tourism organisations meet and exceed customer expectations.	**2B.P3** Explain how three travel and tourism organisations meet and exceed customer expectations. **See Assessment activity 6.2, page 163**		
Learning aim C: Understand the importance of customer service to travel and tourism organisations			
1C.4 Outline customer service skills relevant to two travel and tourism organisations.	**2C.P4** Explain customer service skills relevant to two travel and tourism organisations. **See Assessment activity 6.3, page 173**	**2C.M3** Compare customer service skills relevant to two travel and tourism organisations. **See Assessment activity 6.3, page 173**	**2C.D3** Recommend and justify improvements to poor customer service for one travel and tourism organisation. **See Assessment activity 6.3, page 173**
1C.5 Describe the impacts of excellent and poor customer service on travel and tourism organisations.	**2C.P5** Assess the impact of excellent and poor customer service on travel and tourism organisations. **See Assessment activity 6.3, page 173**	**2C.M4** Compare, using relevant examples, the impacts of excellent and poor customer service on two travel and tourism organisations. **See Assessment activity 6.3, page 173**	

How you will be assessed

This unit will be assessed by a series of assignments set by your teacher/tutor. You will be expected to show an understanding of what customer service is. For example, you may be asked to create a poster for staff in a travel and tourism organisation which states what the customer service aims are in that organisation, and how they will be delivered.

You will also be expected to show an understanding of the needs and expectations of different types of customer. For example, you may be asked to make a presentation explaining the needs which disabled travellers may have and how those needs are met.

You will be expected to show an understanding of how customer service is delivered by different sizes and types of travel and tourism organisations. For example, you may be asked to write a report on how three different travel and tourism organisations try to exceed customers' expectations.

Additionally, you will be expected to show an understanding of the skills needed to deliver excellent customer service. For example, you may be asked to role play two customer service scenarios in a small group.

Finally, you may be asked to write a report which assesses the impact poor and excellent customer service can have upon the success of travel and tourism organisations.

Your assessment could take the form of:

- written work
- presentations
- role plays.

What is customer service?

Introduction

Every day we experience **customer** service. It might be when we buy something in a shop, or when we travel on a bus, or go to a musical festival, or visit a swimming pool. So, before you go any further, you need to decide what customer service is.

In a small group, suggest short phrases that complete the sentence: 'Customer service is . . .'

Definition of customer service

Your group probably offered quite a few words and phrases that help define **customer service**. Perhaps they included:

- meeting the customers' needs every time
- exceeding the customers' needs
- being attentive and helpful
- being concerned and sincere
- making the customer happy to return
- having the customer enjoy the experience.

The definition is a reminder that a business must provide customer service before, during and after a customer buys a product or service.

The importance of customer service

Customer service is important because:

- you need customers to buy products or services from you
- you need customers to be so pleased with you that they keep buying your products or services
- customers tell others of their good experiences and they will, in turn, start to buy from you
- it can cost five times as much to win a new customer as it does to keep an existing one loyal
- you want the security, personal development and buzz which comes from providing excellent customer service.

The 3 Ps of customer service

There are three components to customer service.

- **Product or service.** This is the item you are buying. It may be an inclusive holiday, or a visit to a theme park, or car hire. Does it give you what you expected?
- **Processes and procedures.** These are what you have to use to buy or use the product or service. It might be how you are able to select and purchase it, for example, by visiting a travel agent or using the internet. It might be about how you can use it, for example, can you check in for your flight on the internet or at a self-service kiosk at the airport, or a check-in desk?
- **Personal behaviour.** This is the human behaviour of the people you had dealings with when buying or using the product or service.

Product and service   Processes and procedures   Personal behaviour

The 3 Ps of customer service.

Case study

Jan Carlzon was the Chief Executive Officer of a major airline. He realised that the reputation and success of the airline depended upon how highly the passengers rated their contact with staff, for example when a passenger made a reservation, when they checked in for their flight, when they boarded the aircraft, when they spoke to cabin crew, or when they retrieved their baggage. The contact with staff could be for any reason and by any method, lasting for several minutes or just a few seconds.

He called these contacts **'Moments of truth'**. He recognised that the airline had to do everything it could to make them successful. He said that 'Moments of truth' were the moments that in the end would decide whether an organisation would succeed or fail.

1 What did Jan Carlzon mean by a 'Moment of truth'?

2 What might the 'Moments of truth' be for:
- a travel agency
- a car hire company
- a Tourist Information Centre
- a hotel?

The aims of customer service

Customer service is not just something which is nice to have, it is essential to the organisation in achieving its aims. These aims may vary depending on the organisation, but will usually include:

- meeting customer needs
- meeting organisational targets, such as visitor numbers, bookings, sales
- increasing profits
- creating new business
- encouraging repeat business.

Activity 6.1   What are their aims?

List the names of some travel and tourism organisations; think about the organisations that have been discussed in previous units. On the internet, type in their name and 'aims objectives' in your search engine. How many of the organisations mention customer service in their aims and objectives?

Later you will discover some of the ways organisations develop and use their aims to operate their businesses.

▶ Different organisations in the travel and tourism industry

Introduction

Within the travel and tourism industry there are many different sizes and types of organisation. Write down the names of 12 travel and tourism organisations of various sizes and types. You will explore them further in a later activity.

Some organisations are very large with integrated businesses, while some are small independent companies. Some provide the main goods and services, while others supply the support services. They include:

- **attractions,** such as theme parks, heritage sites, activity centres
- **accommodation,** such as hotels, villas, campsites, holiday centres
- **transport operators,** such as airlines, ferries, train operators, coach companies
- **secondary services,** such as tourist offices, airport representatives, travel insurers, passport offices.

▷ Size of organisation

The size of the organisation is likely to have an impact upon the way it provides customer service. The European Commission defines the sizes of organisations in the following ways.

Small organisations

These are organisations with fewer than 50 employees and an annual **turnover** or annual **balance sheet** not exceeding €10 million.

Small organisations may know many of their clients as regular customers, which enables them to give a more personal style of service. They may focus upon a **niche market**. For example, they may sell walking holidays or gastronomy tours. This provides a focus to the source of their potential customers, e.g. through the Rambler's Association or Cookery magazines.

Key terms

Turnover – is the money brought into the business through sales.

Balance sheet – is a statement of the financial assets minus the financial liabilities of an organisation.

Niche market – a narrowly defined group of customers which forms a small, but profitable section of the market.

Activity 6.2 A niche market

Use the internet or visit some travel agents. List examples of niche markets you find which are being targeted by organisations.

Medium organisations

These are organisations with 50–250 employees and an annual turnover not exceeding €50 million or an annual balance sheet not exceeding €43 million.

Medium organisations may have more than one outlet and may offer a wider choice of products and services.

Large organisations

These organisations have more than 250 employees and a larger annual turnover or balance sheet than medium organisations.

Large organisations may depend more upon systems and technology to help provide customer service compared to smaller organisations using the same technology, for example internet booking facilities or loyalty cards, but with the right approach and staff they can still provide a personal service.

▶ Types of organisation

Public

This is the non-commercial part of the industry which, though they still must make a profit, aim to provide a supporting service or to educate. Examples include Tourist Information Centres (TICs), VisitBritain, Go Belfast and the World Tourism Organization.

Private

This is the commercial part of the industry, for example TUI, Marriott Hotels, Virgin Atlantic, Blackpool Pleasure Beach Ltd and National Express. These companies exist to make a profit for their owners or shareholders.

A large, private sector hotel. Would you like to visit this type of hotel?

Other

Other types of organisation include the voluntary sector which relies upon donations and entrance fees and is often staffed by volunteers, such as the National Trust, Youth Hostel Association and English Heritage.

Activity 6.3   Sizes and types

In the activity at the start of this topic you named organisations of various sizes and types. Put their names into the correct boxes in this table.

Organisations	Public	Private	Other
Small			
Medium			
Large			

Add any more organisations you have thought of.

⏏ Take it further

Research two travel organisations of different sizes and types. Compare and contrast their main customer service aims. Why are they the same or different?

Although the size and type of an organisation may influence the style of customer service provided, the same customer service principles apply.

Assessment activity 6.1

2A.P1 | 2A.M1 | 2A.D1

You have volunteered to help a travel company in your local area called 'Pitch up and Stay'. This was set up two years ago and specialises in camping and caravanning holidays in the UK. A lot of their customers have heard about them through word of mouth, but the company is now expanding rapidly and they want to set same benchmarks for good customer service. You offer to carry out some research to help improve its understanding of customer service.

- Research three travel and tourism organisations that offer camping and caravanning holidays to find out about their main aims when it comes to customer service and present your findings in detail. See if they have any specific benchmarks such as answering the phone in a set number of rings or dealing with complaints in a set time frame.
- Select two organisations and compare their aims and benchmarks. Are there similarities? Are there ways that their customer services aims differ?

Tips

- When you start, keep your research wide by looking at organisations that are quite different from one another. For example, one could be private and small; another could be public and large.
- You should include plenty of examples when you are comparing the aims of the different organisations.
- You will need to present your findings in your own words rather than copy information from the internet. You will need to include references for the website addresses and other sources of information you used in case the owners wish to go back to these sources for further information.
- Think about the best way to present your findings. You could produce a short presentation or you could write a report.

Customer types

Introduction

It is easy to think that customers are just those who buy products or services from an organisation, but it is important to understand that, while they are the external customers, everyone in an organisation also has internal customers.

Imagine you are an assistant in a travel agency. Who are your customers?

Internal customers

Internal customers are those who you directly or indirectly work with to ensure excellent service is given to external customers. They may include:

- colleagues and staff with whom you work closely
- supervisors and managers
- directors and owners
- staff at other locations
- suppliers.

All of them are links in the customer service delivery chain which will deliver service to the external customer. You rely on them to do their jobs well so that you can do your job well. Equally, they rely upon you to do your job well. Only if everyone is doing a good job can the customer service delivery chain stay unbroken. You do not want to be the weak link which breaks that chain.

Customer service is only possible if everyone in the organisation (whether or not they have direct contact with the external customer) aims to give customer satisfaction.

Do not be the link that breaks the customer service delivery chain.

A holiday representative on a coach tour cannot give excellent service to the external customer unless:

- the reservations staff are accurate when taking bookings
- the coach operator provides a smart, mechanically sound coach
- the coach driver is dressed smartly and a good driver
- the hotels have prepared for the arrival of the passengers
- the holiday representative has been provided with information about the places they will visit.

External customers

External customers are those outside the organisation who buy the organisation's products or services.

New customers

When your organisation is first created it will only have new customers, but it must continually aim to attract new customers, otherwise it will shrink and die. New customers will probably be unfamiliar with the products and services you offer. Your organisation will also be unfamiliar with the needs, wants and desires of new customers. The new customer is willing to try your organisation and so your organisation needs to better understand the customer.

Existing customers

If the new customer is pleased with your organisation, it is to be hoped that they will become a repeat or existing customer. Your organisation needs to continue to deliver the products and services which the customer wants. This may change over time as the customer changes their needs, for example because their business needs or leisure interests change. External changes may also impact upon what your customer wants, such as advances in technology or as new destinations are developed.

Individuals

Your customers may be individuals travelling on their own. If proposing a holiday to an individual traveller, discover whether they will know someone else on the holiday. If not, find out discreetly if they want to be on their own or if they would prefer to be with others. Select the holiday carefully to reflect their needs and wants. While on holiday, they may appreciate you, as a holiday representative, talking with them from time to time. They might welcome you introducing them to other guests, but remember they may prefer to remain on their own.

Groups

Other customers may be in a group. Some groups are organised, e.g. a school party or orchestra. Organised groups normally have a leader who can tell you the group's needs and assist you in communicating with the group. They will usually make sure the group is in the right place at the right time and may hold the group's tickets and passports. Working with the group leader will help you enormously, but don't forget that each member of the group has their own needs, so make sure these are met as well.

Other groups do not have a leader, for example those who happen to be on the same visitor attraction tour or inclusive holiday. They may have never met before. You need to be alert to their individual needs, so watch for those who look concerned or seem to want to ask a question.

Think about the type of customer who would go on this type of holiday.

Families

Families are an important sector of the travel and tourism industry and form a major part of those taking vacations, particularly during school holiday periods. They will usually let one of the family take the lead, but don't forget to include all of the family in what you do and say. Talk to the children – share their excitement about going on holiday.

Couples

Couples may be travelling just as a couple, or as part of a group. They may want privacy or they may want to join in with others. It is part of your job to find out what they prefer and to provide it.

Special interests

Travellers may be taking holidays to enjoy their leisure special interests, for example waterskiing, botany, dancing, steam trains. The type of leisure interest they have will influence their needs and choice of holidays.

Business travellers

Business travellers want quick and efficient service. They need the facilities and support normally available to them in their business environment. At airports they will value the use of a business lounge, where there are communication facilities, newspapers and refreshments. They also need particular facilities and services at hotels.

International business travellers often have to cope with jet lag. They may have flown to Sydney which is 11 hours ahead of the UK. Their watch says it is 3 p.m., but their body will be telling them it feels like 4 a.m. That can influence their needs and when those needs occur.

Remember though, even business travellers need to relax, so they may become leisure travellers as well, and expect the customer service appropriate to those leisure interests.

Activity 6.4   What I want my hotel to provide

Make a list of the facilities and services an international business traveller might need from a hotel.

WorkSpace

▷ Debbie Roche

Cruise Line Purser

Having obtained good grades in my BTEC Travel and Tourism course I applied for a job with a cruise line.

After a season as a shore-based Customer Service Assistant I was promoted to the position of Purser on board one of our cruise ships.

In a typical day I undertake many varied tasks. Much of my time is spent with the passengers, working on the reception desk giving information and advice, exchanging currency, helping passengers with any problems they may have and resolving their complaints.

Often I work on the shore tours desk, recommending and booking tours for our passengers and selling maps and postcards.

At other times I tour around the ship chatting to passengers and helping in whichever way I can. It's always nice to be able to talk to the passengers and it's a good way of learning to understand their needs so that I can help them more effectively.

I found it all a bit confusing and daunting at first, but the crew work well together and we have fun in our off-duty hours. The work can be tiring, particularly as it is shift work and we are often working to a deadline, but I really get a buzz helping people enjoy themselves. Another plus is that I am seeing a lot of the world and learning about other countries and cultures.

Think about it

1 What are you learning in this unit which will give you the background skills and knowledge to do Debbie's job?

2 What further skills and knowledge might you need to develop to do Debbie's job?

Did you know? ❓

Of the overseas journeys taken by UK residents, the share taken by those aged 65 or over has been increasing more than any other age group:

- 2006: 9.03%
- 2008: 9.20%
- 2011: 10.45%

(Source: Office for National Statistics)

Key terms 🔑

Culture – a set of beliefs, values, behaviours, habits, traditions.

Ethnicity – being part of a group with a shared history, sense of identity, or cultural roots.

Age groups

You will have the pleasure of meeting people from every age group from infants to the elderly. Each will respond to different customer service approaches. Children will be delighted that there are facilities and services just for them, like play areas in travel agencies and airports and kids clubs at resorts, but they also appreciate someone they can turn to who can help them have fun and give them assurance at appropriate times. Some adults like child-free zones when travelling or at their destination. Parents appreciate help with their infants and young children. Those of an older generation may appreciate a slightly more formal style of delivery, for example always being referred to as 'sir' or 'madam'.

Culture and ethnicity

Your customers will have different **cultures** and different **ethnicities**, particularly if you are working in the inbound travel sector. People of different cultures or ethnicities may have different needs and wishes from each other. Respect their values and wishes. Learn about the beliefs, customs and traditions of other nationalities and religions. Ignorance can lead to offending customers unintentionally. However, if you are able to demonstrate you understand their culture or ethnicity, they will be impressed by your customer service.

In what ways might children have different needs from those of the elderly?

Those with additional physical needs

Approximately one in five people in the UK have some form of disability. Clearly your aim, partly reinforced by law, is to respond to their needs and interests. This may mean creating suitable holiday packages for them, arranging appropriate hotel facilities and transport, and ensuring that the accommodation, equipment, processes and procedures in your organisation meet their needs.

Do not forget that some people are physically disabled, while others have a learning disability. Also, their disability may not always be obvious. You might recognise that someone is blind, but how easy is it to know that someone is deaf? They may ask you to repeat things to them, but is that because they don't speak your language or is it because they are hard of hearing?

Just checking ✓

1 What is an internal customer? Give some examples.
2 What is an external customer? Give some examples.

▶ Needs of different types of customer

Introduction

All customers share a common set of needs. They want you to:

- make them feel important, which means valuing them and treating them as an individual
- know your products and services
- listen, show empathy and understand how they feel.

However, they are individuals. They all have their own needs, wants and desires. Some are practical, some are emotional. Think of your family and friends. In what ways will their needs differ from each other when they are on holiday?

We all tend to say we need something, but do we really need it? Is it a want or a desire rather than a need? Think about a passenger who has asked you about going from London to Paris. He may need to get from London to Paris tomorrow by midday. He may want to go by train, although there are the alternatives of making a ferry crossing or flying. He may have a desire to travel in business class. So, if you are a travel consultant, you must discover which are his needs, which are his wants, and which are his desires, and tailor your selling and customer service techniques to recognise the difference. There is no point in trying to sell him business class on a flight if it does not get him to Paris by midday.

The travel and tourism industry is a people business. People will seek information, safety, advice, products and services, and other specific help from you.

Discussion point

In a small group discuss what you **need** to get from studying this course, what you **want** to get from studying it, and what you **desire** to get from studying it.

▶ Accurate information

Customers expect to be given accurate information. That means you need to know your products and services and how they meet the needs of the customer. What type of holiday, which destination, what sort of transportation and accommodation would meet their needs and what information can you give them to help them decide, for example how much it will cost and when it is available.

Apart from providing information in advance to help your customers make their purchasing decisions, they will also need information when they are in a particular situation, for example:

- Can you give me directions to...?
- At what time is the next show starting?
- Can I take my surfboard on the flight?
- What is the weather forecast for this afternoon?

It needs to be accurate. Telling someone it will take about one to four hours to get somewhere isn't accurate enough. Neither is it accurate enough to say the cost includes breakfast – is that a continental breakfast or a full, cooked breakfast? Telling a customer

Research how airlines have been using technology to keep customers informed about their travel plans.

their train leaves at 9 o'clock can be misleading; do you mean 9 o'clock in the morning or 9 o'clock in the evening? That is why the travel industry uses the 24-hour clock. Practise using it.

Information needs to be timely. There is no point calling a customer on the day of departure to tell them that they will need a visa for the holiday they booked with you two months ago.

Technology is of increasing value in providing information to customers and in keeping them informed. The internet, smartphones and social networks all have their part to play. However, users of technology, whether it be the provider or the customer, must ensure they use the technology appropriately. Some customers are becoming over-familiar with websites and don't read them properly. As an example, some people click that they have read the terms and conditions on a booking website, without having done so, and then discover that there is no refund if the booking is cancelled. Some social networks are becoming overloaded with worthless information meaning that important information may be missed. Play your part by emphasising important information to your customers, perhaps by a second communication, using a different communication method, for example, a follow-up email.

Link

The 24-hour clock is covered in detail in *Unit 5: Factors Affecting Worldwide Travel and Tourism*.

Activity 6.5   How to tell them

On your own, list two appropriate ways for a cruise ship company to communicate with their customers in each of the following situations.

1 What cruises they are offering; when and where to.

2 The price and availability of a cruise.

3 On the day – the ship has diverted to another port because of weather and passengers must join it there.

4 During the cruise – the entertainments programme for the following day.

5 At a port – the tender boats are ready to take passengers from the ship to the shore.

▶ Health, safety and security

Health

Did you know?

The Health and Safety at Work Act (1974) requires all employers and employees to ensure a healthy, safe and secure environment for the public and employees.

Your customers rely on you to keep them healthy, safe and secure while in your care. You share that responsibility with your employer. Be observant. Report anything which could be a hazard, for example a wet floor in a hotel or a strong current at a beach resort.

You should also alert customers to overseas health requirements. Many countries have mandatory or recommended health requirements. This information is available from a number of sources, including the Foreign & Commonwealth Office (FCO), country embassies and travel clinics.

Since 2000 there have been at least three major worldwide health alerts which caused restrictions to travel, changes to travel plans, and stricter controls and procedures:

- Severe Acute Respiratory Syndrome (SARS) which affected 37 countries in 2002/3
- avian flu which spread across many countries in 2003
- swine flu which became widespread in Mexico and elsewhere and threatened to spread across the world.

In each case, those in the travel and tourism industry were kept informed by the World Health Organization, government health departments and other agencies, and were able to inform their customers about how it would affect their travel and holiday arrangements.

Safety

The Health and Safety at Work Act (1974) places a responsibility upon employers and employees to ensure the safety of ourselves and others.

You will see hotels display evacuation procedures in every bedroom and hear coach drivers tell their passengers to wear safety belts. Cruise lines have practice lifeboat drills for all their passengers. Airlines give mandatory safety briefings before every take-off.

Security

Security is ever present, perhaps never more so than in the travel and tourism industry. Access to many forms of transport, hotels, and numerous tourist attractions is monitored, using methods such as closed circuit television, security guards, and body and baggage searches. Remember to play your part by being vigilant and reporting anything suspicious.

Activity 6.6   Health, safety and security

Explain the health, safety and security needs travellers on an African safari holiday may have before, during and after their holiday.

▶ Assistance

Different people need different types of assistance. These needs may change in different circumstances. A business woman may not need help with her wheelie suitcase, but may need help with heavy baggage if travelling on holiday. A passenger may not need help in their own country, but may need help with the language at their holiday destination. Parents may need help with their young children and the elderly may need help climbing stairs at a visitor attraction. Watch for people who may need assistance and provide it the best way you can.

▶ Advice

Customers will look to you for advice. They will consider you to be the expert. A travel agent may be asked about the suitability of a destination for a young family or how best to obtain a visa. A train manager may be asked which is the best side of the train to sit to get the best view. A hotel receptionist may be asked how best to get to a venue because the customer has missed the coach. A holiday resort representative might be asked to recommend a restaurant. This is where your knowledge, problem-solving skills and expertise will help provide excellent customer service.

Take it further

The Foreign & Commonwealth Office website provides a lot of advice and information for travellers. Select a country and investigate the advice and information travellers are given about that country. To access the website for this, visit Pearson hotlinks. You can access this by going to www.pearsonhotlinks.co.uk and searching for this title.

This kind of organisation would need lots of safety procedures. Can you think of any others that would need the same?

Products and services

Make sure you know what products and services your organisation offers and what the benefits of them are. Learn about your competitors' products and services so that you can emphasise to your customers what your organisation offers that your competitors don't.

The customer expects that the product or service they purchased delivers what your organisation promised. The 3 Ps (Product, Processes and Personal behaviour) must all be delivered. Your organisation, and you, must do everything possible to ensure that what the customer bought and is expecting is what is being provided. Are their needs fully met? For example, are you available to them at the times and places they have been promised?

This is not just about whether their flight and hotel is as booked, it is also about the personal customer service you are providing. Are you knowledgeable, friendly and responding appropriately to what they have to say? Is the service you are giving at least to the level the customer expected?

Specific needs

Some customers have special needs. It may be because of a disability. They may need an easy access room, or a wheelchair to take them to and from their transport. They may need an induction loop to help them hear in public areas, or an escort because they are partially sighted. They may have a dietary issue which requires them to have a special meal on their flight.

Special requests are often made to increase the customer's enjoyment. For example, a bride's friend may have asked you to provide a bottle of champagne in the hotel room for a honeymoon couple, or a parent may have asked you to arrange a birthday cake for their child.

Such special needs and requests are very important to your customer, so make sure they are provided. Remember the customer service delivery chain.

Responding to customer needs

Introduction

There are many methods we can use to communicate, they are mostly either some form of written communication, or verbal. You will need an understanding of the options you can use, and how to use them.

List the methods you could use to communicate, for example by phone or email.

Written requests

Much communication is via email and organisations' websites and other technology, such as text messages. However, some customers continue to communicate by letter and written booking forms. It is up to your organisation and you to respond by the appropriate method.

The style, and sometimes the information, can differ depending upon the method of communication, as the Nicky House case study (below) shows.

Case study

The Nicky House Hotel received the following email from a potential customer:

From: SDrudge@bumblemail.co.uk
To: Enquiries@NickyHouse.co.uk

We are considering staying at your hotel.
What availability do you have for two in early June?
What are your rates?
Will your swimming pool be open?
Sarah Drudge

It also received the following letter:

22 Cosy Road,
Anytown,
England
Tel: 01234 567890

The Proprietor,
Nicky House Hotel,
Elsewhere-by-sea,
England

25 April 2013

Dear Sir or Madam,

My girlfriend and I are interested in staying at your hotel in early June. Please let me know what availability you have and what your rates are. We would also like to know if your outdoor swimming pool will be open. We stayed near Elsewhere-by-sea last year and some friends have since recommended your hotel.

Yours faithfully,

Christopher Pritchard

Nicky House has double and twin rooms with sea view available 01–14 June for £100 and a twin room overlooking the garden available 01–07 June for £90. There are no single rooms available. Rates are per room per night including full, cooked breakfast. The heated swimming pool will be available from 01 June.

1 Send an email replying to Sarah Drudge's email.
2 Write a letter replying to Christopher Pritchard's letter.
3 What are the differences in the information and style of the email and letter you received?
4 What are the differences in the information and style of the replies you sent?
5 In what other ways might you have responded to the email and letter?

Email

Nicky Penman sent this email reply to Sarah Drudge's email:

> **From:** Enquiries@NickyHouse.co.uk
> **To:** SDrudge@bumblemail.co.uk
>
> Dear Ms Drudge,
>
> Thank you for email.
>
> At present, we have double and twin sea view rooms available from 1st June to 14th June. We have a twin room overlooking the garden available from 1st June to 7th June. We do not have any single rooms available in June.
>
> The rates are £100 for a sea view room and £90 for the garden view room. These rates are per room per night and include a full, cooked breakfast.
>
> Our outdoor heated swimming pool will be available from 1st June.
>
> If you require any further information please feel free to call me. You may also like to look at our website where you will find more information about our hotel, the area and nearby attractions.
>
> I look forward to hearing from you when you have decided about your dates and the room you would like. I could hold a booking for you until 14th May without a deposit.
>
> I hope you decide to stay with us.
>
> Nicky Penman
> Proprietor
> Nicky House, Tel: 04000 900700, Web: www.nickyhouse.co.uk

Nicky's reply has answered all the questions Sarah Drudge asked and has done so in a style which reflected hers.

Letter

In his letter, Christopher Pritchard gave some background information which would help Nicky make her response more personal. For example, he said he would be with his girlfriend and that they had visited the area before. He also said friends had recommended the hotel.

Nicky does not know exactly what accommodation Christopher wants (one double room, one twin-bedded room or two single rooms). It is important not to make assumptions. He has not said what his exact dates are, so Nicky has tried to cover the likely periods in her reply.

Nicky sent this reply:

> Nicky House Hotel
> Elsewhere-by-sea, England
> Tel: 04000 900700
> Web: www.nickyhouse.co.uk
>
> Mr Christopher Pritchard
> 22, Cosy Road
> Anytown
> England
>
> 27th April 2013
>
> Dear Mr Pritchard,
>
> Thank you for your letter of 25th April, received today. I am delighted that your friends recommended us to you and that you plan to return to our beautiful part of the country.
>
> We have a choice of double and twin bedrooms which have a sea view, or a twin bedroom which overlooks the garden. All are available at present from 1st June to 14th June apart from the room overlooking the garden which is only available from 1st June to 7th June. We do not have any single rooms available in June.
>
> The rates are £100 per room per night for the sea view rooms and £90 per room per night for the room overlooking the garden. These rates include a full, cooked breakfast.
>
> I am pleased to tell you that our outdoor swimming pool, which is heated, will be available from 1st June.
>
> If you require any further information please feel free to call me. You may like to look at our website which will tell you more about our beautiful hotel and the stunning area we live in, together with information about nearby attractions.
>
> I look forward to hearing from you as soon as you have news on the dates you wish to visit us. I will be happy to hold a booking for you until 14th May without a deposit.
>
> I look forward to having you both stay with us.
>
> Regards,
>
> Nicky Penman

Nicky's reply demonstrates that she was responding to all parts of Christopher Pritchard's letter and was providing him with the information he needs. She was also encouraging him to make a booking, both by enthusing about the hotel and area, and by offering to hold a booking without a deposit until shortly before he visits.

Did you notice from the case study that the information Sarah Drudge gave in her email was less than Christopher Pritchard gave in his letter? People are often briefer when sending emails than when writing letters. You should reflect that difference in style in your reply while ensuring that you are still giving the information required.

Did you also notice that Christopher Pritchard gave his telephone number in his letter? That gave Nicky the opportunity to phone him with her reply. That makes the contact more personal. Also, it enables her to give a more expansive reply and provide more information about her products and service. She can use more of her selling techniques to convince him to make a booking while on the phone. She would need to make sure that she had gathered all the information she needed to give in advance and that she had prepared herself for a two-way conversation.

In both her email and her letter Nicky has offered alternative ways to communicate, i.e. using the website or telephone.

Booking forms

Until recently, tour operators included a booking form in their brochures, but now travel and tourism organisations encourage customers to make their bookings online through their websites. Organisations must design their booking forms so that they:

- are easy to read
- ask all the questions which the organisation needs to be answered
- provide the information the customer needs
- are clear and unambiguous.

Activity 6.7   Website booking

Find the websites for three tour operators. Choose a holiday from each website and make a dummy booking to experience the booking process you are taken through.

1 What made them easy to use?

2 What made them difficult to use?

3 What facility was there to identify any extra needs the customer might have?

▶ Verbal requests

Earlier in this unit you read about Jan Carlzon's 'Moments of truth'. Most of those moments happen when there is a verbal contact between the customer and someone in the organisation.

Verbal requests might be face to face. For example, a customer may discuss their needs with a consultant in a travel agency, or with an escort during a coach tour, or a holiday representative at a resort. Verbal requests might also be by telephone, perhaps to a call centre or a hotel reception, or to a visitor attraction.

In all cases, staff must listen carefully to what the customer is saying or asking and be prepared to respond helpfully, knowledgeably and clearly.

Verbal requests might occur when customer's are using the product or service, for example, when asking about a car's equipment or for driving directions.

▶ Recognising unstated needs

Sometimes customers don't realise they have a need – using your experience and staying alert will help you realise that the customer might need something. For example, as a travel consultant, you might realise that someone will need a visa for the

Discussion point

In a small group, decide what reasons there might be for customers' needs to be unstated. Think of some examples.

holiday they are booking, so you should tell them and help them obtain it. As cabin crew you might notice someone does not have their seatbelt fastened, so you need to remind them.

Other times, customers may know that they have a need, but feel too sensitive about asking, or think that no one can help. Perhaps you are a hotel receptionist and notice you have to repeat everything you say to a guest; could it be they are hard of hearing or is it that they do not understand your language very well? Either way, you need to help them.

Perhaps a waiter on a cruise ship may notice someone is not eating their dinner. If he asks, he may discover the person is vegetarian and does not want to eat the beef on the plate in front of her but is too shy to tell anyone.

What additional skills do you think would be useful for waiting staff working at travel and tourism destinations?

It may be that someone does not ask because they have decided they will just cope on their own. For example, a parent with a baby may not ask to be boarded onto the aircraft first, or a guest with mobility problems may not ask if they could have a ground floor room. They would likely be delighted if you noticed they might have that need and that you offered to help them.

Recognising unstated needs is an important part of your customer service delivery skills. Be alert to your customers and watch for those times when they may need help but are not asking for it.

TOPIC B4

▶ Exploring expectations of different types of customer in the travel and tourism sector

Introduction

All customers have certain expectations when it comes to the products and services they are being offered. In a small group, discuss why you and your organisation would want to exceed the customer's expectations.

▶ Meeting expectations

Your customer has been convinced to buy your product or service. You have given them expectations of what that product or service will provide. Your customer also has expectations based upon previous customer service experiences and what their culture and ethnicity expects. Remember, you are giving your customers experiences and those experiences must meet their dreams and expectations.

Did you know?   **?**

In Northern Europe, greetings are quite formal, e.g. a handshake. In Southern Europe, greetings are likely to be less formal, e.g. hugging and cheek kissing.

Activity 6.8   Food, glorious food!

What dietary needs should you be aware of and check about before offering food to:

1 Jews

2 Hindus

3 Muslims.

Customers expect the information you provide them to be timely and accurate. They expect their journey to be punctual. They expect their hotel room to be clean. They expect their family to be looked after well. They expect their excursions to be fun and interesting. They have many expectations! Your organisation, and you, must clearly understand their expectations and make sure they are met.

Everyone in the customer service delivery chain, whether they have direct contact with the customer or are working behind the scenes, must work hard to meet customer expectations. The product must be good, the level of service must be as expected and the organisation must be efficient. If one person does not do their job to the best of their ability, the customer service delivery chain will be broken and the customer's expectations won't be met.

▶ Exceeding expectations

Think of a time when you bought something. Perhaps you went to a shop to buy it. The shop looked the way you expected it to look. The shop assistant sold the product to you at the price you expected. The product worked the way you expected.

Is that good enough? Are you likely to rush off to tell lots of your friends how brilliant that shop is, or how great the product is? Probably not.

What you must try to do is **exceed** your customer's expectations. Remember the importance of the aims of customer service that you looked at earlier. You have to find ways to ensure that the customer continues to buy from you and to be so pleased that they tell their friends about your service. That is the only way that your organisation, and you, will be secure and able to develop.

You must look for opportunities to impress. Anticipate the customers' needs and meet those needs before the customer has to ask. Personalise the experience, perhaps by using their name or chatting to their children about their holiday. Go that extra mile by solving their problems imaginatively.

Think of the halo effect. You might bend down to talk to a child, so that you can be at their eye level. You might ask the name of the toy they are holding. The child will enjoy the experience, but there are other people watching you who are being impressed by what you are doing. That is the halo effect.

Case study

John was a cabin crew member escorting children who went to school in the UK and were flying to Hong Kong where their parents lived, to start their holidays.

During the flight, John checked all the children's passports and noticed it was Fiona's eighth birthday that day. He had all the crew sign a card that he found in the amenities store. The Captain also made an announcement: 'Ladies and gentlemen, thank you for travelling with us today, and a special hello to Fiona whose birthday it is'.

On arrival at Hong Kong, Fiona spotted her parents across a crowded arrivals hall and ran to them shouting, 'Mummy, Daddy, you'll never guess what SuperAir did for me on the flight!'

Hundreds of people in the arrivals hall listened as she told her story. The halo effect was working.

Imagine how much positive promotion, and how much business, was gained by John going the extra mile.

Exceeding the customer's expectations through your extra efforts will not only keep the customer loyal to you, but it will also give you pride in your work.

1 In small groups, suggest some travel and tourism scenarios when customer service expectations could be exceeded.

2 Can you think of any examples where you have seen the halo effect?

Assessment activity 6.2   English   2B.P2 | 2B.P3 | 2B.M2 | 2B.D2

The owners of 'Pitch up and Stay' learned a lot from you about what organisations are aiming for when it comes to customer service. They would like you to expand your research to include examples of how customer needs can be met and exceeded.

Revisit the three organisations you looked at in Assessment activity 6.1 and look at the ways they have met and exceeded customer expectations. You should focus on three different customer types, including internal and external customers and their needs. Try to be specific. Were there any benchmarks that the organisations met or exceeded?

Next, focus on just two of these organisations and explore how successful each is in responding to customer needs, based on the examples you have presented. Include both similarities and differences.

From your research think of some particular aims and benchmarks that you think 'Pitch up and Stay' could use in their organisation.

Tips

- When talking about how customer needs are met and/or exceeded, you should begin by explaining what the customers' needs were. You should also state how these were communicated to the organisation (e.g. in writing or verbally). Alternatively, you could specify if the customer need was identified by the organisation without communication from the customer.

- Organisations are keen to talk about their success in meeting customer needs. They often have quotes from satisfied customers on their website. You can also find these on review sites such as tripadvisor.com. Remember to make a note of all of your sources of information.

▶ Customer service

Introduction

The enthusiasm, skills and techniques you demonstrate to your customers are vital to the success of your organisation and to your personal future. You have to make sure the customer feels you are part of a great organisation from which they want to continue to buy.

In small groups, discuss your personal experiences as a customer.

- Share a really good customer service experience one of you had as a customer. What made it good?
- Share a really bad customer experience one of you had as a customer. What made it bad?
- What could have turned the bad experience into a good experience?

It is the approach your organisation takes to customer service that will determine whether its products, services, premises and staff deliver in a positive and pleasing way.

▶ First impressions

First impressions are so important as you can never make a first impression twice. The first few seconds of contact your customer has with your organisation and you, are vital. If it is not positive, it is likely to be the only impression they will ever have of you, as they will walk away and are unlikely ever to return. Remember Jan Carlzon and his 'Moments of truth'.

▶ Personal presentation

The first contact the customer has with you may be visual as they come into your workplace. Many travel and tourism employees wear a uniform. This promotes the organisation and creates a powerful brand image. Whether or not you are in uniform, you must make sure your appearance is clean and smart.

Make sure your personal hygiene is good. Take regular showers, check that your teeth are clean and your breath smells fresh. You may be working in difficult conditions, for example in high temperatures or crowded buildings or you may be working long hours, so it is a good idea to have hygiene products with you to use throughout the day.

▶ Environment

Always look at your workplace through the customer's eyes. Think about what impression the customer would get from what they could see, hear and feel?

What would you do if you:

- walked in to a travel agency and the brochure racks were empty and the computers were switched off?
- boarded a train and there was litter on the floor and seats?
- entered a hotel lobby and there was no one at the desk and the date display on the wall showed yesterday's date?

You would probably want to leave as quickly as you could, and take your business with you.

It is your responsibility to make your workplace look good and ready for business. If there is litter on the floor, it is creating a bad impression and so it should be cleared up immediately. The act of doing so will create a positive impression on any customers who see you disposing of it. They will recognise you are someone who takes a pride in their organisation, their workplace and themselves.

▶ Skills and techniques

Patience

You understand your part of the travel and tourism industry. You understand your organisation and how it works. You are familiar with your workplace, the equipment, the processes and procedures and the language used.

However, your customer will be very unfamiliar with it all. They may be uncertain and confused. They may not know what they want or what they need to do. You are there to help them.

That takes patience. Help them to identify and express their needs. Help them with the processes and geography of your workplace.

The questions they ask or things they do may sometimes appear daft to you, but they are not to the customer. You may have been asked that question many times that day, but it is the first time for them. Treat them and their question with respect.

Empathy

Sympathy is recognising and acknowledging someone's difficulty or unhappiness. Empathy goes further. It is actually sharing the difficulty or unhappiness through your response. It is often called 'putting yourself in Tom Brown's shoes' or 'seeing it through the customer's eyes'. It brings you closer to understanding the customer's feelings and situation. That means you can help them better.

Think about your journey to school/college. It is a journey you have probably done hundreds of times. Try pretending it is the first time you have done it and that you are a visitor to the area. You will see things you have never noticed before as you will be seeing it through someone else's eyes.

Active listening

Most of us are not good at listening as we like to talk. We cut across other people when they are talking and get distracted easily.

Active listening is more than casual listening. You must listen carefully to what people say, so that you understand their message clearly and can respond appropriately.

Demonstrate you are listening by using verbal and non-verbal techniques. For example, you might nod your head while saying 'ah-ha' or 'I see'. You might repeat key words or statements, like 'You were on the coach'. You might ask questions that show you have been listening and want to help, like 'You said you had your passport this morning. Where were you?'

Why is active listening so important when you are working in a customer facing role?

> **?** **Did you know?**
>
> A survey asked people why they stopped using products. Some said it was because the product no longer met their needs. Some said they did not like the processes and procedures they had to use to buy the product.
>
> However, 70 per cent said it was because of the behaviour of one or more of the people with whom they had to deal.

Sometimes you will be having a quiet face to face discussion with one person. Other times you will be listening when you may be surrounded by a lot of noise and activity and other people talking to you. In that situation, you may need to ask people to take it in turns to speak, so that you can concentrate on what each of them is saying.

Activity 6.9   Are you listening?

Work in pairs. One of you is the speaker and one is the listener.

The speaker talks for two minutes about something that interests them. Perhaps it is about school/college, or their holiday.

The listener spends the first minute not listening carefully. They might fidget, get distracted, look around or make bored movements.

Then the listener spends the second minute listening attentively. They face the speaker, sit quietly, perhaps nodding to show they have understood.

1 After two minutes, the listener tells the speaker what they remember the speaker saying in the first minute.

2 Then the listener tells the speaker what they remember the speaker saying in the second minute.

3 Finally, the speaker tells the listener how they felt when they weren't being listened to properly, compared with how they felt when they were being listened to properly.

We were given two ears and one mouth. We should use them in that proportion and should always try to listen twice as much as you speak.

Sensitivity

Your customers will be of different types. Some may be of a different nationality or come from a different culture to you. Some may be angry, some may be shy. Some may be elderly, some may be very young. The situations you are dealing with will be varied. You may be having a one-to-one debate with a customer who is booking a holiday or you may be a holiday representative at a resort telling a family about local events. You could be a train company passenger assistant talking with a crowd of angry passengers whose train has been cancelled. You need to adjust what you say and how you say it in different situations, to recognise the customer and the situation.

Whether you are communicating in writing or verbally, always be aware of the need for confidentiality. Customers expect you to treat what you know about them confidentially. Such information must not be shared with anyone else unless you are doing so to meet legal requirements or for valid business reasons, e.g. to meet the needs of the customer.

Language

Language is not just about the words we say. It is also about how we say those words and how we use our body. It is said that just 10 per cent of the impact of our communication comes from what we say (the words), 30 per cent comes from the pitch, tone and volume of our voice (the music), but 60 per cent comes from what our body is doing (the dance).

It is important to choose the right **words** so that what you say is accurate and also understood.

- Do not use long, complicated words and phrases just to impress people.
- Do not use jargon, like 'LOL' or 'Gash' (rubbish collected on an aircraft).
- Do not use slang like 'Gotcha' or 'Right on'.
- We all have mannerisms, like 'Um' and 'Er'. Ask a friend what speech mannerisms you have. Do not allow them to creep in to what you are saying.

The **words**.

Use the **music** of your voice. The way you use your voice has a powerful effect on how effective you are in communicating.

- Varied pitch and tone demonstrates interest, while flat pitch and tone indicates boredom.
- A loud voice is useful in noisy situations or emergencies. A quiet voice can encourage a calm atmosphere, which is particularly useful when dealing with an angry customer.

Be aware of the power of your body language (the **dance**). Look around you now. Do you see enthusiasm, boredom, anger, puzzlement, happiness? What is your body saying to others?

- A smile and good eye contact are good examples of warmth, interest and confidence.
- Folded arms, looking at the ground and chewing are examples of boredom and lack of interest in the people and surroundings.

The **music**.

The words you use and the music of your voice are particularly important if you are talking to a customer on the telephone, because you do not have the 60 per cent impact which comes from your body language.

A further aid to communication is the phonetic alphabet which is widely used in the travel and tourism industry to help clarify what is being said. This is particularly useful if you are talking to someone by phone or radio.

The **dance**.

Activity 6.10	Using the phonetic alphabet		

Some letters sound like others, e.g. 'm' and 'n', and 'b', 'v' and 'p'. To overcome this, a standard phonetic alphabet has been devised which is used worldwide. If working in the travel and tourism industry it is important that you learn it off by heart.

A: Alpha	**H:** Hotel	**O:** Oscar	**V:** Victor
B: Bravo	**I:** India	**P:** Papa	**W:** Whisky
C: Charlie	**J:** Juliet	**Q:** Quebec	**X:** X-ray
D: Delta	**K:** Kilo	**R:** Romeo	**Y:** Yankee
E: Echo	**L:** Lima	**S:** Sierra	**Z:** Zulu
F: Foxtrot	**M:** Mike	**T:** Tango	
G: Golf	**N:** November	**U:** Uniform	

Use the phonetic alphabet to spell words verbally. For example, if you were spelling 'David' phonetically over the radio, you would say 'David – D for delta, A for alpha, V for victor, I for India, D for delta.'

In pairs:

1 Spell your name phonetically out loud.

2 Choose some words and ask your partner to spell them phonetically.

Good teamwork is vital – can you think of any other types of team in the travel and tourism sector?

Many of your customers may not share your first language. Try to learn theirs, even if it is just a few key words. It will help in communicating with them and they will be pleased that you are making the effort.

Teamwork

Earlier we discussed the customer service delivery chain. Every person in the organisation needs to do the best job they can, so that their internal customers can do their job well.

Many travel and tourism roles involve people working in close teams. For example, cabin crew may work in teams of four or more on an aircraft. They work under time pressure, in confined spaces. They depend upon each member of the team doing their job well. That means each crew member having the right skills, knowledge and attitude to look after the passengers and to help their colleagues. This way, the passengers receive excellent service and the morale of the team is raised.

▷ Policies and standards

Policies and procedures

Every organisation creates policies and sets standards to enable it to meet its aims.

Mission statements describe an organisation's purpose and values. It is a major influence on the strategy of the organisation, including the level and style of customer service they wish to provide. This influences the policies and procedures the organisation has. It also influences their recruitment and training policies.

Case study

A ferry company might have the following mission statement:

We will maximise the use of technology to provide low fares that generate increased passenger traffic, while maintaining a continuous focus on cost containment and efficient operations.

While another ferry company might have this mission statement:

We will provide the highest level of luxury, and the most motivated staff of any ferry company in Europe.

The first ferry company is likely to concentrate upon systems rather than customer-facing staff to meet its aims and is unlikely to offer any free services.

Luxury is unlikely unless it is charged for profitably. The company will do all it can to drive costs down and offer the lowest price.

The second ferry company is likely to provide high quality facilities. While it may use technology to provide customer service, it will invest in the recruitment, training and care of excellent quality staff to interface with their customers. It is not their aim to provide service at the lowest price, although it will be their aim to provide value.

1 Look up the mission statements of two contrasting organisations. How are they different?

2 Can you identify the key purpose of each mission statement?

Policies create the framework for deciding what to sell, where and how, as well as how the organisation will interact with its customers and staff. They include **customer service policies** which describe the standards and procedures which will apply in the organisation's relationship with its customers. They often include statements on:

- what information the organisation will provide, and how and when it will provide it
- the performance level they will aim for, for example punctuality, quality, response times
- payment and refund policies
- what they will do in the event of a disruption or failure to provide the product or service
- the compensation they will provide.

Customer service standards setting and maintenance

To assess the quality of the customer service provided, organisations must:

- discover what service factors are important to their customers so that they know what to measure
- decide the standards and levels to be set
- decide how to measure those standards
- measure those standards at appropriate locations and frequencies
- encourage feedback from customers.

Table 6.1 – Customer feedback can be gained in many ways. Some examples are shown here.

Comment cards	These may be displayed at the point of sale or at the point of use. These ask customers to comment on the service they have received. This is qualitative feedback as it captures people's opinions.
Questionnaires	A development of 'comment cards' which also asks customers to grade their satisfaction of key standards. This is quantitative feedback as it places a numeric value on people's responses.
Customer forums/ focus groups	Small gatherings of potential, current, or past customers to share views and experiences. This is an excellent way to gather views on customer service issues.
Customer reviews	These may be requested by organisations from their customers, which they may place in their promotional material. There are also 'independent' review websites on which customers can place their comments, e.g. TripAdvisor or Yelp.
Mystery shoppers	Employed to visit organisations and report on their experiences of them. They may be employed by the organisation itself or by a third party organisation.

An example of an organisation setting customer standards would be if a train operator realised that punctuality is an important factor for its passengers, so it decided to set a standard of 95 per cent of trains operating within five minutes of schedule. It installs equipment which automatically records the time each train passes a location. It decides that the locations will be at every station so that the departure and arrival time is recorded for every train at each station. They can then assess whether 95 per cent of its trains departed and arrived within five minutes of their scheduled time. Feedback from their passengers may also provide more information on the concerns the passengers have and the causes of those concerns.

Armed with this information, the organisation can decide if any action is needed to improve the situation. It may be that there is a poor trend on one route or at a particular time of day. This may lead the organisation to review the scheduling and staffing levels. It may be that it needs to measure more things which might be causing the unpunctuality, like the serviceability of the trains or even the skills of the drivers. This could lead to a change in how frequently the trains are serviced, or some additional training for the drivers.

Activity 6.11   How clean are we?

A hotel has discovered that its customers value cleanliness highly, so they decide to create standards of cleanliness. They ask for your help.

1 In which part(s) of the hotel should cleanliness be measured?

2 The hotel has decided cleanliness will be measured by observation and recorded on forms, using a grading scheme of 1 to 10, with 10 being excellent, but what factors should be measured in the bedrooms?

3 How frequently and when should bedroom cleanliness be measured?

Remember

Despite your best efforts, sometimes customers ask questions you can't immediately answer. It is alright to say 'I'm sorry, I don't know the answer, let me find out for you'. That demonstrates your willingness to help.

However, if you keep saying 'I'm sorry, I don't know the answer, let me find out for you' they will not be impressed; they will decide you are not good at your job. Complaints may follow and customers may be lost.

Impacts

Customers will expect you to know all about the products and services your organisation offers, but also how those products and services can benefit them. To do so, you need to match the customer to the product and service. What are the customer's needs, wants, desires and which of your products and services will best meet them? Customers will be impressed by your recognition of their needs and your ability to offer them solutions.

Good product and service knowledge can lead to sales and to making a customer loyal. In turn this may prompt the customer to tell others how good you are, so that they also start to buy from you. So, do all you can to know your products and services and what they can do for the customer.

Knowing what you can offer increases your confidence. This will help you concentrate on using your skills and techniques to deliver excellent customer service.

Technology

While the human being is vitally important to the delivery of excellent customer service, technological support is also important.

Technological advances are becoming more and more rapid. Computers have revolutionised organisations' ability to manage huge and complex situations. In the mid 1960s airlines began to introduce computerised reservations systems. Without them, the industry could not have grown the way it did.

Since then, personal computers, the arrival of the internet and personal communication systems like smartphones have enabled individuals to access information and make transactions which could previously only be done by organisations. There has been a major move towards people making their own travel and holiday arrangements. Online bookings have become the most popular way to book a journey or holiday. This enables organisations to save on commission charges they normally pay to travel agents and so are able to pass these savings on to the customer by reducing prices; this can improve the customer experience.

Technology is helping to make travellers' experiences more pleasant. Largely gone are the days of two-hour queues to check in for your flight. Now you can check in at home on the internet, or at self-service check-in kiosks at the airport and elsewhere, or by using the barcode facility on your smartphone. Organisations can text you with last minute changes to your arrangements or to warn you of delays. Trains, coaches, aircraft, hotels, etc. have increasingly sophisticated entertainment systems, and improved connectivity for business people.

Activity 6.12	How does technology help?

1 Visit a travel agent. Discover what technological advances in the last five years have helped them improve service to their customers.

2 In a small group, share with each other what technology you have experienced when using transport which improved the experience for you.

TOPIC   C2

Impact of excellent and poor customer service on travel and tourism organisations

Introduction

Customer service is provided by your organisation through its values, procedures, processes and technology. It is also provided by you through your skills, knowledge and motivation. It has the greatest impact upon your development and success, and that of your organisation.

Make a list of what might increase and what might decrease if you give really excellent customer service.

Sales and new customers

Providing excellent customer service will encourage people to buy from you. Yours will be an organisation they like dealing with. Failure to give good customer service will have a bad impact upon sales. People will not buy from you if they can get the same or similar product or service from a competitor who provides better customer service.

Good customer service will encourage customers to start to use your product or service.

Complaints

Failure to provide the product or service which the customer expected will lead to dissatisfaction and complaint. Without a good customer service recovery, that complaint may lead to a loss of custom.

Most dissatisfied customers do not complain; they just stop buying from you. Your organisation will not know why they left; they just know sales have gone down. If customers are unhappy, organisations need to encourage them to tell the organisation so that it can be put right for that customer, but also so that the cause can be avoided for future customers.

If a customer has complained about your product or service and you do a brilliant job in recovering the situation, they may become even more loyal to you in the future. The way the employee responds to the complaint is key to recovering the customer.

Compliments

Everyone likes getting compliments, even organisations. Sadly, human nature is such that people are much more ready to complain than they are to compliment. If a customer compliments you or your organisation it helps one understand what is important to the customers and what is being done well.

Repeat business/brand loyalty

If you only meet the customer when they are using your product or service, there is little you can do about to influence the purchasing stage. However, how you look after them will influence whether they will ever buy anything from you again. Remember Jan Carlzon's 'Moments of truth'.

Organisations work hard to retain the loyalty of their customers, using methods such as loyalty cards which give regular customers discounts on future purchases, free use of lounges, upgraded hotel rooms, etc.

Referred business

You know now that satisfied customers will tell others how satisfied they are, and those people may start to buy from you. That broadens your customer base and makes your organisation's future more sound.

Did you know?

Some travel and tourism organisations have such a strong customer service brand image, that they often do not advertise their products; they advertise their people and their image. TV adverts for Virgin Atlantic often just feature their staff; British Airways use their slogan 'To fly, to serve',

Take it further

Research a travel and tourism organisation you believe does not provide good customer service. Recommend ways in which it might profitably improve its service and become a winner.

Activity 6.13 And the winner is ...

Look at the World Travel Awards website, click on Europe and select three winners. Assess the impact that winning the award may have on their business. To access this website visit Pearson hotlinks at www.pearsonhotlinks.co.uk and search for this title.

▶ Staff turnover and job satisfaction

There is a well-known expression '*Dissatisfied staff means dissatisfied customers*'. If staff are dissatisfied, they are more likely to leave, so staff turnover increases. This is also costly in recruitment and induction training. Good organisations recognise that if they want their staff to give good customer service, they must treat their staff well.

Money often is not the main motivator for staff. If they feel valued, they are more willing to perform even better. They will feel valued if:

- they are given responsibility
- they are recognised when they do a job well
- they are given support, guidance and training to help them develop
- their working environment is good, for example restrooms and catering are provided
- they are asked what they think about their organisation (and their organisation takes action on what they say)
- they have an occasional celebration (perhaps when the first 100 holidays are sold, or if it is someone's birthday).

Most of these actions will cost little or no money and will motivate staff to perform well and remain in the organisation.

Everyone wants to do a job which they consider to be worthwhile and from which they get satisfaction. Customer service professionals get a buzz from pleasing other people, but they also need their organisation to please them. They want to have a pride in what they do and who they work for.

Assessment activity 6.3
2C.P4 | 2C.P5 | 2C.M3 | 2C.M4 | 2C.D3

The owners of 'Pitch up and Stay' are keen to learn more about how they can ensure they are providing a high level of customer service in their business, and learn about the impacts of getting this right or wrong.

Revisit two of the organisations you looked at in assessment activities 6.1 and 6.2. Reflect on why they might have been successful by answering the following questions.

- How did the skills and techniques demonstrated by the customer service teams of the organisations compare?
- Where customer service was excellent, what impact did this have on internal/ external customers and the organisations?
- Where customer service was poor, what impact did this have on internal/external customers and the organisations?
- How and why could customer service in one of the organisations be improved?

Tips

- Make sure you give plenty of examples.
- Customers are often ready to make their feelings known if they are dissatisfied with customer service. Look up the organisations on review sites such as tripadvisor.com. Can you find examples of poor customer service that can be used in your work? Remember to make a note of all of your sources of information.

Introduction

The world in which travel and tourism organisations operate is constantly changing. This might be due to changes in customer behaviour or market trends. There are a number of factors that you will investigate in this unit. You will consider how travel and tourism businesses adapt and change to meet the evolving needs of their customers. You will also discover the range of businesses in travel and tourism and how they are structured.

You will find out how economic, visitor and product trends affect businesses in the sector, as well as how businesses respond to these trends.

You will gain useful insight into the travel and tourism sector, as well as into the wide range of jobs that are available across the sector.

Assessment: This unit will be assessed externally using a 60-minute paper-based examination.

Learning aims

In this unit you will:

A know that there are a variety of types and structures of travel and tourism business organisations and understand how different business functions interrelate

B understand the trends in the travel and tourism sector and be able to interpret these

C understand why travel and tourism businesses develop new opportunities to grow and change their products/services and the outcomes of these changes on the business.

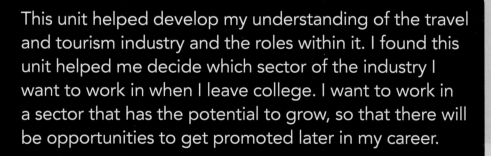

This unit helped develop my understanding of the travel and tourism industry and the roles within it. I found this unit helped me decide which sector of the industry I want to work in when I leave college. I want to work in a sector that has the potential to grow, so that there will be opportunities to get promoted later in my career.

Sandeep, *18-year-old Travel and Tourism Student*

Travel and Tourism Business Environments

7

▶ Types of business ownership

Introduction

Do you ever wonder who owns big businesses and how they are owned? The first part of this unit looks at business ownership in the travel and tourism industry. Make a list of all the different travel and tourism organisations that you can think of.

▶ Common types of business ownership

Private limited company

Private limited companies (Ltd) are owned by shareholders. Shareholders purchase a share (part) of the business. As this is a private limited company the shares will be sold privately, usually to people known to the business. Limited means that there is a limit to the liability that the shareholders in the business have. This means that if the business is unsuccessful, the shareholders' limit of liability to the company's debts is only the amount of money they have invested in the business. The advantage of a private limited company is that it can have multiple owners which provides the opportunity to raise more investment. As the liability is limited the investors are only risking their investments.

The disadvantage is that the business can only sell shares privately, limiting the number of owners compared with a public limited company. However, control of the company is strictly defined as it usually lies with the majority shareholders (people who own the most shares) and so there are few issues regarding who is in control.

Public limited companies

Public limited companies (Plc) are like private limited companies with one major exception: Plcs sell their shares openly on the stock exchange.

This means that anyone can buy shares in any Plc. The advantage of this is the increased ability to raise money from investments. The disadvantage is that anyone with enough money can buy a controlling interest in the Plc.

Franchise/franchisee

A franchise is a business that lets people buy an operating area or outlet to run under their business name and brand. The advantage of a franchise is that the owners gets to operate a business attached to a successful brand. The franchiser will usually provide all the systems, equipment and resources needed to run the franchise. The disadvantage is that the owners have limited control over how their business is run.

Charitable organisations

There are a number of charitable organisations in the travel and tourism industry. Charitable organisations are non-profit making; any money the charity does make gets used in the operation of the charity. A good example of a charity is the National Trust.

Key terms

Ltd – is a private limited company and sells shares privately.

Plc – is a public limited company and sells shares openly on stock markets.

Did you know?

Most Burger King restaurants in the UK are not owned by Burger King, but rather are separate businesses owned by individuals that run the business to the rules and regulations set out in the terms of the franchise agreement.

A charity is controlled by a board of trustees. The advantage of a charity is that it does not make any profit, and therefore pays no tax. However, due to the structure of charities, decision-making can be a slow process; this means that charities may not be as flexible to adapt to change as some other business types.

Other types of travel and tourism business ownership

Sole trader

A sole trader is the simplest type of business to set up. All you are required to do is to tell the Inland Revenue that you will be completing a self-assessment tax return.

This ownership has unlimited liability. The disadvantage of this that the owner of the business is responsible for all the debt of the business. The advantage of this is that all the decision-making is done by the owner, and all profits belong to the owner. The amount of money one person can raise to start the business may be limited compared to other business types.

Partnership

A partnership is when between two to 20 people form a company together. They are usually governed by a partnership agreement that all parties sign. As there are more people involved, you are likely to be able to raise more money to start the business and have a larger range of skills in your business. However, as there is unlimited liability, each partner is responsible for the whole liability of the business including the actions of the other partners. Conflict between partners can also be a major issue. But, since 2002 there has been the option to have limited liability partnerships.

Cooperative

A cooperative is a business that is owned and run by its members, for the benefit of its members. The advantage of a cooperative is that every member gets a say in the decision-making process. This can mean it takes a long time to make decisions as there are a lot of opinions to be heard.

Consultancy

A consultancy could be set up using any of the structures we have already looked at. A consultant is a person who provides expert advice to another business. Consultants are usually used when no one in that business has the skills required for a particular project or issue.

Activity 7.1   Types of business ownership

Complete the table below to check your knowledge of the different types of business ownership

Type of business	Owners	Control	Liability
Sole trader			
Partnership			
Private limited company (Ltd)			
Public limited company (Plc)			
Charitable organisation			

Activity 7.2   Identifying ownership

From the list of companies you identified in the introduction, identify the ownership of each company.

Types of business structure

Introduction

Not all businesses are the same. Some are small, comprising only the owner, while others are huge multinational businesses. Can you think of a way you could group businesses into different types?

Size

Micro-enterprise

A micro-enterprise employs up to 10 people; these are the smallest type of businesses. Due to their size they tend not to operate huge projects. However, they have the advantage of being able to adapt to suit the needs of the customer better than some big organisations. A good example is a small independent travel agency.

Small and medium enterprises (SMEs)

A SME employs between 10 and 250 people. These may be local, national or even international. SMEs make up 88 per cent of all enterprise in the UK. (Source: European Commission on Enterprise and Industry SBA Fact Sheet 2010–2012).

Large business

A large business is one that employs over 250 people. Due to the service nature of travel and tourism, there are a lot of large businesses in the sector; some of which are household names like British Airways or TUI.

Geographical scale of operations

Multi-national companies

A multi-national company, as the name suggests, operates in more than one country. Good examples of multi-national companies include airlines like Virgin Atlantic or a hotel chain like Holiday Inn, which can be found around the world.

National companies

National companies operate across a country. An example is the National Trust which looks after the nation's heritage across the whole of England, Wales and Northern Ireland.

Regional companies

Regional companies operate within a specific area within a country. For example, train-operating companies only operate trains on specific routes in specific parts of the country. Another example is the regional tourist boards that promote tourism and events within a specific region.

Link

See *Unit 1: The UK Travel and Tourism Sector* for more details on the regional tourist boards.

Local companies

These are companies that only operate at a local level. They may have several outlets within an area or just the one. An example would be a bed and breakfast or a local coach company.

▶ Staffing structures

Hierarchical

Most organisations have a hierarchical structure which clearly defines who is responsible for what and for whom. It is expressed as a pyramid with the more senior staff at the top and the junior staff below.

- **Steep hierarchy:** this has many layers of management. The senior management has a lot of control over the organisation, as there are plenty of managers at other levels. As roles are so clearly defined at each level people are often expert at what they do. It is easier to identify training opportunities for each level. Steep hierarchies are slow to adapt and make changes due to the number of layers of management. Communication up and down the organisation is also slow.

- **Flat hierarchy:** this has few layers of management. This makes it harder for senior management to control every element of the business and harder for them to delegate responsibility down the structure. However, communication up and down the structure is rapid meaning that senior management learn quickly what is happening in the organisation. Flat hierarchies are quick to adapt and make changes.

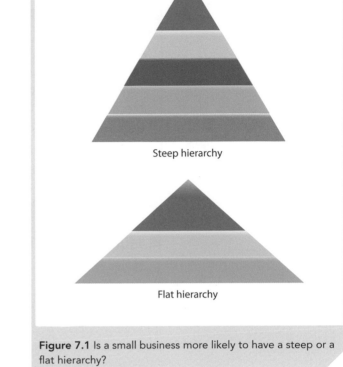

Steep hierarchy

Flat hierarchy

Figure 7.1 Is a small business more likely to have a steep or a flat hierarchy?

Matrix structure

In all hierarchies there are some job roles that do not naturally fit into the hierarchical structure. These are the roles that offer services to others within the structure. For example, a member of the human resources team could be working with senior management on a project one moment and the next could be supporting an apprentice. These departments fit across the business as a matrix, supporting the traditional hierarchy. Other examples include security, health and safety and ICT support services.

Take it further

Review the structure of some local travel and tourism organisations. Discuss with your class whether they are steep or flat hierarchies, or a matrix structure. You may want to look at companies that publish annual reports, as these reports will often include the company's organisational structure.

Assessment practice 7.1

A leading long-haul airline employing 35,000 staff operates with a traditional steep hierarchical structure. Explain one advantage of this structure for this type of organisation. [2]

▶ Business functions

Introduction

All businesses have a number of 'things' they must do to be able to operate. These 'things' are called functions. Functions are usually carried out by departments (depending on the scale and type of business). In this section we will be looking at these internal departments and their functions.

Make a list of all the things you think a business needs to do in order to function. As you go through this section of the unit see how many you managed to list.

▶ Internal departments

Product development

The product development department is responsible for developing existing, and creating new, products for the customer. This includes developing pricing strategies, and might include adding new destinations to their offering or including new attractions that are available at a destination. The department may also need to consider seasonal offerings. For example, the Eiffel Tower in Paris has an ice rink set up every year at Christmas. They will consider the **tangible** and the **intangible** elements of the product.

Customer services

The customer service department will manage customers' requirements and experiences in different destinations, This could be across countries and could involve handling different languages and cultures, as well as time zones. An increasingly important element of working in a customer service department is crisis management. This means dealing with a major crisis for customers abroad, such as a natural disaster or a man-made problem like war or terrorism.

Human resources

The human resources department is responsible for the recruitment and training of staff who work within the company. Their role is to make sure that the company has the right people with the right skills at the right time. This includes the recruitment of overseas and seasonal staff as required. For example, most tour operators will have a holiday representative in a resort to help customers with any issues while they are on holiday.

IT systems

Over the last 25 years, travel and tourism organisations have become more and more dependent on information technology (IT). Travel agencies, tour operators, transport providers and accommodation providers now all use either national or international booking management systems.

How important do you think the look of a web page is to a travel and tourism business?

Finance and accounting

Finance and accounting is the way of measuring financial success or how much profit the organisation has made. Accounting information is also used on a daily basis to help support management in their decision-making. Finance and accounting also manage currency fluctuations when trading internationally, as well as managing the business's cash flow (money flowing in and out of the business).

> ### Assessment practice 7.2
>
> Identify three internal functions in a travel and tourism organisation. [3]

▷ External services

Many organisations will pay for external providers to provide a specific service. This may be due to cost, or time involved, or a lack of specific skills and knowledge within the organisation.

Advertising and promotion

Although many travel and tourism organisations carry out their own promotion and advertising, they will often also use external services for specific elements.

Hotels, visitor attractions, transport providers and tour operators rely on marketing and advertising agencies to help sell their products to customers. Marketing agencies will help develop marketing strategies for companies to ensure that companies make the most of any promotion they invest in. Companies may use advertising agencies to produce print promotional materials or television adverts.

Market research

Market research is both time consuming and costly to collect. Some travel and tourism organisations pay external providers to collect and interpret the research for them, for example customer satisfaction surveys. This is also the case with mystery shoppers, who pretend to be a customer and then give feedback on their experience.

Consultancy services

From time to time a travel and tourism organisation will need to have very specific skills to deal with an issue within their organisation. A consultant will be employed on a short-term contract to work on a specific project. Good examples include brand development, changes in management and public relations. Consultants can be expensive to employ but businesses are paying for a specific skill that they only require for a set period of time.

Accounting/administration

For a smaller organisation it may be more viable to use external services to manage the accounts and some administration. It is common for a sole trader or partnership not to employ an accountant, but rather to use an accountancy firm.

Cost can also be a factor; a number of businesses have outsourced some of their administration and call centres to parts of the world where labour is cheaper.

Online services

Over the last 30 years, there has been a dramatic growth and development in the provision of online services. This is another area that travel and tourism organisations may outsource. For example, a tour operator may outsource the development of their website or any apps their organisation offers.

? Did you know?

Last minute advertising and promotion is increasingly being carried out by specific web-based providers such as lastminute.com and travelsupermarket.com.

Remember

There is a high cost in time, labour and money in collecting market research. Many travel and tourism companies outsource this work so that they can focus on what is core to the business.

▶ Advantages and disadvantages of using external services

There are a number of issues to consider when choosing to use an external service.

Expertise of external functions/services

You need to consider what expertise the external function or service has and how relevant it is to the business needs. Generally, the rarer the expertise, the more expensive it is.

Cost of using external functions/services

External provision can be used to reduce costs, for example using an outsourced call centre. Though the hourly cost of a consultant can be very high, this needs to be compared against the difficulties the business would suffer if they did not have use of the consultant's specific set of skills.

Resources

Compared to the organisation, external functions and services may have more resources that they can mobilise for a project. For example, a market research organisation will have a number of call centre staff to find out customer opinions whereas a tour operator is unlikely to have access to this resource internally.

Impartiality of external functions/services

There may be concerns about the impartiality of an external provider. This could be particularly applicable if a business's competition also uses the same external provider.

Duration in relation to external functions/services

A business needs to consider how long they need to or want to work with external functions/services. Some working relationships may last years, whereas others may only last days.

Businesses have to consider how long they plan to work with external providers as this raises issues about how much sensitive material external providers should have access to and how much a business should rely on them.

▶ Economic trends

Introduction

The current state of the economy affects the travel and tourism sector. In this section we will look at some of these economic trends and what you can interpret from different sources of data. What do you think is the current state of the UK economy? Check with your teacher/tutor to see if you are right.

Employment rates

Travel and tourism products are considered a **discretionary spend**. Take up of holidays will therefore depend on how much people earn and how many people are in employment. Higher employment levels will lead to more holidays being sold, while high unemployment leads to the opposite.

However this is not the full picture. High levels of employment or unemployment in a specific age group will affect the sales of a holiday that is targeted at that age group. At the time of writing, the current high levels of unemployed 18–25-year-olds will affect companies targeting this market.

Disposable income

How much disposable income someone has available, sometimes called discretionary spend, will affect how much they spend on a travel and tourism product. Disposable income is affected by a number of factors: wages, employment levels, costs such as food and housing as well as taxation. The higher the disposable income, the greater the likelihood of a higher spend on travel and tourism products. Equally, the lower the disposable income, the lower the travel and tourism spend. This means that people may choose a different length, type or location for their holiday, if any are taken at all.

Spend per visitor

Within travel and tourism, the average spend per visitor is a good measurement of how a business is doing. Average spend will be affected by how much each visitor has to spend (see the factors mentioned previously). The average spend by visitors on their whole trip to the UK is £600 per visit (Source: VisitBritain).

Higher average spend will have a positive impact on travel and tourism businesses, whereas a lower average spend will have the opposite effect. **Yield management systems** are used by budget airlines and hotels in order to maximise the number of people using the service while still trying to gain as high an average spend as possible.

Currency exchange rate fluctuations

Currency exchange rates are the rates at which you can buy one currency with another, for example how many euros can you buy for £1? A strong pound (where you can buy a lot of another currency) is good for the British going abroad; however it is not good for foreigners coming to the UK. This means that though more British people will go abroad because it is cheaper, fewer foreigners will come to the UK as it is expensive. A weak pound will have the opposite effect.

This fluctuation can have a dramatic effect on the take-up of holidays in affordable destinations. This can be seen in Calais; people from the UK used to travel to France for cheap alcohol and tobacco, but as the euro got stronger against the pound, fewer people travelled, as prices increased. Often the pound is strong compared to new destination currencies, making those destinations attractive.

Key term

Discretionary spend – spending by consumers on things that they want to buy rather than on things they need such as housing or food.

Link

For more information on target markets see *Unit 8: Promotion and Sales in Travel and Tourism.*

Did you know?

In the first quarter of 2013 the House of Commons' library recorded unemployment at 20.5 per cent of 16–24-year-olds. This was down 0.7 per cent on the previous quarter and 1.2 per cent lower than the previous year. How do you think this affects an organisation like Club 18–30?

(Contains parliamentary information licensed under the Open Parliament License v1.0)

Key term

Yield management systems – are computerised reservation systems that are designed to help an organisation get maximum occupancy, while getting as much money from each booking as possible. If a particular flight is busy then the prices will go up, if the flight is not popular the price will go down.

Remember

Exchange rates can go up as well as down.

▶ Product/service trends

Introduction

In this section you will look at how travel and tourism organisations develop products and services to meet changes in consumer trends. You will also look at how to correctly interpret the different sources of data providing you with this information.

Ask an elderly relative or family friend about their childhood holidays. Compare their experiences with your own – what are the differences and why do you think things have changed?

▶ Holiday types

Package

The original package holiday took place in June 1841 when Thomas Cook organised a train trip from Leicester to Loughborough. Package holidays grew massively in the 1950s and 60s with the introduction of affordable air fares. Although still very popular, the traditional package holiday has declined in recent years.

All-inclusive

All-inclusive holidays include three meals a day, soft drinks and most alcoholic drinks, and often other activities are included in the price. They originate from the model originally used by Club Méditerranée (Club Med). Originally seen as quite exclusive, in recent years the all-inclusive option has increasingly been seen as good value and has become a growth sector of the holiday market.

Tailor-made

Tailor-made holidays have been around longer than the package holiday. However, due to the cost of having a holiday tailored to suit individual needs these trips generally became too expensive for the average person. The introduction of the internet has changed this and has led to a massive growth in tailor-made holidays over the last 15 years.

Self-catering

No meals are provided on self-catering holidays, but travellers are provided the facilities to cater for themselves. These have been popular for many years and although they are not currently a fashionable option they remain a good choice for many people.

Staycation

Staycations are a very modern type of holiday. A staycation is where time is taken off from work or school but people stay at home rather than going abroad or travelling to somewhere else in the UK. Holidays are spent on day trips or relaxing at home.

If travelling to a city like Moscow what type of holiday would you be most likely to go on? Research online to find out more.

Take it further

Research Club Med. How and why did they make the all-inclusive model so popular?

Did you know?

The term staycation became popular during the 2007–2010 recession. Their popularity increased due to difficult financial times.

Assessment practice 7.3

Give three reasons why holiday makers might choose a staycation. [3]

▶ Demographic and socio-economic trends

Increasingly ageing population

Due to increased quality of health care and a decrease in the birth rate in most European countries, the average age of the population is increasing. This means that the provision of travel and tourism products and services may change.

Declining youth market

Due to the decrease in birth rates in Europe there is a decline in the number of young people. Over time this will be reflected in a decline in the number of products and services targeted at this market.

Cost-conscious family market

With stagnant wages and increased fuel and food costs, families are becoming increasingly cost-conscious. Holiday companies have addressed this by offering discounted or free children's places on holidays. For example, Disneyland Paris often runs promotions where children under a certain age visit for free if an adult package ticket is purchased.

Affluent empty-nesters

In the UK there has been an increase in the number of affluent empty-nesters. Empty-nesters are couples who have children who have grown up and left home. With an increasingly ageing population, wealthy empty-nesters are a growing group who are likely to be in well-paid jobs or have a lot of savings. This gives them the discretionary income to spend on holidays and other travel products.

▶ Transport

Rise of the low-cost airline

Traditionally, air travel was expensive and exclusive, with a trip on an aeroplane being considered a luxury. This all changed in the mid 1990s with the development of the low-cost or no frills airline. Today, budget airlines account for one-third of all the air flights in Europe and the growth of budget airlines has spread around the world.

Cruising

Before the birth of the passenger aircraft, cruising was the traditional way people travelled the world. After the introduction of the aeroplane, cruising was no longer a viable option, due to the cost and time that it takes to travel by sea compared to travelling by aeroplane. In the past cruising was seen as the height of luxury and cruise ships were like floating palaces. Cruises started in order for people to travel around the world, but the idea was that the cruise itself was a holiday rather than just a way to get to your destination.

Cruises have developed and are now attracting younger couples and families; this has been helped by a new generation of cruise ships specially designed to be more family friendly.

What factors do you think families with young children have to think about when choosing transport?

Low-cost coach travel

Low-cost coach travel has made getting around the UK cheaper. With companies like Megabus and National Express offering tickets for only a few pounds, travelling in around the UK, and increasingly Europe, is a lot more cost-effective and accessible.

Environmentally friendly options

Increasingly, consumers are concerned about their environmental impact on the world.

This has led to a growth in environmentally friendly travel and tourism options. This could be eco-tourism (tourism designed to have as little impact as possible, or no impact at all, on the local environment or people) or staying in a sustainable location (a location which is designed to have little environmental impact). These are discussed in further detail in the cultural trends section. **Carbon off-setting** is used to negate the impact of the holiday on the environment.

▶ Accommodation

Accommodation is the term used to refer to anywhere you sleep on holiday. In this section we will look at some of the key developments in the accommodation sector.

Development of boutique/niche hotels

Boutique hotels are small trendy hotels that are promoted as bringing a unique, location-specific experience to travellers. Boutique hotels appeared in the mid-1980s in New York and London. They tend to be small, with less than 150 rooms, and at the luxury end of the market. There is no clear definition for this style of hotel and the name boutique is now being used as a marketing term by larger hotel chains. Boutique hotels are marketed at younger, trendy and affluent travellers.

Holiday parks

Holiday parks, as we define them today, were created by Billy Butlin in 1936. They reached their heyday in the 1950s and 60s before the introduction of cheap package holidays.

Holiday parks have developed over the years with the growth of companies like Center Parcs re-branding the holiday park as an environmentally friendly holiday, aimed at a more affluent market than the traditional holiday park.

Second homes

As British people started to become more affluent at the end of the 20th century, people began buying second homes abroad. These are often bought in countries like Spain, where property prices are cheap in comparison to the UK.

This means that people do not have to pay for accommodation when travelling abroad. Some people rent their second homes to other holiday makers when they are not using them themselves or let friends or family stay in them.

Research Center Parcs and Butlin's and compare where they are located and how this affects the activities they each offer.

Budget hotels

The growth of budget hotels started in the 1980s in the UK, when Forte Hotels introduced the Travelodge and their popularity continues to increase. They offer clean and safe accommodation for a cheaper price than a full service hotel. Budget hotels are to the hotel industry what low-cost airlines are to the airline industry.

▶ Cultural trends

Culture is constantly changing, due to a number of factors: the level of education of the population, changes in the population and changes in people's perceptions.

Media influences

Over the last 50 years an increase in people's ability to obtain and access information through a variety of different media channels has influenced the rate of cultural change.

With the growth of social media, message boards, blogs and reviews, as well as Facebook, consumers are increasingly researching their holidays and travel plans using feedback posted on these sites. There are now even television channels dedicated to travel and tourism such as Thomas Cook TV and many travel magazines are now available online.

Themed holidays and attractions

Before Disneyland opened in 1955 there existed themed parks and pleasure gardens, the oldest being Bakken in Denmark, which opened in 1583. With Disneyland, rather than just having a group of rides in one location, Walt Disney developed a whole themed world. Since the first Disneyland opened, theme parks have grown in popularity. There are now five Disney theme parks around the world, with a sixth park planned to open in China in 2015–16.

How do theme parks like Disneyland appeal to the whole family?

'Dark tourism'

Visiting a place associated with tragedy, death or suffering, such as New York's 'Ground Zero', taxi tours around the sites of the 'Troubles' in Belfast or visits to cemeteries is known as 'dark tourism'. Although this may seem a strange way to spend your holiday, dark tourism may not be as bad as you first think. Indeed, trips to concentration camps and Anne Frank's house have kept the legacy of the Holocaust in the minds of many generations, hopefully reminding people never to repeat those actions.

Health tourism

Increasingly, people are travelling around the world to receive medical treatment. It is not unusual for people in the UK to travel to Asia or Eastern Europe to have dental or cosmetic surgery. This tourism may be motivated by cheaper treatment, or a better quality of treatment abroad.

Sport tourism

Sport tourism involves either travelling to participate or be a spectator at a sporting event. A good example of this is the many tourists who travelled to London for the

London 2012 Olympics, where millions of tickets were sold. In 2014, Glasgow will host the 20th Commonwealth Games. The city can expect tourists from all over the Commonwealth to attend the games.

Rise of stag/hen parties taken abroad

Traditionally, a stag or a hen party was a party the night before a wedding where, as a rite of passage, the groom would be taken out by his male friends and the bride by her female friends.

The growth of budget airlines has meant that you can travel abroad relatively cheaply so stag and hen parties now often involve a weekend abroad with friends. Popular destinations include Krakow, Riga and Amsterdam.

Eco/responsible tourism

The growth of environmental awareness in the last 40 years is reflected in the growth of eco/responsible tourism. This is where considering the impact of tourism on the environment as well as the local population is the key concern for travellers. Organisations such as Responsibletravel.com organise conservation holidays. A good way to remember what ecotourism stands for is the ecotourist mantra:

> 'Take only photographs, leave only footprints and kill only time.'
>
> (Source unknown)

▶ Seasonal trends

Not all products and destinations will be attractive to customers all year round. For instance, a British seaside holiday taken in February would be very different from one taken in August. This is called a seasonal trend.

Peak and off-peak products and how these change

Some seasonal resorts have short **peak** seasons. For example, Aviemore in the Cairngorm National Park in the highlands of Scotland was originally a ski resort. However, the Scottish ski season can be short depending on the amount of snow. To make money **off-peak**, in the summer, the businesses in Aviemore have developed outdoor adventures, including hill-walking, canoeing, cycling, sailing and rock climbing. A similar approach has been taken by ski resorts in other areas around the world. Another option for seasonal resorts is to offer discounts during off-peak periods or to offer products that are not affected by the season. Center Parcs built domes which house all their facilities, thus providing an indoor area for activities.

▶ Technology trends

Technology is constantly changing, with newer and better versions of products being released all the time. This has had an impact on the travel and tourism industry.

Key terms

Peak – the season which is the most popular time for a product or destination.

Off-peak – the season which is less popular for the product or destination.

Wireless products and services

Wireless products and services have dramatically changed people's access to information. Whereas in the past you would have to ask a guide for directions or an agent for flight or train times, now this is all accessible either through your smartphone or tablet. The growth in 'apps' has also meant that information can be specific for a resort or destination. For example, you can download an app for the Victoria and Albert Museum which gives you access to the museum's collections without having to leave your home.

Social media

As mentioned previously, with the increase in social media there has also been an increase in consumers researching their holidays and travel plans online using feedback from these sites. Increasingly, what a customer thinks will have a direct impact on your business. A large number of travel and tourism organisations have their own Facebook pages and Twitter accounts and invest in managing their social media interaction.

Assessment practice 7.4

Explain two benefits of wireless technology to travel and tourism organisations. [4]

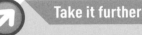

Take it further

Why not check out the Facebook page of some travel and tourism attractions both local and national. Look at the Gunwharf Quays Outlet, the Eden Project and the National Railway Museum Facebook pages to start.

TOPIC B3

▶ Destination trends

Take it further

Current data on destination trends can be downloaded from the Office for National Statistics.

Find out what are the five most common nationalities visiting the UK.

To access the website for this, visit Pearson hotlinks. You can access this by going to www.pearsonhotlinks.co.uk and searching for this title.

Introduction

In this section you look at trends in travel and tourism destinations and how to interpret the available data. Like the other trends you have looked at, some destinations change in popularity over time.

There have been a number of trends in recent years; one of the biggest is the growth in online bookings as opposed to the traditional travel agency route. Conduct a survey asking 25 people how they booked their holiday. What percentage of people booked online?

▶ Countries around the world

You are going to look at the increase/decrease in UK visitor numbers to popular overseas destinations.

Looking at Figure 7.2 you will see that since 2006 there has been a trend of a declining number of visits to most tourist destinations. This is probably due to the global recession of 2007 and the long-term effects of the **recession** and the **credit crunch**.

▶ Visitor attractions

There is a wide range of visitor attractions both in the UK and abroad; this topic will look at the popularity of some of these attractions. There are often increases and/or decreases in visitor numbers to different types of visitor attractions over time.

Key terms

Recession – is where you have two three-month periods in a row where the country is producing less than it produced in the previous three-month period.

Credit crunch – is the term used to explain the difficulty of getting access to credit.

Free entry attractions

Some attractions charge entry, while others do not as they are funded in other ways. Table 7.1 looks at the popularity of free attractions.

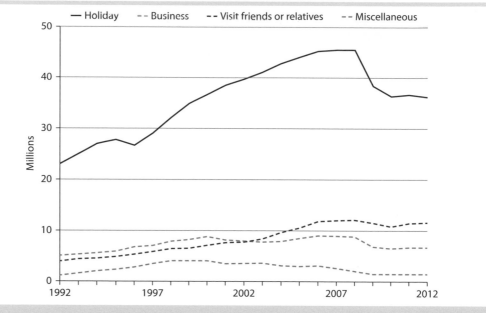

Figure 7.2 Changes in popularity of overseas destinations for UK visitors.

Source: International Passenger Survey (IPS) – Office for National Statistics

Table 7.1 – The top 10 free visitor attractions in England in 2011. Have you visited any of these?

Rank	Name of attraction	2010 Visitors	2011 Visitors
1	British Museum	5,842,138	5,848,534
2	National Gallery	4,954,914	5,253,216
3	Natural History Museum	4,647,613	4,873,275
4	Tate Modern	5,061,172	4,802,387
5	Science Museum	2,757,917	2,894,850
6	Victoria and Albert Museum	2,629,065	2,789,400
7	National Portrait Gallery	1,819,442	1,880,104
8	Old Royal Naval College	1,330,260	1,673,998
9	Tate Britain	1,665,291	1,488,358
10	British Library	1,454,612	1,484,900

Source: www.VisitEngland.com

Paid for entry attractions

Paid for entry attractions are also popular. You can see the popularity of these attractions in Table 7.2.

Another way to consider attractions, rather than just if you have to pay entry, is to consider if they are natural, purpose-built or heritage sites.

Natural attractions

Natural attractions are those that are not man-made. Good examples are national parks such as Snowdonia and the Peak District or lakes and lochs like the Lake District and Loch Ness. Tracking numbers of visitors can be problematic in a national park.

What natural attractions in your local area attract visitors?

Purpose-built attractions

Purpose-built attractions are, as the name suggests, built for a specific purpose. These include both old and new attractions, such as Brighton Pier and Alton Towers.

Table 7.2 – The top 10 paid for entry attractions in England in 2011. Pick one and research the reasons why it is so popular.

Rank	Name of attraction	2010 Visitors	2011 Visitors
1	Tower of London	2,413,214	2,554,746
2	Westminster Abbey	1,394,427	1,899,956
3	St Paul's Cathedral	1,892,467	1,819,925
4	Flamingo Land Theme Park and Zoo	1,268,619	1,427,193
5	Chester Zoo	1,154,285	1,425,319
6	Windermere Lake Cruises, Bowness	1,312,423	1,350,081
7	Royal Botanic Gardens, Kew Gardens	1,140,690	1,188,933
8	Stonehenge	1,009,973	1,099,656
9	ZSL London Zoo	1,011,257	1,090,741
10	Houses of Parliament and Big Ben	967,371	1,054,151

Source: www.VisitEngland.com

Activity 7.3 How popular?

Look at the visitor numbers in Tables 7.1 and 7.2 and work out the percentage change between 2010 and 2011. Why do you think this change happened? Think about the type of attraction and what region they are in.

Heritage attractions

These are attractions that attract visitors due to the history or heritage associated with the site. The UK has a large number of heritage attractions, ranging from stately homes and palaces to industrial heritage sites. If you look at Tables 7.1 and 7.2 you will see a large number of heritage attractions at the top of the lists.

▶ Domestic and international visitor numbers

When considering tourism, we also need to consider internal (domestic tourism), inbound (international tourism) as well as outbound tourism.

Figure 7.3 shows the different purposes that overseas visitors have for coming to the UK. You can see that there has been an increasing trend in the number of visitors coming to the UK for holidays since 2001. It is worth noting that visitor numbers in 2001 were affected by people's concerns over travelling after the Twin Towers disaster (9/11) and again were affected after the London train and bus bombings in 2005 (7/7).

After the economic downturn in 2007/8 business travel dropped off dramatically. This type of travel has been slowly growing again in the last two years.

Discussion point

- What event in 2011 do you think increased the popularity of Westminster Abbey by over one third?
- What effect has the development of the staycation had on visitor numbers?

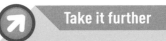

Take it further

Find out more about the National Parks on their website. You can access this by going to www.pearsonhotlinks.co.uk and searching for this title.

- How many national parks are there?
- How many visitors do they have each year?

Link

Read more about National Parks in *Unit 2: UK Travel and Tourism Destinations.*

Take it further

From Figure 7.3 you will notice that there was a downturn in visitor numbers in 2001/2 and again in 2007/9. Why not use the internet to see if you can figure out what caused these downturns.

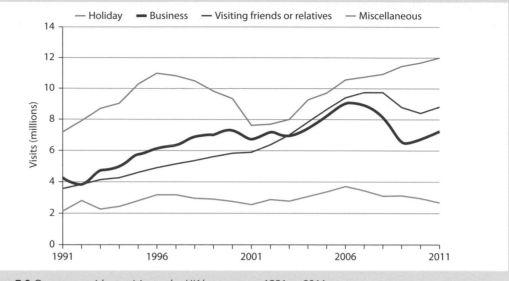

Figure 7.3 Overseas residents visits to the UK by purpose, 1991 to 2011.

Source: International Passenger Survey (IPS) – Office for National Statistics

Domestic tourism is growing as the economy changes. Since 2007, there has been an increase in domestic tourism as people are trying to save money by holidaying at home rather than travelling abroad. Special events such as Prince William and Kate Middleton's wedding and London 2012 have helped this trend.

Learning aim C   TOPIC   C1

▶ Why businesses need to respond to new opportunities

Introduction

In Topic B3 you looked at the trends and changes that are happening in the travel and tourism industry. Businesses need to be able to adapt to these changes so that they can provide customers with products that suit their changing needs. In this section you will look at why and how businesses respond to these changes and the opportunities that may arise from them.

One of the major developments offering new business opportunities for airlines in the last five years was the development of new aircraft, specifically the Airbus A380 and the Boeing 787 Dreamliner.

Research each aircraft and identify what is the advantage of each over other aeroplanes.

▶ To increase market share and maximise shareholder benefits

Holidays are not a new idea so there are very few or no new customers for travel and tourism organisations to attract. In order to gain new customers a travel and tourism organisation needs to attract customers from another organisation. This is described as increasing their market share. The aim of most businesses is to increase profit; the larger the market share the larger the chance of businesses making a profit.

To minimise business risk, avoiding product life cycle decline

As the manager of a travel and tourism organisation you have an obligation to protect the owners' investment. Therefore you are responsible for minimising the business risk while also evaluating and taking necessary risks to make a profit for the owner. One way of avoiding business risk is to manage your product's life cycle, as shown in Figure 7.4. Every product has a life cycle similar to the life cycle of a plant or an animal.

How fast the product goes through each stage will be different for each product. There are two main ways of avoiding decline. You can withdraw the product from the market or you can invest in the product in order to revitalise it. This can be expensive and you need to consider the value of investing in a declining product.

To create new products/ services and appeal to existing and new customers

As new opportunities arise there is chance for a business to develop a new product or service to satisfy the needs of both new and existing customers. A good example of this is Thomson introducing the Boeing 787 Dreamliner for its long-haul routes in 2013. The Dreamliner is being promoted as being cleaner, having larger seats and more space, thus addressing a number of the concerns of the travelling public.

Increase profitability

Profit is the money made by the company. The larger the profit, the larger the return to the owners (shareholders). As investors invest mainly to make money, an increased profitability will be popular with the shareholders. This also gives the organisation more money to reinvest, for example by purchasing new aircraft.

Competition

Most travel and tourism organisations are competing to offer their products/services to the same customers. In this constantly changing environment we need to be aware of what our competitors are up to.

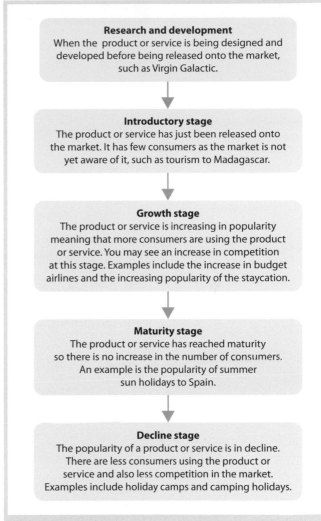

Research and development
When the product or service is being designed and developed before being released onto the market, such as Virgin Galactic.

Introductory stage
The product or service has just been released onto the market. It has few consumers as the market is not yet aware of it, such as tourism to Madagascar.

Growth stage
The product or service is increasing in popularity meaning that more consumers are using the product or service. You may see an increase in competition at this stage. Examples include the increase in budget airlines and the increasing popularity of the staycation.

Maturity stage
The product or service has reached maturity so there is no increase in the number of consumers. An example is the popularity of summer sun holidays to Spain.

Decline stage
The popularity of a product or service is in decline. There are less consumers using the product or service and also less competition in the market. Examples include holiday camps and camping holidays.

Figure 7.4 The Product Life Cycle. At what stage of the cycle do you think a service like a cross-channel ferry is?

Case study

Merlin Entertainments is Europe's number one and the world's second largest visitor attraction company, with more than 100 attractions and hotels in 22 countries and on four continents – 32 of them in the UK, the company's home country. Merlin's iconic brands include: SEA LIFE aquariums, Madame Tussauds, LEGOLAND, Dungeons, the London Eye and UK resort theme parks – Alton Towers, Chessington World of Adventures, LEGOLAND Windsor and Thorpe Park.

Thorpe Park is a resort theme park near Chertsey in Surrey. It started life as a gravel pit owned by Ready Mix Concrete (RMC). In 1970, RMC decided to turn the area into a leisure attraction based on the history of the British people as a maritime nation. Officially opened to the public in 1979, Thorpe Park then included a model world, World War I aircraft display and the Mountbatten Pavilion (now renamed the Dome).

In 1998 RMC sold the park to The Tussauds Group. After a fire in 2000 where many of the original rides were destroyed, The Tussauds Group, began a programme of investment in a number of exciting new rides including Tidal Wave, Vortex and Detonator. In 2007, Merlin Entertainments bought The Tussauds Group, and since then have continued to invest in Thorpe Park to turn it into 'the nation's thrill capital'. They have added state of the art rides such as Nemesis Inferno, Stealth, Colossus and most recently SAW The Ride and Swarm. In addition they have launched an exciting programme of events throughout the season and, in 2013, opened new accommodation on the site called Crash Pad.

1 Why do you think that Ready Mix Concrete wanted to open a leisure attraction?

2 Merlin's strategy is to invest in every one of their attractions every year. In the resort theme parks like Thorpe Park this includes opening a major new ride or attraction, like the £20m Swarm ride, at least every three years. Why do you think they do this?

3 What are the benefits of opening accommodation at Thorpe Park? Why do you think they chose the 'Crash Pad' concept rather than conventional hotel accommodation?

Reacting to competitors

Businesses need to react to what their competitors are doing. For example if a competitor is investing a lot of money into advertising its products/services, then a business needs to be aware of this as it will affect its sales. But rather than just being aware, travel and tourism organisations need to develop strategies to react to what competitors are doing. When one of the major travel agencies/tour operators advertises heavily its competition will often also advertise to try and attract back any potential customer loss. This is known as protecting your market share.

Assessment practice 7.5

Identify three common business objectives for organisations within the travel and tourism industry. [3]

▶ Opportunities for, and threats to, business development in the travel and tourism sector

Introduction

In this section you will look at some of the common opportunities for, and threats to, business development that the travel and tourism sector may need to respond to.

Looking at the area that you live in, identify what business opportunities there are for a new travel and tourism organisation. You also need to consider what might threaten the success of this business.

▶ Changing aspirations and consumer needs

Consumer needs and aspirations are constantly changing. As customers become more well-travelled, their aspirations and needs change. For example in the 1960s, a week's holiday in Spain was considered exotic, whereas the same today is considered commonplace. To go somewhere exotic you would need to consider a destination that is much further afield.

▶ Competitor behaviour

New competitors

New competition will mean that there are more organisations competing for the same customers. New competitors are likely to be small to start with, although this is not always the case. A new competitor is likely to set out to target a specific part of the market and could produce a product/service that is tailored specifically to the needs of that part of the market. For example Holiday Rejoice is a travel agency set up in Aldershot to cater for the local area's Nepalese community.

What would you consider an 'exotic' location?

Decline in competition

Due to the nature of business, not all organisations survive. Some will become bankrupt, some will be taken over by other organisations and others will merge with another organisation. Decline in competition may be a good thing for business as there are fewer organisations competing for the same customers. However, mergers and takeovers mean that although there may be less competition, competitors may be bigger with more resources at their disposal.

Link

Look at *Topic B3* for a reminder of the definition of a recession.

New products and services offered by competitors

Due to developments and trends, competitors will develop new products and services. These new products and services may have a direct impact on other businesses. Organisations need to consider how, or whether, they will compete with this new product/service.

For example British Airways restructured their pricing on European flights after the growth of budget airlines that offer travel to similar destinations for a fraction of the price.

Economic recession

An economic recession will have a number of effects on a travel and tourism organisation.

Downturn in bookings

During a recession, people feel they have less job security and so are less likely to spend their money. One discretionary spend that a lot of people reduce is the number of holidays that they take. For large travel agents this could lead to an oversupply of products to the market. In 2007 and 2010 this downturn in bookings had a dramatic effect on major travel agents.

Downturn in visitor numbers

Visitor attractions also can face a problem in a recession; as with holidays, a visit to an attraction is a discretionary spend. In the recent recession this problem was exacerbated by London 2012. Visitor attractions were gearing themselves up for a busy trading period, but during the games, people either stayed at home to watch the games on television or visited the games themselves. Indeed, many people avoided London during the games as they were concerned about congestion.

Downturn in turnover

When the numbers of bookings decrease and the numbers of visitors decline, this leads to a reduction in turnover, i.e. the amount of money coming into the business. This will have an effect on the profitability of the business and could in some cases mean that a business ceases to trade.

Foreseen events

When events are planned we call them **foreseen events**.

National events

These are events that affect the whole of a nation; they may include a public holiday and may attract tourist involvement in the event. Good examples are St Patrick's Day celebrations in Ireland and the USA or Bastille Day in France.

International events

These are events that affect a number of different nations at the same time, such as Christmas Day or Eid, or they may involve an international audience and performers, i.e. the Llangollen International Musical Eisteddfod. This could mean an increase in tourism to a local area or event.

Cultural events

These could be religious events or equally could be a traditional event such as the Changing of the Guard at Buckingham Palace. Other cultural events may include festivals such as Glastonbury Festival or the London Proms.

Sporting events

These can be about any type of sport. For example, the 2014 Commonwealth Games in Glasgow will include a variety of different sports and will see visitors arriving from any of the 54 Commonwealth states. Major sporting events can have a dramatic effect on an area. Consider the development of Stratford and East London for London 2012, with the development of the stadium and the re-development of the area.

Look at the Proms programme online and think about how the organisers appeal to different audiences.

Heritage events

Britain is known all over the world for its history and heritage. Indeed these are often the major reason given by foreign tourists for visiting Britain (Source: VisitBritain, 2011 report). Visiting a Welsh Castle, staying in a Scottish Castle and visiting Buckingham Palace were three of the most popular attractions. Major heritage events like a royal wedding will also lead to an increase in tourism.

▶ Unforeseen events

Unforeseen events can have a dramatic effect on tourism. In recent years there has been a large number of unforeseen events that have affected the UK tourism Industry.

Natural disasters

Examples of natural disasters include volcanic eruptions, earthquakes, tsunamis and extreme weather. There has been an increase in these types of events and a relationship has been identified between climate change and the frequency of these events.

These events will have a dramatic effect not only on the local area, but also on the visitors who are staying there. Emergency management has become an important element of major tour operators' planning.

Human-influenced events

Other events that affect tourism can be due to human influence such as wars, riots, industrial unrest/strikes and acts of terrorism. These will not only affect the tourists already in the country, but will also have an effect on visitor numbers in future years. Major attractions in London showed a drop of between 7 and 15 per cent in visitor numbers after the 7/7 bombings in 2005.

▶ Exchange rate fluctuations

An exchange rate is the rate at which you can buy a foreign currency. This does not remain constant, but changes all the time. This constant change is called a fluctuation and can impact businesses. How strong the pound is, and how much foreign currency a pound buys, will have an effect on a tourist when they are considering travelling abroad. As discussed previously, a strong pound will buy more foreign currency, which

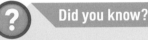
Did you know?

The British royal family is also the royal family for a number of Commonwealth nations including Canada and Australia. When the royal family visit other countries it is often a major tourism event.

Key term

Unforeseen events – when events occur without any warning.

Take it further

Why not research into the effect of Hurricane Sandy on the north-east coast of the USA in October 2012. How did this affect tourism to New York?

Discussion point

What do you think the effect was of the 2011 summer riots in London and other major UK cities on tourism numbers in 2012?

makes going abroad cheaper. However, it means that the UK is more expensive to an incoming tourist. A weak pound would have the opposite effect; it would be expensive to go abroad from the UK, but cheap for foreign tourists to visit.

▷ External costs

External costs are outside the control of the travel company, they include food, fuel and accommodation prices. These costs depend on the demand for the product; an increase in demand or reduction in production will increase prices, whereas the opposite will reduce these costs.

Fuel has a different effect; as most goods need to be transported from place to place, the higher the fuel price the higher the transport cost, which in turn increases the selling price offered to the customer.

▷ Local and national government intervention

Local and national governments may intervene to either stimulate or suppress demand for tourism.

Taxation

Taxation can have an impact on the travel and tourism industry. Domestic and inbound tourists need to consider the Value Added Tax (VAT) that will be added to the cost of accommodation in the UK. Some cities have a tax on hotel rooms that is paid at the end of your stay, such as New York's Hotel Room Occupancy Tax. Airline Passenger Duty was introduced in 1994 and is a tax charged to people travelling out of the UK by air. This affects the tourist destinations that people can afford to travel to. Some countries are affected by UK taxation, such as the Caribbean, and changes to taxation affect whether people will travel to these destinations.

Immigration policy

A country's immigration policy will affect how easy it is to migrate to that country. Immigration is important for a country's economy so skilled workers can relocate to that country. Immigration may have an effect on tourist numbers as people will visit friends and families who have emigrated. Immigration also helps add to a country's culture, which in turn can make the country more attractive to tourists.

Investment in infrastructure

The internal structures that support a nation, such as roads, railways, ports, airports, internet, gas, electricity and water supply, make up the infrastructure of a country. By investing in infrastructure, a government is making it easier for people to move around, which in turn makes it easier for tourists to travel to and around their destination.

Funding of promotional organisations/materials

National and local governments promote both domestically and internationally. How much they fund the promotion of the country will have an effect on the number of tourists who visit. However, as you will see in Unit 8, it is not just how much funding that is important, but also who the promotion will target and the quality of the message. VisitBritain promotes the UK in general, then there are national tourist boards that promote each of the countries individually (England, Northern Ireland, Wales and Scotland), as well as regional tourist boards in England promoting specific areas.

Assessment practice 7.6

Assessment practice 7.6

Give three examples of how the government can influence demand in the travel and tourism industry. [3]

▶ Developments in technology

Technology is constantly changing and new developments will affect the way we work and the communications we use.

Wireless products and services

Developments in wireless products and services have led to an increase in not only access to the internet and information, but also where and how we can access this information. This has led to quicker and easier communication between businesses and their customers; a number of visitor attractions now have downloadable visitor guides as well as other apps that increase the richness of the visitor experience.

Social media

The growth of social media has provided another communication channel to pass information on to existing or potential customers. Interestingly, using social media to sell an organisation is not very effective, but developing an organisation's social media presence and using it to send a specific message or idea can have a positive effect.

▶ Social attitudes

Ethical issues

The social and ethical structure of the UK is constantly changing. Increasingly, consumers are taking into account the ethical behaviour of a company before they make a purchase. This has led many travel and tourism organisations to develop more ethically balanced products and services.

Cultural issues

Increasingly, people in the UK are looking for something more than just summer sun on their holidays. There has been a growth in holidays that celebrate other countries' cultures which include activities such as visiting local communities and attending celebrations of local culture.

Environmental issues

There has been an increase in the number of people who are concerned about environmental issues in relation to travel and tourism. Customers are considering environmental issues before they purchase a product or service.

This has led a number of companies to consider the environmental impact of their products and services. Some companies are now offering carbon off-setting schemes for consumers who are concerned about their carbon footprint.

Why do you think people are becoming more aware about the environmental issues affecting where they travel?

▶ How businesses respond to new opportunities and threats

Introduction

In this section you will look at how businesses change and innovate to respond to new opportunities and threats.

To see how much travel and tourism organisations have changed look at pictures from Butlin's in the 1960s compared to today. You can view some of these images on the Butlin's Memories website as well as the current Butlin's website. To access the websites for these, visit Pearson hotlinks. You can access this by going to www.pearsonhotlinks.co.uk and searching for this title.

- What differences do you notice between the pictures?
- Why do you think that Butlin's has changed?

▶ Changing the structure of the business

One way to respond to changes in the business environment is to change the structure of the business. Below are some of the ways of changing a business structure.

Takeovers

A takeover is when one business or individual purchases another business, and therefore takes over the business. This will be a complete takeover of the control and management of the business. Takeovers can be a quick and effective way to expand a business quickly.

Mergers

This is when two or more businesses combine their assets to create a new business, usually leading to a bigger business. Mergers are a way to expand into an area that you have little or no experience in. For example, two tour operators who focus on tours to different geographical locations may merge to offer a wider range of tours.

Vertical and horizontal integration

Another way to develop a business is to integrate their products and services with another business. This can be done through takeovers and mergers like we have just looked at.

- **Vertical integration:** this is where a business integrates with a business that either supplies it, or is a supplier to it. It is called vertical integration as the businesses are integrating up and down the product delivery chain. For example, Thomson, the tour operator, also owns Thomson, the travel agency and Thomson, the airline.
- **Horizontal integration:** this is where a business integrates with one that offers a similar provision. It is called horizontal integration as the businesses are integrated across the product delivery chain. For example, Thomas Cook also owns Club 18–30, Neilson and Direct Holidays.

New subsidiary companies

Another approach is to develop a new subsidiary company that will be part of the parent company and so benefits from the experience and expertise of the parent

By merging, tour operators can offer customers more opportunities to travel further afield.

company. The new company will be seen by consumers as a different provider. This approach works particularly well when an established company is trying to develop a new product or service for a new market. For example a tour operator may develop a new subsidiary company to handle its new tailor-made holiday provision.

Assessment practice 7.7

Identify and explain one advantage of vertical integration for an organisation within the UK travel and tourism industry. [3]

▶ Developing new markets

New customer types

Customers' needs and expectations are constantly changing. Sometimes these changes create new customer types who are looking for a specific product to suit their needs.

For example, there has been an increase in tourists who are concerned about the environmental impact of their holidays. These customers who wish to travel on 'green' holidays are a new customer type. Tour operators have been developing tours to satisfy the needs of this new type of customer.

New destinations

Some customers are always looking for something new and different. In recent years there has been a growth in the number of long-haul destinations that can be visited from the UK, leading to the development of new destinations. Examples in the last 25 years include China and Dubai.

New accommodation types

In recent years there has been a range of new accommodation types coming onto the market. Developments in the types of accommodation that are available to customers will lead to the development of new products and services.

For example, theme parks have started to develop resort hotels within their parks to encourage people to travel further to visit or to stay longer. In Dubai, the Burj Al Arab, a 7 star hotel, is often voted the world's most luxurious hotel, offering a level of luxury that most hotels cannot offer.

▶ Introducing technological innovations

Developments in technology have led to innovations in the way that customers and organisations communicate, as well as the development of new products and services.

Apps

Apps (applications for smartphones, tablets, etc.) are a great way for tourist organisations to communicate with their customers. Train and bus operating companies have downloadable interactive timetables. Visitor attractions have interactive visitor guides that visitors can download to enrich their experience. Apps are useful for businesses as they mean that they can offer a more enriched experience to their customers.

? Did you know?

The world's first underwater resort, Poseidon, is being developed in Fiji which, if money for the project can be raised, will offer customers an entirely new holiday experience.

Link

You can read more about the Burj Al Arab in *Unit 4: International Travel and Tourism Destinations.*

Bluetooth® technologies in theme park rides

Disneyland Resort and Walt Disney World have introduced Bluetooth® technology to help customers find their way around the parks. The app provides the user with a map of the park and also pinpoints their location. It also gives the user information about the length of queues at the rides and can be used to book the ride in advance to reduce queuing times.

Booking systems

Electronic booking systems have been around for a while. Modern booking systems not only record bookings, but also help to manage the number of customers and the booking price in order to boost sales.

For example, if a customer books a flight on easyJet on a popular day the computer system will charge them more than if they had booked on an unpopular day.

E-marketing

With the increase in the popularity of electronic devices, smartphones, tablets and other mobile devices, there has been a rapid increase in electronic marketing. E-marketing has developed from pop-ups and banners on a website to sophisticated targeted communication, through text, emails and apps.

Electronic and mobile ticketing and promotion

A number of providers are now moving away from the traditional printed ticket towards using tickets that can be downloaded online or text tickets that can be viewed on smartphones. This reduces the costs involved both in printing and posting the tickets as well as saving the customer time. Examples of companies that use this type of ticketing include easyJet and National Express coaches.

▶ Cutting costs

Businesses cannot force people to buy their product or service so there are limits to how much they can control their sales. However, they do have the ability to control their costs. Cutting costs is one way to improve the profitability of the business.

Economies of scale

Economy of scale means that the more frequently a task is completed, the cheaper the unit costs become. For example, if a business purchases a large amount of stock they can negotiate a larger discount than if they were only ordering a small amount.

Outsourcing to take advantage of cheaper labour costs

Another way to reduce costs is to pay another organisation to carry out the work. Labour costs vary in different parts of the world, and indeed in different parts of the UK. A classic example of this is the number of call centres that have outsourced that area of their business to companies in India to take advantage of their lower labour costs.

Moving functions overseas

This is similar to outsourcing as businesses move their operations overseas to take advantage of the lower labour costs. The difference from outsourcing is that you are keeping the work in-house, rather than paying another company to complete the work.

WorkSpace

▶ Jayne Wells

Owner, Travel North

After completing a BTEC First Diploma in Travel and Tourism, I trained as a travel agent in a large international travel agency. After five years I was promoted to assistant manager, before leaving to start my own agency.

In the travel agency I realised that the number of people booking holidays online was increasing rapidly and saw an opportunity to open my own online agency, focusing on providing holidays for people who were travelling from the north of England. I chose the north as a lot of packages meant travelling to London airports and I thought that the specific focus of my agency would work well.

I set up a private limited company with myself and my parents as shareholders and, with a friend's help, set up a website. I researched a lot of the package holidays that were leaving from airports in the north of England and started to put together my own packages.

Promoting my website was difficult as there is so much competition online. However, I had a meeting with a Google advisor who explained how I could use their search engine to get my site appearing near the top of their search results. Social media will be really useful for my agency so I have set up a Facebook page that customers can use to leave comments for the company and also to communicate with each other. An exciting development is that I am currently in negotiations with GroupOn to offer some discounted products; this is a great way to be competitive with my prices.

Though my agency has only been operating for a few years we are getting a good reputation for both the way we look after our customers and also for providing a new service for people based in the north of England.

When I was at college I did not know what I wanted to do; now I can't see myself doing anything else.

Think about it

1 Why do you think Jayne decided to set up the company as a private limited company rather than any of the other ownership options she had?

2 What is Jayne's agency's unique selling point?

3 What are the benefits to Jayne of having only an online presence and not having a bricks and mortar agency?

4 Jayne had no idea what role she wanted within the industry. Have you considered which sector you might like to work in? Or what function you might like to have in the industry?

BTEC
Assessment Zone

This section has been written to help you to do your best when you take the examination. Read through it carefully and ask your teacher if there is anything that you are still not sure about.

How you will be assessed

For this unit you will be assessed through a one-hour written examination. The examination paper will have a maximum of 50 marks. The number of marks available for each part of a question will be shown in brackets, e.g. [2], with the total for each question being shown at the end of the question.

There will be different types of question in the examination.

A Questions where all of the answers are available and you have to choose the answer(s) that fit. *Tip: always make sure that you read the instructions carefully. Sometimes you may need to identify more than one correct answer.*

Examples:

> John Luke Travel is a small tour company that specialises in taking sports fans to events. John started the company by himself in 2005 after he found it hard to get to some events he would have liked to attend, but did not want to drive to. John has no full-time employees, except himself, but he does have five drivers who work part-time, mainly on weekends. John hires minibuses and coaches from other companies and sells tickets to fans who want to attend events such as football away matches, athletic meetings and some horse racing events.
>
> John Luke Travel has which type of business ownership? [1]
>
> A Public limited company
>
> B Partnership
>
> C Sole trader
>
> D Co-operative
>
> Answer: C
>
> Which **two** of the following would be considered an opportunity for John Luke Travel? [2]
>
> A Glasgow hosting the 2014 Commonwealth Games
>
> B Decrease in rail fares
>
> C Improved transport links
>
> D Increase in customer demand
>
> E An increase in competition
>
> Answers: A and D

Disclaimer: These practice questions and sample answers are not actual exam questions. They are provided as a practice aid only and should not be assumed to reflect the format or coverage of the real external test.

B Questions where you are asked to produce a short answer worth 1 or 2 marks. *Tip: look carefully at how the question is set out to see how many points need to be included in your answer.*

Examples:

> There has been a significant increase in people taking their holidays in the UK rather than travelling abroad, sometimes known as domestic tourism. Explain **two** possible reasons for the growth in popularity in domestic tourism. [4]
>
> **Possible answers:** A growth in unemployment, leading to some households having less disposable income.
>
> Currency exchange rate (the weak pound), making foreign travel more expensive so fewer people can afford to travel abroad.

C Questions where you are asked to provide a longer answer – these are worth 8 marks. *Tips: make sure that you read the question in full, and answer all of the parts of the question you are asked. It is a good idea to plan your answer so that you do not forget anything and remember to check your answer once you have finished.*

Example:

> Lifestyle Travel, specialising in European holidays, and Simpson's Tours, offering trips around the world, are the only travel agents based on the high street of the market town of Exwood, Cheshire. Recently there has been a development in their provision of services, Simpson's Tours closed their high street branch and launched themselves as a web-based only travel agent.
>
> Discuss the opportunities and threats of this development for Lifestyle Travel. [8]
>
> **Answer:** Some customers don't have access to the internet, so Lifestyle Travel could market themselves as the only high street travel agent in Exwood. However, it is possible that Simpson's Tours would be able to offer their products at a discount because they save costs by being online only, so they could potentially increase their profit. Lifestyle Travel could also launch a website and offer similar online services, but they would have to be careful about the costs involved; however by operating both a high street travel agent and a web-based service they could potentially increase their market share. Also, Lifestyle Travel could target new markets by offering different products or services, for example they could offer holidays to long-haul destinations. An opportunity for both organisations could be to go into partnership; this could benefit both organisations because the customers could access their joint products and services in a number of ways, so this could increase sales. Also there would be very few costs involved because neither organisation would need to alter the way they operate.

Hints and tips

- **Use the time before the test.** Make sure that you have got everything you will need. Check that your pen works and that you read the instructions on the front of your examination paper. Try to make yourself feel comfortable and relaxed.

- **Keep an eye on the time.** The examination will last one hour, and you should be able to see the clock in the examination room so that you will know how long you have got left to complete the paper. As a rough guide, allow 1 minute for every mark on the paper. This means that a question worth 5 marks should take you around 5 minutes to complete.

- **Read the questions fully.** Make sure you read the question through enough times to be sure that you understand what you are being asked to do. It is easy to misread a question and then write an answer which is wrong. Check you are doing what you are being asked to do. This is where many students lose marks.

- **Plan your answers.** For longer questions it is worth spending a minute or two to write down the key points which you want to include in your answer. If you are being asked to evaluate, you will need to think about positive and negative points. Using a plan will allow you to make sure you include both in your answer.

- **Check your answers.** Once you have answered all of the questions on the paper, you will probably have a few minutes to spare. Use this time to check your answers and maybe fill in any blanks which you have left. You should try to answer every question on the paper.

- **Read through longer answers.** Read through your longer answers to make sure your answers makes sense, and you have answered the question fully.

- **Make sure you have completed the front of the paper.** Once the examination has ended, check that you have written your name and candidate number on the front of the paper. This is important so that you will gain the marks for your work.

How to improve your answer

Read the two student answers below, together with the feedback. Try to use what you learn here to improve your answers in your examination.

Question

Parkside travel is a small independent travel agency that has been owned and run by Sue and Andy Hill for the last 20 years. They have a very good reputation locally for looking after their clients and for their customer service.

Andy has decided that it is time to develop an online presence. The plan is to include an online booking service, web brochures and e-ticketing.

Explain **two** benefits to Parkside Travel of having an online presence. [4]

Student 1's answer

The first benefit I can think of is that Parkside Travel's customers will be able to see what products they have 24/7. This means that customers can choose and pay for a holiday without having to go to the travel agency. This could benefit Parkside Travel as they will be able to sell products even when the travel agency is closed.

The second benefit I can think of is that, by being online, Parkside Travel will be able to sell and promote their products and services to a wider customer base, i.e. not only people in the locality of the agency. This will hopefully lead to more bookings as the customer base is bigger.

Feedback:

Student 1 has identified two benefits of having an online presence. Firstly that the customer can access the product 24 hours a day and that customers do not have to be in the local area, unlike if they were using the agency. [2 marks] Each of the benefits has been explained in terms of the direct impact on Parkside Travel. More sales due to increased access to the products and services and more sales as an online presence provide a wider customer base as more customers can see the products and services compared with just in the agency. [2 marks]

Student 2's answer

Parkside Travel's website will be able to have images and moving graphics, containing lots of information. This is better than a brochure that is just printed on paper.

Parkside Travel's website could be seen by people from all over, whereas the agency is only accessible to local people. These means that they could have loads more customers from all over the world.

Feedback:

Student 2 has also identified two benefits of having an online presence, [2 marks]. However Student 2 did not explain why having moving graphics and images and lots of information on their site would be of a benefit to Parkside Travel. If Student 2 had explained that the interactivity of a website is more interesting and stimulating to customers than a paper brochure and that information can easily be updated, and that this would then lead to an increased interest in Parkside Travel, then the second mark would have been achieved. Student 2 did explain the benefit of having a wider customer base so would overall achieve 3 marks for this answer.

Assess yourself

NFC (National Flag Carrier) Airlines is a large European national airline that flies to over 60 different countries around the world from their Central European hub.

They have been an airline since the 1960s, and although they were originally state owned, they have been a public limited company for the last 15 years.

They employ over 25,000 staff and have a fleet of over 30 aeroplanes ranging in size from the Boeing 737-400 to 2,787 super jumbos.

Question 1

What is the business structure of NFC Airlines? [1]

A   Micro-enterprise

B   Small and medium enterprise (SME)

C   A large business

D   A multinational company

Question 2

A budget airline, Cheapstar Airlines, specialising in European short-haul flights, has started up in the same country as NFC airlines. Explain **two** of the expected effects this will have on NFC business. [4]

1   ....

2   ....

Question 3

Identify and explain two other threats that may affect NFC business. [4]

1   ....

2   ....

For further practice, see the Assessment Practice question on pages 179, 181, 184, 189, 194, 199 and 201.

Introduction

Every day we see hundreds of promotional messages from companies, all trying to sell us their products or services.

In this unit you will look at what makes a particular promotion memorable, what makes us want that particular product or service, why and how it is made to seem desirable and what makes us actually buy the product or service.

You will also look at how and why travel and tourism businesses promote and sell their products and services. You will also learn the language that is used in the marketing industry as well as review a wide range of promotional methods and materials.

Finally, you will have an opportunity to put everything that you have learnt into practice by designing your own promotional materials aimed at a specific market.

Assessment: This unit will be assessed through a series of assignments set by your teacher/tutor.

Learning aims

In this unit you will:

A investigate how travel and tourism products/services are sold

B understand the promotional techniques and materials used by travel and tourism organisations

C plan and create effective promotional materials for travel and tourism target markets.

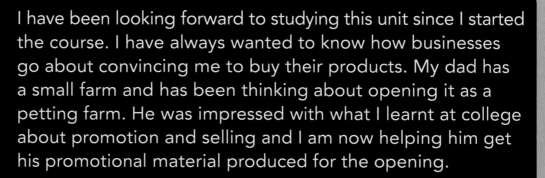

I have been looking forward to studying this unit since I started the course. I have always wanted to know how businesses go about convincing me to buy their products. My dad has a small farm and has been thinking about opening it as a petting farm. He was impressed with what I learnt at college about promotion and selling and I am now helping him get his promotional material produced for the opening.

Joanne, *16-year-old Travel and Tourism student*

Promotion and Sales in Travel and Tourism

8

BTEC
Assessment Zone

This table shows what you must do in order to achieve a **Pass**, **Merit** or **Distinction** grade, and where you can find activities in this book to help you.

Assessment criteria			
Level 1	**Level 2 Pass**	**Level 2 Merit**	**Level 2 Distinction**
Learning aim A: Investigate how travel and tourism products/services are sold			
1A.1 Outline how promotion and sales are supported by the aims and objectives of two travel and tourism organisations.	**2A.P1** Explain how promotion and sales are supported by the aims and objectives of two different travel and tourism organisations. **See Assessment activity 8.1, page 220**		
1A.2 Outline the target markets of two travel and tourism organisations.	**2A.P2** Describe the target markets of two selected travel and tourism organisations. **See Assessment activity 8.1, page 220**	**2A.M1** Explain how a travel and tourism organisation has developed/adapted their products/services for a specific target market. **See Assessment activity 8.1, page 220**	**2A.D1** Analyse the impact of new technology on how two travel and tourism organisations sell their products/services. **See Assessment activity 8.1, page 220**
1A.3 Outline the selling channels used by two different travel and tourism organisations.	**2A.P3** Describe how two different travel and tourism organisations sell products/ services, including use of new technology, to their target markets. **See Assessment activity 8.1, page 220**	**2A.M2** Explain why two travel and tourism organisations use a variety of selling channels, including use of new technology, to reach their target markets. **See Assessment activity 8.1, page 220**	
Learning aim B: Understand the promotional techniques and materials used by travel and tourism organisations			
1B.4 Outline how two different travel and tourism organisations promote their products/services to their target markets.	**2B.P4** Explain how two different travel and tourism organisations use a variety of promotional techniques and materials to appeal to their target markets. **See Assessment activity 8.2, page 226**	**2B.M3** Explain how the use of different promotional techniques and materials can increase the appeal of travel and tourism products and/ or services. **See Assessment activity 8.2, page 226**	**2B.D2** Assess the effects that different factors can have on the choice of promotional techniques and materials used by travel and tourism organisations. **See Assessment activity 8.2, page 226**
1B.5 Outline factors that influence the choice of promotional techniques and materials by two travel and tourism organisations.	**2B.P5** Describe the factors that influence the choice of promotional techniques and materials by two travel and tourism organisations to appeal to their target markets. **See Assessment activity 8.2, page 226**		

Learning aim C: Plan and create effective promotional materials for travel and tourism target markets

1C.6 English	2C.P6 English	2C.M4 English	2C.D3 English
Outline, with support, a plan of a piece of travel and tourism promotional material.	Plan a piece of travel and tourism promotional material to meet specified message and budget. **See Assessment activity 8.3, page 234**	Plan a piece of travel and tourism promotional material explaining how it meets the specified message, budget, timescale and selected target market's needs. **See Assessment activity 8.3, page 234**	Plan and create travel and tourism promotional material within agreed budget and timescale, and evaluate how it meets the needs of, and appeals to, a selected target market. **See Assessment activity 8.3, page 234**
1C.7	2C.P7	2C.M5 English	
Create a piece of travel and tourism promotional material with support.	Create a piece of travel and tourism promotional material designed to appeal to a target market. **See Assessment activity 8.3, page 234**	Create a piece of travel and tourism promotional material demonstrating a clear message, correct language use and design quality appropriate to a selected target market. **See Assessment activity 8.3, page 234**	

English Opportunity to practise English skills

How you will be assessed

The unit will be assessed by a series of assignments set by your teacher/tutor. You will research two travel and tourism organisations. From your research you will identify how their products and services are sold, who their target markets are and the promotional techniques and materials they use to promote to these target markets. Finally you will plan and create effective promotional material for a specified travel and tourism target market.

Your assessment could be in the form of:

- written reports
- presentations
- promotional plan
- promotional materials.

The best way to find out about different travel and tourism organisations is to visit them. Talk to the staff and management involved in their promotions, making sure that you have planned questions before to ensure you ask everything you need to know. You may find that your teacher/tutor organises these visits or that you will organise them yourself.

▶ Importance of organisational aims and objectives to travel and tourism promotion and sales

Introduction

Promotion and sales can support a number of travel and tourism aims and objectives. Sometimes these aims and objectives may conflict with each other within an organisation. In this topic you will look at some of the major aims and objectives of travel and tourism organisations.

Make a list of what you think would be your main objectives if you had your own business. Compare your list with the aims and objectives that are discussed in this unit and see if they are similar to yours.

▶ Financial

Finance can be seen as a measure of the success of a business, some of the key financial objectives are shown below.

To make a profit

Most businesses exist to make a **profit** for their owners. After all, why would you invest in a business if you were not going to have any return for the money invested? This means that most businesses will have making a profit as a primary objective.

Increase sales

Increasing sales will mean more business for the organisation and hopefully a larger profit. Promotions help to stimulate sales, as potential customers become aware of your product or service. Improving employees' sales techniques can also increase sales.

Reduce losses

If a business is not successful, it might set an objective of reducing losses. Loss reductions are achieved through the reduction of costs. This has included reducing the number of employees, which in turn reduces the wages that the business has to pay.

Break even

Some organisations, mainly in the charitable sector, are not required to make a profit, but to **break even**. Break even occurs when a business has made enough money through product or service sales to cover the costs of producing them and running the business. Ensuring that an organisation breaks even is often an organisational objective. Even if an organisation only aims to break even, and so not make a profit, they will still run on the same corporate principles as private sector companies, such as operating within budgets. This is because they still need to be able to compete with these private sector companies.

Key terms

Profit – is the money that businesses make from their sales after the costs of making their sales have been taken out.

Break even – the point where the business makes neither a profit or a loss.

Manage assets

For many travel and tourism organisations, such as hotels and airlines, their assets, i.e. what they own, can be extremely expensive and need to be taken into account by the business when considering their finances. Costs such as the refurbishment of hotels and the ongoing maintenance of aeroplanes are a key factor in how a business manages its yearly finances.

With the growth of green/eco tourism, governments are starting to look more closely at the management of their tourism assets as these assets are what attract tourists to their country and so are important to their economy.

▶ Strategic

Strategic objectives give structure to the long-term direction of the organisation.

To expand

One way to increase sales is to increase the amount of trade that your business is doing. This can be done by opening new outlets in new locations or by merging with, or taking over, other businesses in an area where your business is not well represented.

Diversify

Diversification is where you offer an increased range of products aimed at a wider customer base. For example, if your tour operator does not offer holidays aimed at teenagers, then it could diversify into that market.

Compete

Most travel and tourism organisations are in competition for customer spend. Competition strategies can either be focused on a specific competitor or a specific target market. A competition strategy can help a business to focus on what it offers and how this differs from what competitors offer or from the needs of the customers.

Generate consumer loyalty

Another strategy is to generate **consumer loyalty** for your product or service. Loyal customers will choose to reuse your product or service. This has the advantage of reducing your promotional costs, as it costs less to encourage repeat customers to reuse products and services. Businesses generally make more money from loyal customers than they do from new customers, so generating loyalty is very important for a business' success.

▶ Physical resources

Organising resources

Aims and objectives will be set to help organise the resources of an organisation. For example, an aeroplane is an expensive asset and it is important that the airline maximises its usage in order to make as much money from it as possible.

It is also important to plan the refurbishment and development of physical resources, particularly in the case of accommodation where it will need to be updated and renovated over time, due to natural wear and tear.

Did you know ?

In 2013 Boeing had to ground 50 of their Dreamliner aeroplanes so that their battery systems could be replaced. How do you think this affected their planned 2013 budget?

Did you know ?

Governments are increasingly protecting their assets. In the UK this includes the classification of Areas of Outstanding Natural Beauty and of National Parks and the preservation of historic buildings.

Outside the UK, examples include increased protection of game reserves in Africa and the development of World Heritage sites such as the Taj Mahal in India and Yellowstone National Park in the USA.

Key term

Consumer loyalty – where consumers continue to buy or use a product or service.

How do you think this doorman offers good customer service?

▶ Human resources

Staff performance

Individual and team aims and objectives will be used to help identify the expected performance of a team or individual and then will be used to measure their performance. Individual targets are set not only to help the individual achieve their goals but also to help the department obtain their targets. Successfully meeting these goals will then help an organisation achieve their strategic targets.

Customer service

Aims and objectives for customer service within a company often include how issues are handled and the timeframe involved. For example, many companies have a policy that any complaints must be dealt with in a set timeframe.

▶ Corporate responsibility

This is the responsibility that an organisation has to the environment and society. In recent years this has become important to organisations, as consumers have started to consider the behaviour of organisations when planning holidays. Examples include the boycotting of, and even protesting about, a particular company's products or services.

Promotion of responsible tourism principles

- **Economic responsibility** means maximising the benefits for the local community with minimal impact on local livelihoods, including paying a fair wage and price for goods locally.
- **Environmental responsibility** means minimising the environmental impact of tourism. This can cover a wide range of issues such as over-consumption of resources, carbon emissions and ensuring the development of tourism infrastructure such as airports and roads does not negatively affect the environment.
- **Social responsibility** is concerned with the effects of tourism on the local community; minimising the negative effects while maximising the positive effects of tourism.

Many companies develop a **mission statement** which shows the public how they are meeting these three principles. This allows the public to make an informed decision about the products and services they choose when travelling.

Key term

Mission statement – the public statement many organisations work towards to provide a specific culture for their customers.

Take it further

The development of HS2, the high speed train link between Birmingham and London has raised a lot of debate. Using the internet, research the arguments both for and against the HS2 project and discuss with your group.

Activity 8.1   Organisational objectives

List five different common organisational objectives and explain how organisations may achieve these.

Target markets

Introduction

As everyone is different, with different needs, wants and desires, it is not possible to develop one product that will satisfy everyone in the market. Companies develop different products targeted at different groups of the market; these are called **market segments**. Make a list of the different ways you can think of to segment a market.

Age

Some products are designed and targeted at specific age groups.

However, this is not the most accurate way of grouping people together; just because they are the same age does not mean that they have the same needs and wants.

Gender

Other travel and tourism products are targeted specifically at one particular gender. There are a number of holiday companies like Venus Adventures that specialise in women-only holidays and adventures.

Socio-economic groups

Socio-economic grouping is a way of segmenting the market on the grounds of social background and income. This classification system divides the market into six social economic groups. Table 8.1 gives examples of the types of career in each class.

Table 8.1 – The different social economic groups defined by the travel and tourism sector.

Group	Type of job role	Example of job
A	Professional	Air traffic controller or airline pilot, director of a tour operator
B	Managers	Hotel manager, travel agency manager
C1	Supervisors	Shift supervisor,
C2	Skilled manual	Chef, aircraft engineer
D	Semi-skilled manual	Aircraft dispatcher, airport security
E	Unskilled manual	Baggage handler, cleaner

Lifestyle

Segmenting the market by lifestyle means that you need to look closely at the family circumstances of people, as well as the activities that they undertake, it is slightly more complicated then segmenting by other means. Your needs change as you go through the stages of the family life cycle as shown in Table 8.2.

Key term

Market segment – a specifically defined group of customers that have similar needs and wants, that a product or service can be developed for.

Did you know ?

Some companies specialise in age-defined groups.

- PGL have been offering adventure holidays to school groups and children since 1957.
- Club 18–30 produce holidays targeted at 18–30 year olds.
- Saga holidays specialise in holidays for the over 50s.

Table 8.2 – Stages of the family life cycle.

Bachelor
Young and single with limited or no family responsibility
Newly married
Young and married with no children
Full nest 1
Family with youngest child under school age
Full nest 2
Family with youngest child of school age
Full nest 3
Children are still at home but are now working
Empty nest 1
One partner working and children have left home
Empty nest 2
Both partners are now retired
Solitary survivor 1
One partner left who is still working
Solitary survivor 2
One partner left who is retired

At each stage of the life cycle a person's income and responsibilities change, and each change is significant because it will affect the type of holiday chosen at each stage. This means that the way that organisations promote their products or services to people at each stage has to vary considerably. For example, someone at the bachelor stage will be looking for a very different holiday to a family who have small children.

Other lifestyle choices also need to be considered. For example, does the person live in a rural or an urban environment? This may dramatically change the person's access to services and also what type of products and services they may require.

▶ Ethnicity

Another method of segmentation is on the grounds of ethnicity. There are a number of travel agencies in the UK that specialise in travel to one or two destinations, focusing on the needs of an ethnic community. This could be providing holidays to a specific destination for religious grounds or travel to visit friends and relatives from the person's country of origin. For instance, El-Sawy Travel specialise in Hajj and Umrah packages for practising Muslims.

▶ Geographical locations

Local

Some travel and tourism providers may focus on providing goods and services to the local market. Some local tour operators and coach companies offer trips and tours to local events or to other locations. For example, a weekend coach trip from the North East to London may be a popular option; but may not be so popular for people from the home counties.

National

Some travel and tourism providers have a national appeal. For example, people will travel from all over the UK to go to Alton Towers in Staffordshire.

International

Other travel and tourism providers have international appeal. Examples are World Heritage sites, such as Kew Gardens, the Tower of London and Durham Cathedral.

The size of the audience that your product or service appeals to will affect how and where you promote it. You are likely to promote further afield if visitor profiles in the past show that people have travelled from all over the UK.

Take it further

The Blue Reef Aquarium in Portsmouth focuses most of its advertising and promotion on people who live within an hour's drive from the aquarium. Research the methods they use to reach a local market.

▶ Common and special interest

Another way that you can segment the market is to focus on common interest groups; two good examples are sport and hobbies. We will look at each of these in turn.

Do you think the promotions that the Blue Reef Aquarium use would make you want to visit?

Sport

There are a number of providers that offer products and services for customers interested in following a particular sport. This could include providing transportation and accommodation as well as tickets for a spectator to follow their favourite sport or sporting team. For example, football fans go on tours to see their club/side play in important matches abroad.

Hobbies

Many people like to participate in their favourite hobby while

Think about your hobbies and research if there are any holidays that would let you learn more about them

on holiday or even learn a new skill. This has led to the growth of special interest holidays. It is now possible to learn to cook in France, paint in Spain or pony trek across America. These holidays include other tourists who have the same hobby or interest so you can enjoy your hobby with like-minded people.

Case study

Sport Abroad has over 35 years' experience of delivering supporter tours, sporting holidays and event hospitality. This makes them one of the UK's leading sports tour operators. They provide tours for tournaments including the Rugby World Cup, British and Irish Lions Tours, Rugby Sevens series, the Ashes series and the Cricket World Cup.

Sport Abroad is so successful because they have made it their mission over the last three decades to learn as much as they can about the people who are travelling on their tours. By listening to their travellers and tailoring their services to meet their needs exactly, Sport Abroad has built all their overseas sports tours on the following four principles:

- Guaranteed match tickets.
- The finest hotels.
- The best airlines.

- Small groups of like-minded supporters.

(Source: www.sportabroad.co.uk)

Research these principles further at Sport Abroad's website. You can access this website through Pearson hotlinks. Go to www.pearsonhotlinks.co.uk and search for this title.

1 Why do you think Sport Abroad, part of the TUI Group, trade under their own brand rather than the TUI brand?

2 Sport Abroad sells special interest holidays to sporting events. If you were planning a special interest tour for a cookery holiday what would you consider to be important for your clients?

3 If Sport Abroad wanted to expand their range of products what other events do you think would be good for Sport Abroad to expand into?

▶▶ Selling channels and the impact of technology

Introduction

A selling channel is how the organisation sells their product or service to the customer. Examples of selling channels include travel agents and travel websites.

Make a list of all the different channels where you could buy a product or service. Check your list with a friend to see if they have any different ideas.

▶ Chain of distribution

This is the traditional chain that a product or service would go through from the producer of the product or service until it gets to the customer. Retailers have two different ways to sell to the customer – either face to face or communicating via telephone or internet. The chain of distribution is shown in Figure 8.1.

▶ Face to face

Face to face sales tend to be used when selling complex products and services to the customer. The benefit is that you can explain the product and service and also react to the customer's body language and facial expressions, **overcome objections** and explain the parts of the product or service that the customers are interested in. The disadvantage to the organisation is the cost of employing staff who are available for a face to face discussion.

Travel agents

Travel agents are a good example of face to face selling. Travel consultants identify the customer needs and offer products or services that suit the customer's requirements. They are often found on the high street and customers will often go into the shop specifically to speak with someone after previously looking at information online, in a brochure or in the shop window.

Ticket office

A ticket office serves a similar role as a travel agency, providing products and services to the customer. Examples include the ticket office at your local train or bus station or in an attraction such as a theatre or theme park. Ticket offices generally do not provide such a wide range of products or services as a travel agent and tend to be linked to a specific type of product or service.

Reception

Staff at a hotel reception can explain the range of products and services that are available in the hotel and in the local area, to the customer. This could include different accommodation choices or services that the hotel offers like treatments within their spa facilities or the food and beverage provision of the hotel.

Producer
Organisation or persons that produce the product or service

↓

Wholesaler
Organisation that sells the product or service in bulk

↓

Retailer
Sells the product or service to the customer

↓

Customer
Person who purchases the product or service

Figure 8.1 The chain of distribution

Key term

Overcoming objections – this refers to addressing a customer's worries and concerns about a product or service. This may be done by explaining the product or service or even by offering a different, more appropriate product or service.

▶ Telephone and online

Over the last 30 years travel and tourism organisations have increasingly been offering customers access to their products and services over the telephone and, more recently, online through computer and mobile communication devices, such as smartphones and tablets. This benefits travel and tourism organisations as they do not have to have as many high street locations, which reduces the organisation's operational costs. Customers also benefit by being able to access the organisation's products and services from any location and, sometimes, by getting the product for a cheaper price.

Call centres

These offices handle large numbers of calls from customers. They handle complaints and customer service issues as well as selling products and services to the customers.

Booking websites

The internet is now the primary location of most travel and tourism organisations. Websites are used as a selling channel and to promote the products and services of the travel and tourism industry.

An advantage of websites is that they are accessible to the customer 24 hours a day. Organisations can communicate information to the customer quickly, including special offers and other promotions.

▶ Impact of new technologies

New technology has had, and is continuing to have, a dramatic effect on the way that people buy and look for products.

Broadband and mobile internet

The ability to access high speed internet services both at home, and increasingly when travelling, has dramatically changed customers' expectations of their access to travel and tourism organisations' selling channels.

Customers expect to be able to access the internet while they are travelling; in shops, at airports and in hotels. This is used by customers not only to show holiday pictures or to conduct business, but also to purchase additional travel and tourism products and services. For example, customers are likely to review trips and tours online before booking even while on holiday.

Social networking sites like Facebook and Twitter are also being used increasingly by travel and tourism organisations as a way of communicating with their customers.

Self-service machines

Self-service machines have reduced the need to have areas staffed 24 hours a day. A number of UK railway companies now have ticket machines where a customer can buy their ticket. Hotels are also using self-service machines to reduce the time taken to check out of the hotel.

If you were booking a last-minute trip to Paris would you be more likely to book online or go to a travel agent?

 Take it further

Sites like TripAdvisor and Yelp are an effective way for tourists to make informed decisions about their holiday activities. For example, restaurants in tourist destinations may ask their customers to post a review on the site if they appear happy with their meal. Pick a location and using sites like these, research where you would like to visit.

? **Did you know ?**

Self-service check out machines are particularly popular in city centre business hotels where the machines can offer an express check out facility. Why do you think this is?

Mobile phone apps

As smartphones become more popular, travel and tourism organisations are using 'apps' (applications) to communicate with customers. This improved communication is being used to encourage customers to remain loyal to the organisation.

Apps are also being developed to enable customers to use their mobile phones to pay for goods, as well as to make bookings and to give feedback to companies.

Some travel and tourism organisations are developing apps to enrich the customer's experience. For example, some museums now offer downloadable audio guides and extra information about their exhibits.

Digital television

The arrival of digital television has led to a dramatic increase in the number of available channels. Some travel and tourism organisations have developed their own television channels that they use to communicate with their customers, as well as to sell them their products and services. Smart television (television that has internet connectivity) is being used to enable customers to purchase travel and tourism products and services through their televisions.

Computerised screens give more flexibility to organisations in the ways that customers can interact with the websites. The increase of smart television, as well as the increase in smartphones and tablets, is opening up new channels for travel and tourism organisations to interact with their customers.

Take it further

Find out what apps you can download for local travel and tourism organisations. Evaluate how good they are and what needs they satisfy.

Assessment activity 8.1

2A.P1 | 2A.P2 | 2A.P3 | 2A.M1 | 2A.M2 | 2A.D1

Your local tourist board wants to conduct an investigation into promotion and selling in the travel and tourism industry in your local area. They have asked whether your group could assist them in their research. They have broken down the investigation into a number of different tasks and have asked you to present your findings as a presentation with supporting notes.

Task 1

Agree with your teacher/tutor the two local travel and tourism organisations you aim to investigate.

Give information about the aims and objectives of each organisation and how these relate to promotion and sales activities.

Task 2

Look at the products/services that are offered by your two chosen travel and tourism organisations, and consider how these have been developed/adapted for a specific target market.

Task 3

Review how the two organisations sell these products/services, including how they use new technology. Does their use of technology have an impact on how they reach their target market?

Tips

- When choosing your two organisations you need to consider if the organisations will have enough products or services to give you enough information for this assignment.
- Organise a visit to your chosen organisations where possible. If you telephone beforehand you may be able to organise an interview with a manager or a member of the marketing team.
- If you are going to interview someone make sure that you review the new techniques they use and prepare your questions beforehand so that you know what you need to ask and find out for your assessment.

Promotional techniques and materials in travel and tourism

Introduction

In this section you will look at how travel and tourism organisations promote their products and services to their customers. Promotion is vital so that customers are aware of the products and services that the organisation offers.

Make a list of all the different methods of promotion you come across on a day-to-day basis. Compare your list with others in your class.

Promotional techniques

Advertising

Advertising is a promotion where you pay another party to have your chosen message displayed on their media. Examples range from newspaper advertising, to billboards, to pop ups and banners on websites and sponsored adverts on sites such as Google and Facebook.

Organisations have control over the message that is being communicated, but the cost can be high. On some media it can be difficult or expensive to change the message, such as on a television advertisement.

Direct marketing

Direct marketing is marketing that is directed specifically at the individual. Direct marketing includes direct mail – sometimes known as junk mail; direct email – sometimes known as spam; as well as telephone calls and even door-to-door distribution.

Direct marketing focuses on the individual rather than a large market segment. The message can be tailored to the needs of the individual rather than trying to appeal to everyone. Developments in computerisation mean that it is now easier to tailor mail, emails and even text messages to the needs of the individual.

Public relations (PR)

Public relations is less about selling a product and service than about developing the customer's image and perception of the organisation and its products and services. Organisations in recent years have been involved in developing their websites and social media to communicate the organisation's image. For example, the Eden Project in Cornwall promotes its environmental awareness and its recycling schemes to develop a green image. Any activity that is designed to make the consumer perceive the organisation in a better light could be considered PR.

Remember

We see thousands of advertising messages, catchphrases and slogans every day; it can be difficult to make a message stand out from the others. It is worth considering how much notice people take of advertisements and whether the placement of an advert is reaching your specific target market. For example, is a TV advert airing at the right time? If advertising to teenagers you may want your advert to appear during a show like *Hollyoaks* rather than a political affairs show.

Did you know ?

To improve their public image some organisations have become involved with raising money for charities. For example, Cathay Pacific set up the Sunnyside Club, a charity to help improve the lives of mentally and physically ill children in Hong Kong (Cathay Pacific's home country).

A stand advertising the Philippines as a holiday destination at the World Travel Market. What do you think they will display on the stand that will attract trade?

Displays

Displays are used to promote products and services. These are usually used at trade events, such as the World Travel Market.

Shop windows are also a display area, and are used to encourage customers to come into shops, such as travel agencies.

Sponsorship

Sponsorship is where an organisation pays an individual or event to be associated with the organisation. Sponsorship can be on a large scale such as sponsoring a sporting team or event, or on a small scale such as being involved in a local project. Sponsorship will not directly increase sales, but will increase the customer's awareness of the organisation's brand. This will mean that customers may consider the organisation when they are deciding on making a purchase.

If sponsoring a television show organisations can link to a certain audience. P&O Cruises sponsored the third season of *Downton Abbey* and so advertised their product to huge audiences during the show's run.

Sales promotion

A sales promotion is where a discount or some additional product or service is offered to encourage customers to buy the product. These may have a time restriction on them. For example, it is quite common for tour operators to offer free places for children on family holidays to encourage early bookings.

It is worth remembering that by discounting a product or service the organisation will not make as much profit from that product or service.

Sales promotions are also used to sell products or services that have not been sold. Hotels discount room prices when the hotel is not busy, similarly travel agencies will offer heavy discounts for holidays that are due to depart in the near future.

Brochures

A brochure is a booklet with lots of details of the products and services available. Most travel agencies will use brochures to help customers make a decision about their choice of holiday. They are useful as customers can take brochures home with them and consider their choices.

▶ Promotional materials

Advertisements

The travel and tourism industry uses a wide range of advertising materials.

- **Television** advertising, like the ad breaks you see in your favourite programmes, has the benefit of moving images and sound. However the customer does not have a hard copy of the information so have to rely on their memory. This is an expensive way to advertise, both in the cost of air time and also in product costs.

Discussion

Sponsorship can be expensive, such as sponsoring a major event like a sporting event or a festival, but it does not have to be. With your friends, discuss what worthy causes you would sponsor in your local area if you were the manager of a local travel and tourism organisation. You need to consider what the benefits of the sponsorship would be to your company.

It can be difficult to target a specific market, although with the increased number of channels on satellite and cable television this is getting easier as channels will often now target specific audiences, such as *E4* and teenagers.

- The **radio** may seem an old fashioned way of advertising; however it is worth considering that in the UK we spend longer listening to the radio than we do watching the television. It is common to repeat your message and brand a number of times within an advertisement on the radio so that the customer can remember the message as there are no visual aids.

- **Leaflets** usually consist of a page or two of information. They are used heavily by tourist attractions and services to promote their offerings to customers.

- **Billboards** are also known in the UK as advertising hoardings. These are the large signs that you may see on major roads and in towns and cities promoting products. Although they are very visual, most customers will only look at a billboard for a few seconds. This means that you have to have a short and clear message for the customer to consider. The exception to this is where customers may be staying in the same place for a while, such as on a train on a bus or at a bus stop. Here you can communicate a more complex message as the customer has time to read and consider the message.

- This is where you pay a **newspaper or magazine** for space to communicate your message. The cost depends on the circulation of the magazine or newspaper, where your advert is in the publication and how much space you require.

- A number of large tourist destinations use **promotional DVDs** and downloadable content to promote their destinations or attractions. They can communicate a lot more information to the customer through this format, such as taking them on a virtual tour of the resort or attraction. In recent years this provision is being offered on an increasing number of organisations' websites.

- **Merchandising** is when products and services are advertised through branded items that are given away or even sometimes sold to customers. Most hotels and conference centres will give away pens and notepads to their delegates and customers. These giveaways will carry the organisation's brand as well as their contact details, i.e. telephone numbers or website address. Disney has a chain of stores around the world which helps to promote not only their films and DVDs, but also their themed resorts.

- Organisations will pay other **websites** to advertise on their sites. For some sites, such as Facebook, this is the main way they generate revenue. Due to the personal information that social networking sites keep about their users, it is possible to target specific advertising at specific groups.

Advertisements on websites are called **banners,** whereas **pop-ups** appear when you first access a website.

Direct mailshots

Direct mail is sent directly to the customer in the post. Direct mail is commonly referred to as junk mail. A well-targeted direct mailshot can have a high success rate in converting to sales. This is particularly true if the customer has had previous contact with the organisation. For example, a number of theatres send out mailshots directed to previous customers, listing the forthcoming attractions that might be of interest to them.

Take it further

What do you do when the ad breaks come on the television? Does this change the effectiveness of the companies' advertising?

Visit your local tourist information centre. Have a look at how many leaflets they have for tourists to choose between. Consider how you would get your leaflet to stand out amongst all the competition for the customer's attention.

Did you know ?

Advertising in magazines and newspapers can be a good way to communicate a message to a specific market segment, as each newspaper and magazine will appeal to different groups of people.

Key terms

Banners – these tend to appear either across the top, bottom or down the side of a website.

Pop-up – a form of online advertising that literally just pops up when you first access a website.

Take it further

Check out the following websites to see examples of press releases.

- Surfers against Sewage is a pressure group with an interest in improving the quality of UK beaches and sea shores.
- Thomas Cook Press Centre produces a number of press releases regarding their business.

To access the websites for these, visit Pearson hotlinks. You can access this by going to www.pearsonhotlinks.co.uk and searching for this title.

Did you know ?

Most towns and cities will use a celebrity to turn on their Christmas lights. They appear, not only to encourage more people to visit the town for the ceremony, but also to encourage them to stay afterwards and spend their money in the town's shops and restaurants.

There are many attractive travel photos to show in shop windows. Which has been your favourite so far in this book?

Emails

These are used in a similar manner to direct mail, but are sent electronically. Email has the advantage of being able to include hyperlinks to the organisation's website, as well as being cheaper than direct mailshots as there are no printing costs or postal charges. Like direct mailshots they can be easy to ignore or just delete. Direct emails are sometimes referred to as spam.

Loyalty schemes

Loyalty schemes are designed to encourage repeat custom. These schemes may be set up either by a company to encourage repeat usage of their product or with a consortium of companies working together, like the Nectar card. A number of airlines have customer loyalty schemes, for example British Airways Executive Club. Credit cards often allow you to collect points to stay in hotels, such as Marriott credit cards.

Press releases

A press release is when a company releases information to the press. This is a good way to inform customers of new products, or changes to existing products and services. Press releases may be published as stories or may encourage the media to investigate a particular issue. This is a very cheap way of communicating with the customer although the organisation has little control over how the press release is used once it has been released.

Celebrity appearances

Celebrities can be used to endorse a product or service. With the growth of celebrity culture, the idea of using the same products and services as a famous celebrity is appealing to customers. Celebrity appearances are similar to sponsorship; however they may only appear at a one-off event.

Shop windows

As mentioned previously, window displays are used to encourage customers to enter shops, such as travel agencies. As well as showing the holidays they offer and any current promotions it is not uncommon for travel agencies to display the exchange rates they offer if they have a bureau de change in their store.

Displays at exhibitions

A number of travel and tourism organisations do promotions at exhibitions, for example at large international events such as the World Travel Market held in London every year. Tour operators and National Tourist Boards from around the world meet at this event to promote their products and services. On a smaller scale, exhibitions can also be events such as local wedding fairs where hotels may have a promotional stand.

Displaying logos

Sponsorship is where an organisation pays another company to display their logo. By sponsoring an event or a sporting team, the organisation gets associated with the event or team. For example, Arsenal is sponsored by the Emirates group.

Special promotions

These are used to encourage customers to buy a product or service. They may have time limits attached to them to encourage customers to book early. For example, hotels may offer a free meal or access to their spa facilities if a trip is booked before a certain date. Increasingly, organisations are also offering discounts for booking online.

Buy one get one free offers (known as a BOGOF) are another good example. For example, Southwest Trains runs a '4 travel for the price of 2' offer.

Competitions

Competitions are used to generate interest in a product or service. It is also a good way of getting a customer's personal details to add to companies' databases for use with direct mailshots and emails.

Holiday brochures

Brochures are a traditional way to promote holidays. They contain a lot of information to persuade the customer to buy the product and service. However, once they are printed and distributed they cannot be updated so quickly contain out-of-date or wrong information. They are expensive to produce due to printing costs and can take a lot of time to create. Most tour operators produce a brochure which is then distributed to travel agents or directly to the customer.

Online brochures

These are the same as paper-based brochures, but are available on the internet. They are usually uploaded as Adobe PDF files, so that the customer cannot alter the information. They are easier to update and can also include moving images and sound. It is not uncommon to include a tour of the destination and its attractions within some online resort brochures.

Can you find any special promotions or competitions online to visit New York?

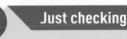

Just checking

You have looked at a wide range of different promotional methods and media. Make a list of the different methods you have looked at and identify the strength of each method.

TOPIC   B2

Hollywood

▶ Factors which affect the choice of the promotional techniques and materials used

Introduction

Now you need to consider when you will use each of the different promotional techniques and methods that you have covered previously.

Describe what you think is the best way to promote to the following people and why:

- a 16-year-old girl
- a 70-year-old man
- a couple in their mid-20s planning their wedding.

Cost and budget

Some promotional methods have a higher cost than others. An advertisement in a local newspaper will be considerably less expensive than advertising on a television channel. Every promotional campaign will have a budget, i.e. an amount of money within which you have to work, and some organisations have a larger budget than others. Your budget and the cost of the different types of promotional methods will affect which method you choose to use.

Sponsoring a major sporting event or team may be feasible for a large national or international organisation, but would be less feasible for a small local business.

Target markets

A target market is the group of people that you wish your product to target and will dictate which methods or media will be most effective. Some methods are more effective for one target market than another. Local advertising is fine if you only need, or want, to communicate to a local market, but has limited benefits on a larger scale. For example, a visitor attraction may realise that their customers tend only to come from the local area and therefore promote only to the local market.

Some groups have preferred media that they communicate through; social media such as Facebook and Twitter appeal more to a younger age group. National newspapers have different political viewpoints and appeal to different market segments.

Did you know ?   **?**

There are now even television channels that are targeted at different markets. For example Ledger Holiday, who provide tours around battlefields, advertise on the History Channel.

Assessment activity 8.2   2B.P4 | 2B.P5 | 2B.M3 | 2B.D2

Your local tourist board was impressed with the work you did on investigating how travel and tourism products/services are sold. They have extended the project and have asked you to continue your investigation into the two businesses that you looked at earlier.

They are interested in understanding the promotional techniques and materials used by travel and tourism organisations. They have broken down the investigation into a number of tasks and they have asked that you present your findings as a report.

Task 1: Review how your two chosen travel and tourism organisations use a variety of different promotional techniques to increase the appeal of their products and services to their target market.

Task 2: Consider the factors that influence the choice of promotional techniques and materials and the effects these different factors can have on the target market.

Tips

- Another meeting with the organisation's management will give insight into their reasons for the promotion that they do.
- Consider why each piece of promotional material is aimed at that specific target market.

The features that make promotional materials effective

Introduction

You have looked at the different types of promotional materials that travel and tourism organisations use to promote their products and services. However, in the very competitive market of travel and tourism trying to get the customer to pay attention to your message rather than that of other providers means you need to understand the features of the promotional material that make it effective.

When watching television (not BBC channels!), keep a notepad and pen close at hand. When the advertising break is on, try to identify what in the advertising is or is not making it an effective promotion.

Needs of the target market

Promotional material needs to address the **needs** and **wants** of the target market. You will remember from earlier that the target market is the segment of the market that you have designed the product or service for. The product should be designed specifically to address the needs of your target market. Not only do you have to address these needs, but you also have to communicate your offering effectively to the target market.

Placement

Marketing departments need to consider where they plan to place their promotional materials. The promotional material needs to be where the target customers are most likely to see it.

An advertisement on the London Underground might be a great place to promote a weekend break abroad, but probably not the best place to promote a weekend break in London itself.

Information provided

The marketing department also needs to consider the information that they are providing in their promotional material. Different promotional material will give you different opportunities to communicate different amounts of information to your target customers. A billboard may only have a few words or a sentence on it, whereas a holiday brochure will be crammed full of information.

Message

You need to give thorough consideration to the message you are trying to communicate. It could be that you want to highlight a **unique selling point (USP)**

Key terms

Customer needs – are the requirements a customer has, e.g. children's meals at a hotel.

Customer wants – are the requirements that the customer would like to have, e.g. a hotel with a beach.

Remember

The behaviour of the target customers will dictate the best medium to use to communicate to them. For example, banners on Facebook may be a great way to communicate to 16–25-year-olds, but possibly not the most effective way to communicate with the over-65 market.

Key term

Unique selling point (USP) – is what makes your product or service different from other products or services in the market.

of your product or service that makes it different from, or better than, that of a competitor. You must make sure that your message remains clear and that the rest of the promotional material reinforces the message you are trying to communicate.

Language

The language in the promotional material must attract both the interest of the target customer and encourage them to take action, i.e. buy the product or service.

There are several ways to achieve this. Most promotional material includes a lot of verbs (doing words) so that it is dynamic and encourages customers to take action.

Another approach is to write the promotional material in a way to make the customer feel that they are already experiencing the product and service. Hotels do this by writing their wedding brochure more as a diary than a brochure. Customer comments will also help reinforce your message.

Some organisations also encourage customers to take action by highlighting the limited number of places available, stating that a product is selling fast and stating that an offer only has a limited timeframe before it finishes.

Take it further

Next time you are watching television watch the commercial break and see how many products and services have offers with a limited time frame.

▶ Design of the material

Layout

The layout needs to be eye-catching, so that it catches the target customer's attention. It also needs to have a logical layout so that the customer can follow the order of the promotional material.

Style

The style of the promotional material should be in line with the message that you are trying to communicate and will reflect something about the product or service that you aim to offer the customer. For example, a product that is aimed at young children should be child-friendly, using a bold typeface with nice clear language. Whereas a product aimed at adults may use a more elaborate typeface.

| Activity 8.2 | Attractive promotions |

Collect some promotional material that you find eye-catching, and try to identify what it is about it that made it attractive to you. Think about those features when you design your piece of material for your assessment.

Take it further

Compare the style and layout of two brochures – one aimed at family holidays and the other for an adult-only resort like Sandals or Warner hotels.

Colour

The colours you choose will conjure up ideas and images for the customer. Red is the sign of danger, but also can reflect excitement. Holiday brochures tend to be yellow and blue, a colour that reflects the golden beaches and clear blue seas of the holiday destination they sell. Similarly, ski holidays and honeymoon brochures tend to be white.

Images

Images are used a lot in promotional materials as they can communicate a large amount about a product or service. In travel and tourism we are lucky that we have a very photogenic range of products to sell. If you visit a local tourist information centre or travel agency, you will see a large number of images that are used to communicate their products and services. A well-chosen image can generate interest, and desire for a product or service.

What does this picture say to you?

Straplines

A strapline is a phrase that is associated with a product or service. Organisations spend a lot of time and effort in developing a strapline that communicates an image they want the customer to remember about their product or service.

These straplines stay in the consumer's mind due to the number of times they are repeated, not only on their promotional materials, but also in their stores and on their products and services.

Novelty

Some organisations use novelty as a way of generating interest and making their product and service stand out from their competitors'. For example, Thomas Cook had a television advertisement where a man pulls the valve out of the tyre of the coach taking him back to the airport. This implies that a Thomas Cook holiday is so good you will not want to leave. This simple idea is executed with humour and so is likely to stay in the audience's mind.

Branding/logo

A brand, or logo, is an image that is associated with an organisation. Originally brands were used to reassure the customer about the quality of the product or service. Organisations have spent fortunes over the years developing their brands and communicating their image to customers to make themselves easily identifiable. For example, the easyJet's bright orange aeroplanes are instantly recognisable. Most major international airlines would similarly be recognisable for different reasons.

The branding or logo should be used by the organisation to give a consistent message across its product range, and should also be used in store and in all communications, including on their website, on emails and on letterheads.

The colour of the logo is often used throughout an organisation, such as on uniforms. Logos are usually positioned at the bottom of promotional material, often on the bottom right of the page, as this is the last thing the customer will see.

Activity 8.3   Straplines

Try to think of as many straplines for products and services as you can.

Compare them with a friend and see who can get the most.

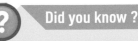 **Did you know ?**

Don't just book it. Thomas Cook it.

This is a very famous strapline that was revived in 2008 after a 15-year break as it was still so recognisable to customers.

Activity 8.4   Researching logos

Research the logos for a couple of major travel and tourism organisations, for example, Thomas Cook or Virgin Atlantic. See if the colours of the logo are used as a base for their uniforms, etc.

What messages are the logo and colour scheme giving about the company?

Just checking

What seven things do you need to think about when designing promotional material?

▶ Planning the creation of promotional materials

Introduction

All promotional material needs to be planned so that everything that is needed is ready when it is needed. You will now look at some of the major areas you need to consider when planning promotional materials.

Before you start learning about planning promotional material, consider what would happen if there was no plan at all.

▶ Timescales

Table 8.3 – Things to consider when planning promotional material.

When does the promotional material need to be available?	Build in interim deadlines so that you can see if you are still reaching your deadline and assess your progress at certain points.
	Ensure you remember the production time.
How long will it take to prepare the promotional material?	Think about the length of the material and what its purpose is.
	A newspaper article might be produced quite quickly. Other materials, such as websites or brochures, may take much longer.
How long will the promotional material be needed for?	Decide how long you will spend planning the material. If it is only going to be used for a short time, like a leaflet for one event, you will not want to spend a long time planning it.
	Think about how much money you will spend on the material.
	How long it is needed for will also affect the method and style of design you choose.

Budget

Every business activity will have a budget. The budget is how much money you have to run the project, in this case to produce a piece of promotional material. Budgets are usually set by the organisation's management and should be considered as a constraint within which you must work.

Different travel and tourism organisations will have different budgets to promote their products and services. A large organisation like Virgin Atlantic will be able to afford to spend a lot on promoting their products, whereas a small local tourist attraction would have much less and would choose lower cost methods of promoting themselves.

TOPIC C3

Hollywood

Creating promotional materials

Introduction

In this section you will be looking at creating promotional materials and some of the things you need to consider. Collect a range of promotional materials by visiting your local tour operator, or photographing any advertisements that you like, or even collecting some of the leaflets that may have been delivered to your door. Try analysing them to see how they were created. What do they have in common? For example are the same colours used? Are there any similarities in the layout?

Techniques and materials

There are a huge range of techniques and materials that you can use in promotion, from the traditional billboard advertising to the use of social media and smartphone applications.

Media

There is a wide range of media that you can use to promote your product or service. Costs vary dramatically from an advertisement in a small local paper or magazine to an expensive advertisement on national television. The media that you choose for your promotion should be relevant to the target customers, and should make use of a medium that the target customers would use.

Some media are very specific and targeted at individual or small groups, such as direct mail and cold calling, whereas other media are aimed at a mass market and will target a large number of people, for example a billboard or a television advertisement.

Link

Read more about how organisations use new technology to communicate with customers in *Topic A3*.

Take it further

Use the internet to look up the following websites and try to identify how they have used creativity to generate the image of the organisation:

- Cadbury World
- Severn Valley Railway.

Key term

Stakeholder – is anyone who has some interest in the business or project. This can include customers, suppliers, staff and even people who live locally to the business or project.

Did you know ?

You could use a 360 degree evaluation. This is where you get feedback from everyone involved in a project as well as the group the promotion was aimed at.

Technology

Developments in technology have changed, and will go on changing, the way we communicate with our customers. The internet provides a new selling and promotional channel for businesses to communicate with their customers. These new channels of communications need new forms of promotional materials. A banner or pop-up on a website may look different to a print advert, and will most likely need different technology to create. This is something to consider when developing promotional materials.

Developments in smartphones now give customers mobile internet access and the ability to access apps (applications). This is particularly relevant if you develop an app that your customers can use. This will require a whole new set of technological skills and organisations will need to consider this before they proceed.

Creative skills

You need to use your creative skills when you are developing your promotional materials. As stated earlier, it can be difficult to get your promotion to stand out from the crowd. By being creative, you can make your material more noticeable. This is increasingly important online to make pop-ups and banners stand out and, crucially, to stop people automatically closing them.

However creative you are being, you need to remember your target customer and always design with them in mind.

▶ Evaluation of materials

All promotional materials need to be evaluated. You can then identify both what was good about the promotion, so that you can reuse the ideas, and also what did not work as well so that you do not make the same mistakes again.

- **Using feedback from teachers/tutors, peers and other stakeholders** – Feedback can be a valuable source of information to help you to evaluate your promotional materials. Other people may see things that you have missed, or even see it from a different perspective.
- **Clarity of message** – You need to evaluate how clearly your message was perceived by the target customer. You can use feedback to assess how clear your message was and whether the customers understood the message.
- **Use of language** – You need to evaluate the language that you used in the promotional materials. Did the language used communicate the message well to the target customer? Different market segments need to be communicated with differently and what may seem fun to one group of target customers may seem rude or even patronising to another.
- **Market placement** – You need to evaluate how effective your promotional material was at placing your product or service within the market. Even if the material was effective you may have designed the promotional material to target a specific market segment, and inadvertently targeted another market segment.

If you were using this image what sort of language would you use on your promotional material?

You may consider building into your promotional material some way of evaluating how successful it was. For example, a number of advertisements offer a discount if they quote a promotional code. The number of times this promotional code is used will be recorded to assess how effective the promotional campaign has been.

- **Design** – Did the design make the material attractive to the target customer? Did it encourage customers to look at the material and even to make a purchase? You also need to consider the design elements that were successful, so that you can use these in future campaigns. You could develop a theme that can be carried through your campaigns.

- **Timescale** – Did you manage to complete all the preparation stages within the set timescales? If deadlines were missed why did this happen and what will you do to prevent this in the future?

  You also need to evaluate whether the advertising was published as agreed, i.e. did the newspaper advertisement appear when planned and was it the right size?

- **Budget** – You need to evaluate your success, or otherwise, in completing the promotional material within the given budget. If you met the budget, did the budget give you enough room to be able to achieve everything you planned and were you able to use the media that you wished?

  If you did not meet the budget, what made you go over-budget? Was the overspend worth it?

Hollywoo

Assessment activity 8.3 — English 2C.P6 | 2C.P7 | 2C.M4 | 2C.M5 | 2C.D3

A local business has heard from your local tourist board about the quality of work you have done on promotion and selling. They have asked you to help them plan and produce a piece of promotional material to help in a future campaign.

The business wants to promote the opening of a new family attraction at a local farm. The attraction is offering tourists the opportunity to see how a real farm works as well as having talks and workshops about the different animals, which they hope will encourage school and college groups to visit. There will also be a petting zoo and a cafe for people to visit. They hope that the petting zoo will attract families with young children. The new attraction is due to open in two months. The organisation is very excited about this new development and has given you a budget of £500.

Task 1

Produce a plan for your piece of promotional material. Your plan needs to show that you have responded to the organisation's brief. You will need to show that you have:

- understood the message they are trying to get across to their target market
- understood who the target market is and have designed promotional material that will appeal to this audience
- planned a piece of promotional material that you can deliver within the timescale and the budget.

Task 2

Your plan has been approved and you have been given the go-ahead to create your piece of promotional material. You will need to ensure that this gets the organisation's message across to the target audience using appropriate language and a design that will appeal to them. You will need to create this to the agreed budget and timescale.

Task 3

Report an how you did. Did the promotional material you produced meet the organisation's needs, and did it appeal to the target market? How closely did you follow your plan?

Tips

Before you start producing the material you need to:

- identify what your target market is and what their needs are
- consider the restraints that you may have for the promotional material such as time and budget as well as equipment; i.e. in some schools and colleges you may be able to produce a television advertisement as you have the facilities to do so while in others you will not
- try getting the feedback from a focus group (small group of the target market) to see if there is anything they could suggest to improve your material once you have designed your material
- remember to plan your promotional material and identify all the issues that you have considered in its preparation.

WorkSpace

▶ Nisa Gurung

Designer, Endeavour Travel

I came to the UK from Nepal about 6 years ago to study travel and tourism. I have travelled a lot and I have always wanted to be a member of cabin crew.

However, during my studies I realised that I found the promotional part of the course the most interesting. After finishing college I managed to get a job working in the head office of a large international long-haul tour operator in their publicity department.

After a couple of years working in the customer service team I have moved to the brochure design team. I now design the pages of the promotional materials for all their products. This gives me an opportunity to put all the designing and promotional skills I learnt at college to good use and if my old tutor is reading this I still know where to put the logo!

I am currently working on a family friendly summer sun brochure which mainly covers holidays to Spain and Greece. I know a couple of the resorts well as my company sent me on a familiarisation trip last year.

I also get to work on a variety of different promotional materials which means I am involved with lots of different parts of the business. One of the challenges in my role is thinking about how to make adverts look appealing to different audiences. Working out how to do that often means I have to be really creative!

It also feels great as last year all our hard work paid off and we won an award for the design of our brochures. It feels really good to be recognised for our hard work.

Think about it

1 Where should Nisa put the logo on the page?

2 What could Nisa do to make sure the family friendly nature of the brochure comes across to the customer?

3 What is the benefit to the organisation of sending their staff on familiarisation trips?

Introduction

There are many industries in the travel and tourism sector, providing a wide range of different employment and career opportunities. The travel and tourism sector is one of the largest and fastest growing in the world, therefore constantly changing and consisting of many companies and associated job roles.

In order to do well in the highly competitive and attractive travel and tourism industry and secure one of the exciting job roles it has to offer, you will need to know the opportunities available, the requirements of those jobs and the qualifications and experience required to secure one of those roles.

Identifying realistic career opportunities and knowing the different job roles will help to provide you with the first insight into the many possibilities within this sector. The recruitment process can be quite specific within travel and tourism, so knowing this process will also provide benefit and increase chances of future employment.

Assessment: This unit will be assessed through a series of assignments set by your teacher/tutor.

Learning aims

In this unit you will:

A know the employment opportunities available in the travel and tourism sector

B examine travel and tourism employment requirements

C understand travel and tourism recruitment and selection, and employment development.

> I love travelling, experiencing new destinations and meeting new people. I would like to work as a member of cabin crew one day but need to build up my knowledge and experience within the travel and tourism industry first. I have always wanted to do this and eventually would like to work for one of the major airlines. I know the role is demanding with long hours, but there are also rewards such as free flights and the fact that every day is different, flying to a different destination with a different group of people. I can't wait to get my wings!
>
> Isabel, *17-year-old Travel and Tourism student*

Travel and Tourism Employment Opportunities

9

BTEC

Assessment Zone

This table shows you what you must do in order to achieve a **Pass**, **Merit** or **Distinction** grade, and where you can find activities in this book to help you.

Assessment and grading criteria			
Level 1	**Level 2 Pass**	**Level 2 Merit**	**Level 2 Distinction**
Learning aim A: Know the employment opportunities available in the travel and tourism sector			
1A.1 Identify two job roles in each of three given travel and tourism industries.	**2A.P1** Describe the key responsibilities of two job roles in each of three given travel and tourism industries. **See Assessment activity 9.1, page 245**	**2A.M1** Explain why selected roles within one travel and tourism industry are offered on a full-time, part-time, seasonal or shift-working basis. **See Assessment activity 9.1, page 245**	
1A.2 Identify the working pattern in relation to two job roles in each of three different travel and tourism industries.	**2A.P2** Describe the working pattern in relation to two job roles in each of three different travel and tourism industries. **See Assessment activity 9.1, page 245**		
Learning aim B: Examine travel and tourism employment requirements			
1B.3 Compare, with support, job specifications in relation to two different travel and tourism job roles.	**2B.P3** Compare job specifications in relation to two different travel and tourism job roles. **See Assessment activity 9.2, page 253**	**2B.M2** Compare the job and person specification for an entry level and a managerial position in a travel and tourism industry. **See Assessment activity 9.2, page 253**	**2B.D1** Contrast the job specification, person specification, statutory and contractual requirements on a staff and a managerial position in two selected travel and tourism industries. **See Assessment activity 9.2, page 253**
1B.4 Describe, with support, person specifications relevant to two different travel and tourism job roles.	**2B.P4** Describe person specifications relevant to two selected travel and tourism job roles. **See Assessment activity 9.2, page 253**	**2B.M3** Compare the statutory and contractual rights and responsibilities for an entry level and a managerial position in a travel and tourism industry. **See Assessment activity 9.2, page 253**	
1B.5 Outline statutory and contractual rights and responsibilities of employer and employee.	**2B.P5** Describe statutory and contractual rights and responsibilities of employer and employee. **See Assessment activity 9.2, page 253**		

Learning aim C: Understand travel and tourism recruitment and selection, and employment development			
1C.6 English	**2C.P6** English	**2C.M4** English	**2C.D2** English
Describe the recruitment, selection and employment entry for a given travel and tourism job role.	Explain the recruitment, selection and employment entry for a given travel and tourism job role. **See Assessment activity 9.3, page 258**	Review the recruitment, selection and employment entry process in relation to a given travel and tourism organisation. **See Assessment activity 9.3, page 258**	Evaluate the recruitment, selection, employment entry processes and career progression opportunities of two selected travel and tourism organisations. **See Assessment activity 9.3, page 258**
1C.7	**2C.P7** English	**2C.M5**	
Outline, with support, two career progression opportunities in the travel and tourism sector.	Explain career progression opportunities relevant to two different travel and tourism job roles. **See Assessment activity 9.3, page 258**	Review the career progression opportunities for a given travel and tourism job role. **See Assessment activity 9.3, page 258**	

English	Opportunity to practise English skills

How you will be assessed

The unit will be assessed by a series of assignments set by your teacher/tutor.

You will be expected to show your understanding of the career opportunities within the travel and tourism sector and research the employment requirements and recruitment process followed.

These tasks will focus heavily on your own research and will be based on scenarios involving working in the travel and tourism industry. For example, you may be asked to imagine yourself working for a specialist travel and tourism recruitment company and you have been asked to update the information and produce a series of leaflets you provide to potential employees for all travel and tourism sectors.

Your assessment could be in the form of:

- information materials such as posters, leaflets or information booklets
- professional presentations
- multimedia presentations
- a research project
- group discussion
- role play
- flow charts.

▶ Job roles within the travel and tourism sector

Introduction

In this topic you will discover the many different types of job roles and opportunities across a variety of industries within the travel and tourism sector. As a starting point, think about all the different job roles you might find within each of the travel and tourism industries and put this information into a spidergram. For example what jobs would you find in the airline and airport industry?

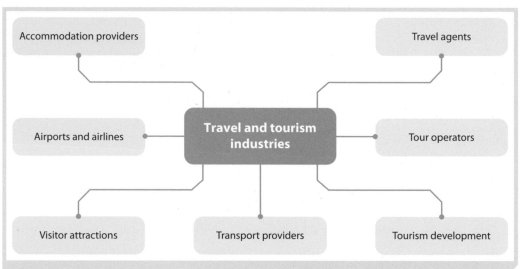

Figure 9.1 Think about all the different types of jobs in the travel and tourism industry.

▶ Travel agents

High street travel agents such as Co-op Travel and Thomas Cook employ travel consultants, also known as travel advisors, as well as foreign exchange advisors in the larger retail shops and a management team usually consisting of a store manager, assistant manager and an overall area manager. The store manager will have overall responsibility for the running of the retail store as well as the staff employed there. Travel agents will also have trainees and apprentices: junior consultants who are new to the role. An average-sized travel agency will employ between five and 10 staff, consisting of senior travel consultants, travel consultants, junior or apprentice consultants along with an assistant manager and the manager. There are also a number of head office roles in administration, human resources, accounts and marketing.

Travel agents will sell a variety of travel products to the public and businesses and these will range from package holidays, flights, accommodation, and transport such as flight links. They also sell **ancillary** services such as foreign exchange, travel insurance airport hotels and parking and attraction tickets. Ancillary services add value to sales for the agency and add value to the experience of the customer. By providing these additional services, customers can book everything they need in one place. It also helps the travel agency remain competitive in a highly competitive market.

Key term

Ancillary – additional products and services offered by travel agents.

Tour operators

Tour operators, including First Choice and Thomson, organise tours and package holidays, which they distribute in a number of ways. Many of the tour operators' products are sold through travel agents, but they also sell directly to the public by telephone call centres and the internet.

There are many job opportunities working for a tour operator, and many people are employed to create the package holidays. For example, they need buyers to source the products and components which make up a package holiday. This will involve booking flights, organising transport for resort transfers, and checking the accommodation. Other job roles within a tour operator will include quality controllers, operation managers and the people who create the marketing material such as web designers, editors, writers and photographers. There are also the customer service and reservation agents who will answer enquiries, deal with any problems or issues, make bookings and send out travel tickets and itineraries where required. In larger operators there is usually a training department that supports the training requirements of the company.

Overseas resorts will have another team of representatives, consisting of:

- resort managers and representatives
- children's representatives and entertainers
- transfer representatives and airport supervisors
- ski representatives in the ski resorts.

They will be the people who take ultimate responsibility for looking after the holidaymakers while they are in the resort and dealing with any problems, issues or queries that may arise during the duration of their stay.

Airlines and airports

The staff working for an airline such as British Airways or Virgin Atlantic can be divided into ground crew (**landside and airside**) and air crew (airside). There are a range of different job roles depending on the airline's size. Air crew include the pilot and co-pilot (first officer) who have overall responsibility for the flying of the aircraft and for the safety of everyone on board. Airlines will employ an average of six cabin crew on a standard flight which could include senior cabin crew, and a cabin manager or **purser**, who will look after and maintain the safety of passengers during the flight.

The ground crew within the airport will include check-in agents, customer service agents, information assistants, baggage handlers, dispatch and airport management. Some airlines will employ companies called ground handlers, to carry out the ground side of their operation. This is particularly common for smaller airlines that do not have a base of operations in one airport. The ground handling companies take the responsibility of employing a range of people at the airport to handle the ground operations.

There are also other employers at the airport who employ, for example, the airport cleaners and security staff.

Discussion point

If you wanted to go on a package holiday abroad with your family, what people would be involved? Think about all the people involved in putting the holiday together, then all the people involved in your own holiday experience from the time you book, while at the airport and while on holiday.

Key terms

Landside – the area within an airport before the security control point.

Airside – the area within an airport after the security control point.

Purser – the most senior cabin crew onboard a flight overseeing the other cabin crew members. The purser also completes the flight reports.

Did you know?

Many travel organisations pay their sales employees commission on the sales they make in order to attempt to motivate staff and increase sales. Therefore good sales staff can earn a lot of money. For example, Travel Agents and Airlines pay their travel consultants and cabin crew commission on sales made.

▶ Accommodation providers

There are a wide variety of accommodation providers such as Keycamps, from campsites and caravan parks such as Haven, to villas and 5-star hotels. The accommodation industry tends to divide itself into **serviced** and **non-serviced** accommodation. Serviced accommodation offers food and additional services such as beverage provision, leisure facilities and business facilities. This provides jobs in reception, conference, banqueting, events management and housekeeping. Other jobs within serviced accommodation include chefs, waiters, porters, concierge as well as management positions in each of the areas as well as general management.

Activity 9.1 — Jobs in accommodation

You work as a recruitment officer for a specialist travel and tourism recruitment company and you have been asked to research the prospective jobs available with some of the local accommodation providers within your area for a client.

Using a variety of resources, such as the internet, brochures, leaflets and educational visits, research the local accommodation providers in your area and identify what career opportunities they have available. Once you have established the jobs available, provide an overview of the types of hours/shifts involved in each job and identify the experience and qualification you would require for each position.

▶ Visitor attractions

There is a wide range of visitor attractions in the UK including theme parks such as Alton Towers and Chessington Adventure and museums like the Natural History Museum. There are other attractions such as Madam Tussauds, Sea Life Centres, and the London Eye. These all provide a vast variety of job roles. There are some general career pathways in areas such as customer service, ticket office personnel, security and management posts. Other job roles include, for example, tour guiding, where visitors are shown round an attraction. Tour guides need to be highly skilled in customer service and have a detailed knowledge of the attraction. There is also a wide range of roles that depend on the type of attraction.

Museums, galleries and stately homes may have curators who are responsible for the collections, as well as restorers and conservation workers who maintain the exhibits. Most visitor attractions have gift shops and tea rooms which require retail staff and catering staff. Theme parks will also require maintenance and engineering staff as well as ride operators and ticketing staff. Some visitor attractions also have an education officer who is responsible for arrangements during school and college trips such as at Cadbury World in Bournville. For example, they may provide information or study packs, give a presentation or a specific education tour as an additional service to education groups and in order to support learners with their studies.

Activity 9.2   Theme parks

In order to further develop your knowledge and understanding of the job roles within visitor attractions, think about your nearest theme park. Previous experience of visiting a theme park would be most beneficial; or taking the opportunity to visit one as a group would provide valuable information.

Think about all the different types of job roles that there would be in order to ensure a visitor attraction operates smoothly, from the moment you buy an entrance ticket and arrive on the car park, while you are there enjoying the rides, up until the time it comes for you to leave.

Working as a group, or independently, think about the customer journey and draw this on a flip chart. Think about all the staff that you will come into contact with when you visit a theme park and make a list on one side of the paper. Now think about the role each staff member will have to play and add this to the opposite side of the paper. You should now have a detailed list of the job roles along with key responsibilities within a theme park, which will support your assignment work.

▶ Passenger transport operators

There are four main methods of transport: air, rail, road and sea. The main forms of transport are airlines, trains, coaches, ferries and cruise ships.

Train operators such as Virgin Trains and Chiltern Railways employ a range of staff, including customer service staff, ticketing staff on the platform and on the train, who will also provide information on tickets, and at larger stations a station manager.

Private coach companies that are booked for specific trips will employ coach drivers, as well as managerial roles, such as an administrator, who depending on the size of the coach company may also handle the coach bookings and deal with any customer service issues. Larger coach companies may employ separate staff to undertake these roles.

Coach operators that run a service to a scheduled timetable, such as National Express, will employ dispatchers at major coach stations who are responsible for checking customers' tickets, as well as dispatching the coaches. These tickets will be sold online, by telephone or through travel agents, therefore they will also have staff employed in call centres.

Ferries and cruise ships have a range of staff responsible for both sailing the ship and for the passengers onboard. Most employees are required to be 21 years or over, and require qualifications or previous experience. There are many different career opportunities including deck officers, engineers, maintenance staff, entertainers, onboard passenger service staff, retail staff, waiters and chefs. Destination services staff are also employed by cruise operators who deal with shore excursions.

> **Remember**
>
> There are many different types of visitor attractions, including purpose-built ones, such as theme parks like Alton Towers, natural ones, such as Cheddar Gorge, and historical and cultural attractions, such as Stonehenge.

Tourism development

VisitBritain ultimately promotes the UK abroad in order to encourage incoming tourism. VisitBritain employ teams of staff specialising in many areas including marketing, brands, web development and design, finance, information technology, office services, press and PR, market intelligence, digital and new media, quality standards, online shops, human resources and research and evaluation.

The countries in the UK also have their own tourist boards known as VisitWales, VisitScotland, VisitEngland and the Northern Ireland Tourist Board.

Discussion point

There are ten regional tourist boards for each part of England. Can you name the ten tourist boards, then think of the types of jobs available in the regional tourist boards?

Just checking

1　What is the role of a travel agent?
2　What job roles would you find within the airport and airline industry?
3　What types of job roles would you find in visitor attractions?
4　What methods of transport are included under transport providers?
5　What is the main role of a tourist board?

Working patterns in travel and tourism

Introduction

Within the travel and tourism sector there are many different career opportunities and job roles which all consist of different working patterns, mainly due to this being a service-related industry. You would benefit from using the spidergram from the previous topic and complete an investigation into a selected job role. You could start by investigating the work patterns of different job roles across the industries and share your findings through either a short presentation to your group, in-class feedback or peer discussion.

The working patterns of different industries within the travel and tourism sector can vary greatly depending on the type of role and the work being carried out. Many industries are heavily service-based, dealing with customers 24 hours a day and therefore are likely to have shift work in order that customers are provided with a service at all times.

Full-time/part-time

Many of the industries within the travel and tourism sector offer both full- and part-time positions. For example a retail travel agent located within a large shopping complex may employ several full-time employees. However, due to longer opening hours and increased sales on a weekend, there is a need to ensure that both evenings and weekends are staffed appropriately and staffing is increased at a weekend to cope with demand. Employing part-time staff helps to support this balance of employees where extra staff are required. For the organisation, there would be smaller salaries and fewer entitlements, such as holiday pay, compared with full-time members of staff.

Seasonal

Seasonal staff are employed in many of the industries within the travel and tourism sector. Tourism can be very seasonal, i.e. very busy in peak holiday times such as the summer months, but very quiet during term-time in winter periods. Organisations such as accommodation providers may increase their employee levels during the school or summer holidays when bookings are at their highest, but reduce their employees again come the winter. This is known as seasonal work where staff will have a seasonal contract and will be employed for an agreed time.

Shift work

Shift work is common within many industries across the travel and tourism sector, as many organisations deal with customers 24 hours a day. For example, most employees within the airport will be required to work shifts as they have passengers and flights departing and arriving at the airport at all hours. Therefore the majority of jobs within an airport will have to be manned at all times.

What working patterns do you think this employee would have and why?

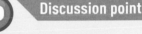
Discussion point

Think about the nature of cabin crew work. If you have been on a flight, what were the cabin crew doing and what would their working hours be considering both short-haul and long-haul flights. List all the things you think cabin crew would be required to do, before, during and after a flight.

Assessment activity 9.1   2A.P1   2A.P2   2A.M1

You are working for a travel and tourism organisation of your choice. You have been asked to update an information booklet that you give out to potential employees that explains potential contracts and working patterns. You will need to include two job roles and their responsibilities from three different travel and tourism industries (six in total) and include the different working patterns for each of your chosen job roles.

You will also need to provide further details as to why certain job roles are offered on a full-time, part-time, seasonal or shift working basis.

In order to support your work, you should use a variety of resources for investigation purposes. You should also present your work in a professional format suitable both for use within the industry and to be given to potential employers.

Tips

- When investigating your chosen travel and tourism job roles across three industries, you will need to ensure you clearly investigate the working patterns for those job roles.
- Try to choose different job roles with different working patterns before you start your further research into the roles and responsibilities.
- Ensure you explain clearly why both full-time, part-time, seasonal and shift work are favourable within certain travel and tourism roles and why.
- You should spell check your work and could include images to provide a professional look to your booklet and enhance your work.

Job specifications for employment in the travel and tourism sector

Introduction

A job specification is written by organisations looking to employ new staff into a specific job role. In order to get an overview of the types of job specifications travel and tourism organisations produce and their content, you could research and locate a sample of job specifications for each of the travel and tourism industries considered previously, and then discuss the requirements with the rest of your group.

Duties and responsibilities

A job specification is a general statement put together by the organisation seeking to employ new staff. It will explain the purpose of the job role and the duties and responsibilities of the job. A job specification will normally also include the job title and department, where the work is performed, the hours, the salary and any commissions or bonuses paid. Some job specifications will also include pension, holiday entitlement and sick pay.

Key terms of employment

Due to the variety of industries within the travel and tourism sector, the hours of work can vary between different industries and different job roles. For example air cabin crew on long-haul fights will work a long shift and then may have two days off.

What kind of benefits do you think cabin crew receive?

Holiday allowance and sickness pay will vary from industry to industry and from organisation to organisation. The minimum statutory holiday entitlement is four weeks for a full-time permanent employee; however, many jobs such as overseas resort representatives are seasonal where staff will be contracted for a summer or winter season.

Pay and employment benefits

The levels of pay in some areas of the travel and tourism sector can be quite low. As travel companies are continually competing on price for their holidays this has lowered margins; and as staff are one of the largest operational costs in the travel and tourism sector, this trend has led to a low salary culture in the travel and tourism sector. Having said that, pay is not the main motivator for many working across the variety of travel and tourism industries as there are a number of perks or employment benefits that many feel compensate for the low level of pay in some job roles. Many travel and tourism organisations, including travel agents and tour operators, offer additional commission on top of basic pay based on sales performance, which means if you are good at selling you can significantly increase your pay at the end of the month.

Employment benefits can come in many forms. Benefits could be the location of the job, for example being a holiday representative working in a variety of countries or cabin crew travelling the world flying to various destinations.

▶ Person specifications for jobs in the travel and tourism sector

Introduction

A person specification states the personal qualities an organisation may be looking for when employing new members of staff. In order to familiarise yourself with what personal qualities travel and tourism organisations are asking for, a good starting point would be to research and locate a sample of person specifications from a variety of travel and tourism organisations using various research materials such as the internet and travel trade newspapers. Specifications can then be compared for their content and layout.

▶ Qualifications

A person specification is produced by the organisation looking to employ new staff for a particular job role. A person specification matches the right skills of a person to the job. It will describe the essential and desirable personal attributes, which includes the qualifications of the prospective employee within a specific job role.

Organisations may seek vocational qualifications specific to the travel and tourism industry such as a BTEC or Diploma in travel and tourism. Most of these vocational qualifications will teach transferable skills which can be used in many different job roles. Organisations may also seek more academic qualifications such as GCSEs, A-levels and degrees.

▶ Vocational skills

Information technology

Information technology is becoming more and more important within the travel and tourism sector and is very much the way of today's world. Travel agents use the internet for both booking holidays and researching destination information. They have specific data systems that allow them to check holiday availability with tour operators for their customers. Therefore, having IT skills is of great benefit when applying for jobs within the travel and tourism sector.

Literacy and numeracy

Having a qualification in English and Maths has great benefits when applying for careers within travel and tourism. Many travel companies want this as a minimum requirement and part of their recruitment process requires candidates to undertake a literacy and numeracy test to prove their competence in spelling and basic calculations.

Discussion point

Think about the various travel and tourism job roles that you have discovered on this course. What do you think motivates the people in these roles to go to work? Use this as a starting point for a class discussion around factors that motivate people to work, and then think about what currently motivates you to study. Discuss your thoughts with your peer group.

Leadership

Leadership qualities are important in many careers within the travel and tourism sector and having initiative is essential for the majority of job roles. Many travel and tourism job roles will involve dealing with customers face to face and taking on some responsibility. Therefore organisations look for these qualities in their employees.

Communication, listening and problem-solving

Communication and listening skills are essential skills for working in any industry within the travel and tourism sector. As travel and tourism is a service industry, it is important that employees can both listen to customers' needs and requirements as well as communicate clearly and appropriately with them. This may also mean being able to adapt both your listening skills and communication skills when dealing with different types of people.

Why is providing good customer service so important when working in the travel and tourism sector?

Project planning and organisational skills

Project planning requires many of the vocational skills needed by someone to be a successful employee within the travel and tourism sector. Organisational skills, planning, problem solving, marketing, team working and customer service skills are all important vocational skills, acquired through project planning; these are all transferable skills to a variety of job roles. These include working as an overseas resort representative or resort supervisor, as airline cabin crew or a purser and in a hotel reception or conference and banqueting.

Customer service

In a service sector like travel and tourism, customers are the most important people. Without customers there would be no business. Customers spend money on the products and services offered and sold by travel and tourism companies, therefore in reality it is the customers who pay the wages of the employees who work for the companies.

The travel and tourism sector is highly competitive; good customer service is what separates a successful company from its competitors. This also encourages valuable repeat business.

Many travel and tourism companies such as First Choice and Thomas Cook have their own in-house trainers providing intense customer service training for all staff members to ensure customer service is consistently high across all areas of the organisations.

▶ Personal skills

Teamwork

Many job roles within the travel and tourism sector will involve team working; a group of people working together effectively will achieve greater things than the same number of people working on their own. It is essential within many of the industries

Link

Learn about customer service in *Unit 6: The Travel and Tourism Customer Experience.*

Remember

All travel and tourism organisations want the best possible employees; these will be those who hold many of the vocational and personal skills. What skills do you already have?

in travel and tourism for employees to work effectively with their colleagues in a productive and professional manner. For example, airline cabin crew work closely with one another, the captain, and ground control to ensure the smooth operation of a flight and to provide service of a high standard to passengers.

Reliability

This is an essential quality for employees within the travel and tourism sector. Will you be where you say you are going to be at the time you have agreed? Many industries such as the airline industry must have reliable staff; if cabin crew are late they will miss their flight; there is no room for being unreliable.

Personal presentation

In any service industry, people's first impressions count. All organisations will want to create a professional image to their customers from five-star hotels, such as the Hyatt Regency, to Haven holidays camps and, therefore, will require their employees to dress smartly. Many travel and tourism organisations will provide their staff with a uniform so that the image they require is portrayed by all their staff; it ensures that staff are smartly dressed at all times.

Commitment

It is essential in any job role to be committed to what you do, to the people you work with and the task you are doing. You must give one hundred per cent at all times to the task at hand and, even when you have worked a long night shift and are tired, you must still give the same one hundred per cent to the job. For example as an overseas resort representative, you may be required to undertake both property visits and evening airport transfers as well as dealing with customers' problems at any time of the day or night. Throughout this you would be expected to provide excellent service at all times.

What other roles can you think of in the travel and tourism sector that require uniforms?

Flexibility

To be successful in many job roles you will need to have flexibility. However, the travel and tourism industry is fast moving and constantly changing therefore being flexible is even more important.

Motivation

The motivation and commitment of employees is key to the success of a good team and therefore a good organisation. There are many motivating factors for working in the travel and tourism sector, such as shares, performance-related pay, i.e. commission, flexible working, competitions, incentives and perks such as free flights, free familiarisation trips and discounted accommodation and the travel factor in seeing different destinations.

Attitude

The attitude of a person is highly important when organisations are selecting new employees to represent their company to customers. For many jobs within the travel and tourism sector, organisations are looking for someone with a positive, proactive and willing attitude.

▮▶ Transferable skills

Part-time work

Experience of part-time work particularly in a customer service role allows valuable experience to be gained, for example in dealing with customers' queries and matching products to their requirements, dealing with issues or complaints if they arise, cash handling and banking, stock taking and working shifts. Part-time work can also develop wider skills in people, such as communication skills, team working and problem-solving which are all valuable transferable skills that would be required to work in most travel and tourism job roles. Candidates with part-time work experience who already hold these skills will have a greater advantage when applying to work in the travel and tourism sector.

Voluntary work

Undertaking voluntary work is another way to build up your transferable work skills. Having the experience of dealing with different people and working with others are all the types of skills travel and tourism organisations will look for in potential new employees.

What transferable skills do you think this employee will gain from her current job role?

▶ Binding rights and responsibilities

Introduction

Employment across all industries within the travel and tourism sector will involve statutory rights and responsibilities. Using either a guest speaker from the travel and tourism industry or a visit to one of your local travel organisations such as a high street travel agent, investigate some of the statutory and contractual rights and responsibilities that current employed staff hold. Further group discussions would prove useful around this topic.

▶ Statutory rights

Health and safety

All workers are entitled to work in environments where risks to their health and safety are properly controlled under the Health and Safety at Work Act 2011, and providing these **statutory** rights is the responsibility of the employer. Workers also have a duty to take care of their own health and safety and that of others who may be affected by their actions at work. Employees must cooperate with their employers and colleagues to achieve this. This means making sure that workers and others are protected from anything that may cause harm; effectively controlling any risks to injury or health that could arise in the workplace. Risk assessments should be carried out that address all risks that might cause harm in the workplace. Employers must also provide staff with information about risks in their workplace and instruct and train them on how to deal with these risks.

Equality

The **Equality** Act 2010 is the law which bans unfair treatment and helps achieve equal opportunities in the workplace and in wider society. The act covers nine protected characteristics, which cannot be used as a reason to treat people unfairly. Every person has one or more of the protected characteristics, so the act protects everyone against unfair treatment. The protected characteristics are:

- age
- disability
- gender reassignment
- marriage and civil partnership
- pregnancy, **maternity** and **paternity**
- race
- religion or belief
- sex
- sexual orientation.

The Equality Act sets out the different ways in which it is unlawful to treat someone, such as direct and indirect discrimination, harassment, victimisation and failing to make a reasonable adjustment for a disabled person. The act prohibits unfair treatment in the workplace, when providing goods, facilities and services, when exercising public functions, in the disposal and management of premises, in education and by associations (such as private clubs).

Key terms

Statutory – a minimum entitlement in line with legislation.

Equality – treating everyone fairly no matter what their background.

Maternity – mothers' rights after having a baby.

Paternity – fathers' rights when their partners are having a baby.

Have you seen any examples of the Equality Act being enforced in the news recently?

Why is it so important that all workers have the right to a holiday?

Employment protection

All employees are protected by the Employment Rights Act 1996 regardless of their length of service. Employees should not be unfairly treated because they have brought to the employer's attention, by reasonable means, a concern about situations at work that they reasonably believe are harmful, or potentially harmful to health and safety; or a situation that they reasonably believe to be of serious danger.

Pay and holidays

Under European Union regulations all full-time employees are entitled to a minimum of 5.6 weeks of annual leave per year. This is four weeks paid holiday annually plus bank holidays. As a reward, some companies may increase the length of holiday entitlement for length of service to increase staff loyalty for part-time workers. Part-time workers are also entitled to a minimum of 5.6 weeks paid holiday per year, although this would amount to fewer actual days of paid holiday compared with a full-time worker as it would be calculated on the number of part-time hours worked. For example if a part-time employee worked three days a week, their annual leave entitlement would be three-fifths of 5.6 weeks which comes to 16.8 days of paid holiday entitlement.

Working hours and conditions

Employees would not usually have to work more than a 48-hour week on average, unless they choose to. However, some sectors will have specific rules on this, for example a coach driver has strict guidance on the number of driving hours. Normal working hours are usually set out in the employment contract.

Maternity/paternity rights

Statutory maternity pay is paid to you by your employer when you take time off to have a baby. You have to qualify for statutory maternity pay by working for an employer for a specific period of time, and how much you get may change after the first six weeks. Statutory maternity pay is paid for up to 39 weeks and is paid in the same way as your wages usually are. Statutory paternity pay is made to the father of a child for up to two weeks.

▶ Contractual rights

Of the employer

The employer will supply the employee with a job description detailing the job role and expectations of the employee as well as **contractual** obligations such as notice period, annual holiday entitlement and working hours and location. The employer will also have contractual obligations such as a notice period to terminate the employment of an employee and procedures to be followed.

Of the employee

The employee will be issued with a job description from the employer as detailed above. If the employee agrees to these conditions of employment then he or she will be required to sign an employment contract therefore agreeing to abide by the terms and conditions laid out by the employer.

Key term

Contractual – a binding agreement.

Assessment activity 9.2

You are looking for a job in the travel and tourism industry. You should look at contrasting job options.

Select two jobs, one at entry level and one at managerial level, within two different travel and tourism industries, four jobs in total. Compare and contrast each job and make a short presentation to show which job role you would consider applying for, you could also say what makes you suitable for that role.

For each job role you should consider the:

- job specification (requirements of the job role)
- person specification (skills and qualifications needed)
- statutory requirements (employer's responsibilities)
- contractual requirements (employee's responsibilities).

Tip

Make sure you check the spelling and punctuation in your presentation.

Learning aim C   **TOPIC**   **C1**

▶ Recruitment and selection in the travel and tourism sector

Introduction

Many of the larger travel and tourism organisations will have their own Human Resource department that will handle the recruitment of new employees. It is vital to any organisation to have the best staff employed in the right positions. A recruitment and selection process is normally used in some form to ensure consistency, fairness and good practice when recruiting new employees. Think about if you have ever been for an interview yourself or filled in an application form for a part-time job – what happened next? Use your own current experiences and well as those of your peers in order to start to think about the recruitment process for the majority of organisations.

▶ Production of documentation

Job description

A job description is produced by organisations looking to employ new staff; this will detail the requirements of the job role being advertised as well as detailing what the person in that job role would be required to do.

Person specification

The person specification describes both the required and the desirable personal attributes required by potential job applicants such as:

- skills
- personal qualities
- qualifications
- experience.

An example can be seen in Figure 9.2.

Remember

First impressions count. Read the application form and closely follow any instructions, for example to complete the form in capital letters or to use black ink. Ensure your application form does not contain any mistakes and crossings out. If shortlisted for an interview, do your homework on the organisation and find out as much as you can about the company. Think about some of the generic interview questions they may ask and rehearse your answers. Ensure you are familiar with your application form and its content in case they ask you something about what you have written. Dress to impress. Smart business wear is always recommended for an interview.

JOB DESCRIPTION	
Job Title: Entertainment Manager	**Reports to:** Area Manager
Hours: Variable/can be extensive according to the business needs.	**Direct reports:** Entertainers and Sound technicians

Job purpose

- To lead, develop and motivate a given team of Entertainers and Sound technicians ensuring that all the company objectives and targets are communicated and reached.

Responsibilities & key outputs

- To oversee the day to day duties of the team ensuring that entertainment opportunities are maximised.
- To ensure that sales targets are consistently achieved.
- To make sure that all entertainment equipment and support material is maintained to the highest quality.
- To install a high level of responsibility and job ownership amongst the team.
- To provide regular updates/feedback to the Operations Director regarding operational, service delivery and staffing progress.
- To actively promote all merchandise and revenue opportunities.
- To monitor the quality of entertainment.

People skills

- The ability to prioritise workloads.
- Good communication and man-management skills.
- Self motivated with the ability to motivate a team.

Decision making skills

- Taking ownership of any challenges resolving problems at resort level.
- The ability to monitor standards.
- The initiative to appropriately escalate problems and incidents to the Operations Director.
- Liase with staff to ensure that service levels and operational needs are adhered to.

Development skills

- To conduct appraisals in line with the company guidelines.

Figure 9.2 This provides a typical example of a job description.

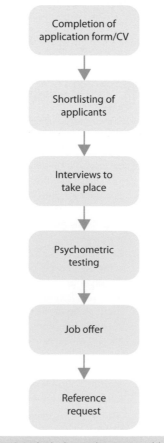

Completion of application form/CV

↓

Shortlisting of applicants

↓

Interviews to take place

↓

Psychometric testing

↓

Job offer

↓

Reference request

Figure 9.3 Think about what you would need to do for each stage of the process.

▶ Advertising

Travel and tourism organisations will advertise job roles in different ways. Some larger organisations such as Thomas Cook or Thomson will advertise through their own website and some will advertise through a specific travel and tourism recruitment search engine or recruitment agency; these are by far the most popular ways to advertise for new employees. *Travel Trade Gazette* and *Travel Weekly* are still used by some travel and tourism organisations to advertise new job roles, but as these are trade newspapers and are therefore received by existing travel and tourism organisations, they tend to be for specific and experienced roles.

▶ Application process

Application method

When applying for an advertised job role, you will be required either to send in a CV or, most likely, to complete the organisation's application form.

Shortlisting applications

After the closing date for applications, the organisation will shortlist applicants for interview using pre-set criteria, depending on what their priorities are for selecting the applicants. Once they decide which applicants they wish to see, these applicants will be invited to come for an interview.

Activity 9.3 Writing a CV

When applying for jobs within the travel and tourism sector, some organisations may ask you to provide a CV, while others ask you to complete an application form. Having a good CV can be a useful record for you, giving a log of the qualifications and experience you have.

In order to start recording your own achievements and experiences, the first thing to do is to make a list of the schools/colleges attended with dates and details of qualifications achieved along with any other achievements such as emergency first aid or Duke of Edinburgh award.

Now think about any work experience or part-time employment you may have had. List the name of the company along with your job title, role and responsibilities. Again include dates of employment.

Now think about any other skills, achievements or experience that may add value to your CV and demonstrate your qualities and experience. Finally, include the names of two referees; this could be your college tutor or school teacher.

Now see if you can put this into a word-processed document and develop a professional looking CV.

Interviews

Within the travel and tourism sector, you could be interviewed by a panel, on an individual one-to-one basis, or you could have a virtual interview over the internet or via phone. Many travel and tourism interviews take place over a whole day and consist of a variety of activities in order for the organisation to view how you handle different situations. Some organisations will also require you to complete a short literacy and numeracy test as part of the interview process. Ultimately, the interview is where the organisation decides if the interviewee is right for the job.

Psychometric testing

Psychometric testing may be used to help an organisation decide which person to employ. Psychometric tests are multiple choice questions with no specific correct answers. Analysing the answers given by the candidate can give an organisation an insight into the person's personality.

Why is it so important to look smart when attending an interview for a role in the travel and tourism sector?

Job offers

If you are successful at interview, you will normally receive an offer of employment by letter. It is common practice for the organisation also to telephone the successful interviewee first.

References

After an offer of employment has been made by an organisation, and accepted by the applicant, two references will generally be obtained, usually from previous employment or education.

Just checking

1 What are the main ways of applying for a job within the travel and tourism industry?

2 What are the key stages in the application process?

3 What procedures would a new employee usually go through?

▶ New employment

Introduction

Newly employed staff within a travel and tourism organisation will be required to gain an understanding of their new job role and the organisation they have just joined. As a starting point, make a list of the things a new employee would need to do in order to familiarise themselves with their new role.

▶ Job role requirements

Induction

On commencement of new employment with an organisation all new employees will be required to undertake an induction process to welcome them. This will ensure they are effective in their work as quickly as possible by familiarising them with both the organisation and their job role.

An induction will include health and safety, an introduction to the workplace, lines of responsibility, the job role and the location of general facilities.

Training

Travel and tourism organisations will provide both in-house training as well as having external training opportunities available. Larger companies tend to offer more of their own in-house training, which will be delivered across their employees. There are many external training courses which an employee may request permission to attend. It they are allowed to attend, they will be required to give feedback to their fellow employees.

Probation monitoring

New employees will undergo a probationary period, normally lasting anything from six to 12 months. At the start of this period the expectations of the role will be outlined, with targets also often being set. Within the probationary period the new employees will have regular reviews with their line manager to assess the quality of their work and to ensure that the new employee is meeting the required expectations within their job role.

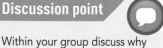

Discussion point

Within your group discuss why you think it is important for all new employees to go through an induction process and how this benefits both the new employee and the organisation.

▶ Career progression

Introduction

There are many job opportunities across the different industries within the travel and tourism sector; you will be unlikely to have just one job role, but rather you will experience a number of different jobs as you develop your abilities, knowledge and experience. A good starting point would be to think about where you would like to be in 10 years' time and how you are going to get there.

Further career development

Training/further study

Many travel and tourism organisations will provide both internal and external training opportunities for employees, some of which could lead to a full qualification such as an NVQ. More specialist roles, such as a pilot, would require specific qualifications such as a **JAA-PPL** license. A role like an air traffic controller would require a high level of numeracy and **NATS** training. The role of an overseas resort representative focuses more on personal skills, such as having good customer service, selling and communication skills and they will have to undertake intensive training in the UK and in a resort before commencement in their role.

Performance monitoring

Many employees within travel and tourism organisations will have to meet targets relevant to their roles. Staff who constantly meet these targets can be recognised for their hard work through rewards and through an appraisal system. Employees with an outstanding performance record are more likely to progress.

Progression opportunities

Many of the travel and tourism organisations are both **vertically** and **horizontally** integrated and therefore own companies within different areas such as travel agencies, tour operators, airlines and accommodation. Both multiple and independent companies have these links. This provides employees with progression opportunities, not only within the industry they already work in, but within other industries. This also allows employees to move to different pay structures.

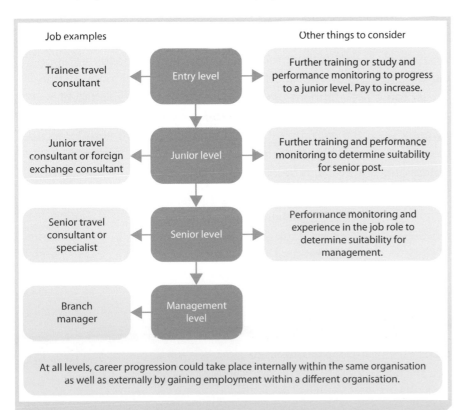

Job examples

Trainee travel consultant — **Entry level** — Further training or study and performance monitoring to progress to a junior level. Pay to increase.

Junior travel consultant or foreign exchange consultant — **Junior level** — Further training and performance monitoring to determine suitability for senior post.

Senior travel consultant or specialist — **Senior level** — Performance monitoring and experience in the job role to determine suitability for management.

Branch manager — **Management level**

Other things to consider

At all levels, career progression could take place internally within the same organisation as well as externally by gaining employment within a different organisation.

Figure 9.4 There are many routes for career progression.

Career pathways

There are many different travel organisations across the industry. Career progression can be both external when working for a company and applying to work for a different company, or internal where you may be applying to work in a different industry but for the same company. For example, an employee working for a Thomas Cook travel agent would have a progression opportunity to work for Thomas Cook airlines.

Case study

Chloe left education with GCSEs and a BTEC in Travel and Tourism, and gained work as a junior travel consultant. After 12 months of hard work and commitment, Chloe repeatedly exceeded her sales target. As a reward the company offered Chloe the opportunity of a familiarisation trip to the Dominican Republic in order to increase her knowledge of long-haul destinations.

Chloe continued to do well and went on to become a senior travel consultant and then three years later she became an assistant manager.

After five years in retail travel, Chloe decided that she would like to do something different. Due to her company also owning an airline, Chloe was inspired to apply for a cabin crew position. By using the skills and knowledge gained from her previous studies and from her work in retail travel she was successful in gaining a cabin crew job.

Chloe has now worked as cabin crew for four years on both short- and long-haul flights. She has recently been promoted to senior cabin crew and is very happy in her job role. Chloe felt that the knowledge from her initial studies on the BTEC Travel and Tourism programme and her experience of retail travel helped her get to where she is today.

1 Does the case study demonstrate internal or external progression?
2 What transferable skills would Chloe have gained in order to support her career progression?
3 Explain how Chloe moved her career path across different industries?

Assessment activity 9.3 — English

2C.P6 | 2C.P7 | 2C.M4 | 2C.M5 | 2C.D2

You have been asked to assist in the re-organisation of the human resources department, and to contribute to a redeveloped recruitment and selection process. You must research current good practice in the recruitment and selection of candidates, as well as information about potential career development within the company and present this information in a professional presentation to a group of senior managers within your company for approval.

You will need to select a travel and tourism organisation and to link your work to a specific job role or roles. You also need to ensure you include the application process and any relevant documentation. To ensure good practice, you will need to review the recruitment process in relation to a chosen travel and tourism organisation. You will then need to evaluate the recruitment, selection, employment entry process and career progression opportunities for two chosen travel and tourism organisations.

You should use a range of resources and your presentation should be delivered in a professional manner. Think about what formal wear looks like. Your presentational slides should also be of a professional format; PowerPoint® could be used here.

Tips

- When investigating the the different stages involved in the recruitment and selection process, you should research and investigate at least two travel and tourism organisations in order to provide depth to your work.

- Ensure you consider the application as well as the recruitment and selection process and include procedures for new employment and career progression opportunities.

WorkSpace

▶ Natasha Emeruwa

Senior Consultant in Retail Travel

I work for one of the leading travel agents and my role includes:

- providing destination information and advice
- matching customer requirements
- selling holidays in the UK and abroad
- selling ancillary services
- administration duties
- liaison with leading tour operators
- meeting sales targets
- customer service issues.

I love working in retail travel as I get to experience some of the destinations I am selling. This means I can provide first-hand information to my customers.

My main role as a senior travel consultant is carefully matching customer holiday requirements to an appropriate destination in order to ensure they have the best possible holiday experience. There's nothing better than seeing a completely satisfied customer who has had a fantastic holiday that you have suggested and booked for them. It's important to value and treat every customer as if they are special in order to ensure that customers will come back to you again to book their next holiday. Customer service is at the forefront of everything I do.

To be successful as a travel consultant in retail travel, you will need to have excellent people and customer service skills, good selling skills, confidence and patience and a good knowledge of travel destinations. Being friendly, approachable and assertive are also very important when working in a service industry like travel and tourism.

Think about it

1 What skills and knowledge might you already have from other units studied or previous experience which would help you to gain employment in travel and tourism?

2 What further skills and experience would you need to obtain your chosen career in travel and tourism?

3 Think about other job roles in travel and tourism that require selling skills.

Introduction

This is an interesting and practical unit where you will work in a team to organise, deliver and review a study visit or trip. This can add to your experience and enjoyment of travel and tourism in a real setting while also giving you the chance to work with others towards a common goal.

After the visit, you will need to review what went well and make recommendations on how to improve in the future. Many jobs in travel and tourism will require you to work as part of a team, and this unit will allow you to practise and develop these important and transferable skills.

As most jobs in the industry require you to work in a team, being a reliable team member is an essential skill. Think of the number of people involved in setting up a conference or arranging a package holiday – these people all need to work together to make these events successful.

Assessment: This unit will be assessed by a series of assignments set by your teacher/tutor.

Learning aims

In this unit you will:

A plan a travel and tourism study visit or trip

B work with others to deliver a travel and tourism study visit or trip

C review a travel and tourism study visit or trip and review own performance.

> My friends and I organised a visit to an O2 concert for a coach load of friends and neighbours. It was a really good experience and taught us a lot about how to get the best value – and also about what not to do! We had to make sure we each knew what our responsibilities were, so the trip fitted together.
>
> Matthew, *16-year-old Travel and Tourism student*

Organising a Travel and Tourism Study Visit

10

This table shows you what you must do in order to achieve a **Pass**, **Merit** or **Distinction** grade, and where you can find activities in this book to help you.

Assessment and grading criteria

Level 1	Level 2 Pass	Level 2 Merit	Level 2 Distinction
Learning aim A: Plan a travel and tourism study visit or trip			
1A.1 Plan a travel and tourism study visit or trip briefly outlining aims, itinerary, costs and resource requirements.	**2A.P1 Maths** Plan a travel and tourism study visit or trip describing aims, itinerary, costs and resource requirements. **See Assessment activity 10.1, page 270**	**2A.M1 Maths** Plan a travel and tourism study visit or trip, explaining its aims, itinerary, costs and resource requirements. **See Assessment activity 10.1, page 270**	**2A.D1 Maths** Plan a comprehensive travel and tourism study visit or trip, discussing in detail relevant legal and health and safety requirements. **See Assessment activity 10.1, page 270**
1A.2 Identify hazards and outline minimisation of risks when planning a travel and tourism study visit or trip.	**2A.P2** Assess hazards and describe minimisation of risks when planning a travel and tourism study visit or trip. **See Assessment activity 10.1, page 270**	**2A.M2** Analyse the legal and health and safety requirements of a travel and tourism study visit or trip. **See Assessment activity 10.1, page 270**	
1A.3 Outline legal factors that need to be taken into account when planning a travel and tourism study visit or trip.	**2A.P3** Describe legal factors that need to be taken into account when planning a travel and tourism study visit or trip. **See Assessment activity 10.1, page 270**		
Learning aim B: Work with others to deliver a travel and tourism study visit or trip			
1B.4 Outline your role and responsibilities when organising a travel and tourism study visit or trip.	**2B.P4** Describe your role and responsibilities when organising a travel and tourism study visit or trip. **See Assessment activity 10.2, page 274**	**2B.M3** Explain your role and responsibilities when organising a travel and tourism study visit or trip. **See Assessment activity 10.2, page 274**	
1B.5 With support, demonstrate your role and responsibilities both before and while on a travel and tourism study visit or trip.	**2B.P5** Demonstrate your role and responsibilities both before and while on a travel and tourism study visit or trip. **See Assessment activity 10.2, page 274**	**2B.M4** Demonstrate your role and responsibilities, showing initiative and working positively at all times with others, both before and while on a travel and tourism study visit or trip. **See Assessment activity 10.2, page 274**	
1B.6 Work with others, with support, during a travel and tourism study visit or trip.	**2B.P6** Work with others during a travel and tourism study visit or trip. **See Assessment activity 10.2, page 274**		

Learning aim C: Review a travel and tourism study visit or trip and review own performance

1C.7 English	2C.P7 English	2C.M5 English	2C.D2
With assistance, review the success of a travel and tourism study visit or trip, using feedback.	Review the success of a travel and tourism study visit or trip, using feedback gathered. **See Assessment activity 10.3, page 277**	Assess own performance, and study visit or trip success, using feedback gathered from relevant sources, recommending improvements. **See Assessment activity 10.3, page 277**	Evaluate own performance, and study visit or trip success, using feedback gathered from relevant sources, recommending valid improvements for the future. **See Assessment activity 10.3, page 277**
1C.8	2C.P8		
With assistance, review own performance, using feedback, following a travel and tourism study visit or trip.	Review own performance, using feedback gathered following a travel and tourism study visit or trip. **See Assessment activity 10.3, page 277**		

English	Opportunity to practise English skills	Maths	Opportunity to practise mathematical skills

How you will be assessed

This unit will be assessed by a series of assignments set by your teacher/tutor. You will be required to plan, participate positively and review a study visit or trip. These visits can be chosen by the centre and every learner must contribute and take an active role. It may be possible to have different groups organising several visits or trips for the whole class.

You must contribute to a comprehensive plan for the visit, including a risk assessment.

You should then produce evidence of your positive contribution to the team during the visit, describing your role throughout.

Lastly, you should then use feedback to review the success of the visit itself and also your contribution to it. You should make recommendations to improve future trips.

Your evidence

This could be in the form of:

- personal contribution to the plan
- observation records
- log books
- diaries
- witness statements
- questionnaires
- surveys
- statistics, e.g. from survey, profit/loss
- videos.

Developing a plan for a study visit or trip

Introduction

Planning a real visit or trip is a skill that will be very useful both in your working and personal life. You will look at how to cost, plan itineraries and consider all the aspects of a successful visit. Think of a visit you have been on yourself – what decisions had to be made before you actually started off?

Choice of study visit or trip

The first decision to be made about your **study visit** or trip is where you are going to go. Your teacher may guide you towards a day trip or trips in the UK or a longer visit within the UK or overseas. As all learners need to take an active part in the organisation of the trip, you may want to make several visits or have a small group take responsibility for all, or part of, a day. Each learner needs to provide evidence of their own involvement and contribution, so this is an important part of the decision process. You must be realistic – you may want to spend a month on safari in Africa, but the cost and time factor has to be taken into account.

You will need to think about the following factors.

- **Where?** The destination chosen should be one where aims and objectives can be achieved, all learners can take an active part and needs to be realistic in terms of journey time and **duration** of trip.
- **When?** The visit should take place at a time suitable for the school/college and possible weather restrictions. The length of the visit or visits should be considered.
- **How?** Transport is expensive, but keeping control of the group is important.
- **Who?** How are the organisers going to take an active part?

Deciding where to go is crucial and should be considered and discussed in detail. You may want to look at several options, carefully researching the cost and transport implications as well as the purpose of the visit. Your teacher will be able to advise on any restrictions, such as the timing or duration of the visit.

Meeting set aims and objectives

Part of the decision will be based on how well the destination can help meet aims and objectives. There may be a variety of aims and objectives for the visit, depending on those taking part, the destination and the activities organised. The success of the trip will be measured against these objectives, so they must be written carefully. They could include:

- **educational aims**, such as gathering information, interviewing personnel, completing a checklist, comparing and contrasting destinations
- **developing organisational skills**, such as designing and completing documentation, researching costs and keeping within a budget, completing accurate risk assessments
- **working with others**, such as working as part of a team, supporting others, providing feedback.

In the above examples, the first part could be developed as the overall **AIM**, and the examples given could be the specific **OBJECTIVES** to achieve that aim.

It is important that you spend some time setting **SMART objectives**, as you will find it much easier to check whether they have been achieved during your evaluation.

▶ Curriculum opportunities

This is a study visit, so you should link it to the themes you are studying in other units. You are studying destinations in the UK for Unit 2, so you could consider focusing on a resort or attraction as a case study. You may like to discuss an overseas resort if you are looking at international destinations in Unit 4 or you could gather information on customer service, linking to Unit 6.

The whole class will benefit from having the same experience at the same time. Visiting an attraction or destination together means that groups can discuss the experience, as well as looking at the destination from a 'professional' point of view.

The visit ought to be fun and interesting – it may be the first opportunity that groups have been able to work on a practical task together.

▶ Suitable destinations

When choosing a suitable destination for your visit, consider how long it will take to travel there and whether you intend to go for a day or longer. The following are other things to consider.

Arrival and departure points

It is important that it is easy for people to reach the intended destination by some form of transport. For example, are there car parking facilities or good rail links? When planning a visit you should ensure that everyone has travel information and knows where they should meet at the start and end of the visit.

Weather conditions

Think about the possible weather at both your arrival and departure points. Is it a good time to visit your intended destination? Will the weather impact on your travel plans or people's enjoyment of the visit? It may be that you are visiting an indoor attraction, in which case weather might be less of an issue.

Distance to be travelled

Most people will not want to travel more than two hours each way on a day trip – otherwise you may spend longer travelling than at the destination. On a residential visit you may want to travel further, but factor in 'comfort' and food stops.

Means of transport

You may want to keep the group together for safety and convenience. The cost of private coaches is high, but may be worth the cost. Group educational tickets by rail may be available. Travel by air is also a possibility, but may not be cost effective and usually requires passengers to have passports, even within the UK.

Case study

Dover Castle belongs to English Heritage. Pre-booked educational groups can visit free, and there are a range of resources available to enable teachers and learners to get the most out of their visit. One adult to every 15 pupils is required for Year 7 and above. (Source: English Heritage Handbook 2012)

Dover Castle is built on top of the 'White Cliffs' of Dover and was built in 1066 on top of a Saxon settlement. It has a Roman lighthouse and was built on the site of an iron-age fort. It also has a Secret Wartime Tunnels Tour in the medieval tunnels underneath the castle.

A trip could be combined with a visit to the docks or a seaside resort.

1. What events does Dover Castle hold to encourage visitors?
2. What sort of resources are available for school groups?

Resources

Your school or college will have a policy about how many staff are required to travel with learners. Their availability may affect the date, time and length of the visit.

The cost of transport also needs to be considered and how much each learner should contribute. You may have access to a minibus, but will need to check availability of the bus and driver.

If you are going to a study centre or outdoor facility, you may need to provide equipment such as tents, clothing, etc. – this could also have an impact on the cost.

Allocation of roles

It is essential that you know who is in charge of what part of the visit. This means you may not only have to communicate with the rest of your team, but other teams as well. Make sure that everyone has a copy of documentation, or can access it online, so that you can still continue to plan even if someone is off sick. You may want to allocate roles within your team, such as marketing, finance, secretary, coordinator. Make sure you know who to report any issues to and the 'chain of command'.

You may need a different coordinator and team during the planning stages and a slightly different allocation of roles during the visit itself. Make sure you record all these decisions and the reasons for them.

▶ Legal and other duties

Your school or college may have an educational visit policy or code of conduct that you must follow. This may mean that some visits are seen as too high a risk, or may be outside the guidelines. Teachers and other staff have a legal duty of care, which will also impact on the visit. The Equality Act requires 'suitable adjustments' to be made so that those with learning or physical disabilities or impairments can participate fully.

There may be a school or college insurance policy, or guidelines for individual personal cover needed – again, this may affect the choice of visit, particularly if overseas. If travelling overseas, each passenger will need a valid passport and visa requirements will need to be checked, particularly if non-EU passport holders are travelling.

▶ Health and safety

This is the most important thing to consider. The visit must stick to the government (Department for Education) and local guidelines as discussed above. Ratios of staff to learners should be reasonable and ensure that learners are adequately represented. Learners may want to draw up an additional code of conduct for the visit, covering use of alcohol, drugs, personal responsibility and behaviour including clothes and curfews. Learners should also be advised about their personal safety and being aware of their belongings.

▶ Itinerary

You will need to produce an itinerary, both for the participants and their parents or carers, showing all the relevant details of contact information, travel arrangements, rendezvous points, food and equipment requirements and timings. You may need to produce a draft version for planning purposes and a final version when all the details have been agreed – quite often close to the departure date. Look at Unit 2 to see all the features of an itinerary.

▶ Finance and administration

The cost of the visit is an important part of the decision. You will need to take in to account:

- transport
- entry to attractions
- food/drink
- accommodation
- any other activities
- equipment.

The total cost may need to be divided amongst the passengers. You will need to have a system to ensure all payments have been made and recorded according to your centre's policy and procedures. You need to be aware of your trip's budget throughout and should always keep a record of all bookings you have made for the trip.

You will need to have records of each participant's contact details, food requirements, passport and visa numbers (if applicable) and any special requirements such as a

---

Activity 10.2   What are my strengths?

Once your team has been allocated, you will need to spend some time deciding who takes on roles within the team. On your own, write a list of your strengths – are you good at maths? Drawing? Writing? Leading other people? Are you well organised and do you give attention to detail? With the rest of your team, discuss the roles needed and allocate them according to each person's strengths.

Take it further

Look at your college or school policies covering study visits. Summarise these and then list any aspects you think could be covered by an additional code of conduct. Discuss these with the participants and draw up a code of 10 points that you feel should apply to the visit to reduce the risks for everyone.

Link

Unit 2: UK Travel and Tourism Destinations may provide ideas for destinations as well as a template for itinerary writing.

Did you know?

Some destinations can provide free entrance for educational groups as well as an education officer or education pack.

ground floor room. You will also need information about who to contact in case of emergency and their contact details.

Parents or guardians will need to sign a 'consent form' for the visit if the learner is under 18-years-old. Confidential information, such as medical conditions or ongoing medication, should be held by the teacher/tutor in charge.

▶ Study visit or trip information booklet

You will need to provide your participants with a booklet explaining what the trip is all about – just like a tour operator's brochure on a smaller scale. 'Sell' the venue and activities as well as giving information about what participants are expected to bring with them in terms of equipment and clothing.

This will also be useful for parents and carers to understand what the trip is all about, so include as much information as possible. You may want to include the draft itinerary.

If one booklet is produced as a group effort, make sure that you record your own contribution to it.

▶ Record of study visit or trip

You will need to record all the decisions you have made as a group, and your contribution to them. You might like to use a simple diary, with an entry for each day that the group meet or make a decision.

You could also use a 'log book' or sheets, which can be completed as an individual or to record group actions and their outcomes. An example is given in Figure 10.1.

Make sure that you don't get behind in completing these – they are essential for providing evidence in your assignment and are much easier to do at the time and not weeks after the event.

Date	Task/ contribution	Actions	Any problems?	Teacher/tutor comments

Figure 10.1 Log book for recording contributions throughout the organisation process.

Activity 10.3 Proposing a visit

You should by now have a proposal for a study visit – have you included all the items we have covered?

In particular, have you considered your centre's policy on visits and checked that all legal and health and safety aspects have been covered?

Do you have SMART objectives, and will the visit allow them to be achieved?

Have you recorded all your actions and decision-making activities?

What sort of qualities do you think you would need to be a tour guide?

Process of risk assessment

Introduction

When planning any form of activity, it is important to think about all the things that could go wrong, how you might minimise the risk of these things happening in the first place, and what you might do to put things right if they happen anyway. This is called 'risk assessment'. You do this informally all the time – think about a trip you may have made recently to the shops or to see a film. In pairs, think of what you did to minimise risks.

Identify possible hazards

You should take each line of the itinerary and consider whether any of the activities contain a **hazard**. These could include the following.

- Travelling to and from the destination – hazards might be late arrivals, accident, sickness of teacher/tutor or learner, missed connections, etc.
- Travelling around a destination or attraction – is there a risk of tripping/falling/getting lost?
- At the venue – are you undertaking any risky activities such as sports or outdoor pursuits? Does the venue contain unfenced high drops? Water hazards?
- Is free time available? What may the hazards be if learners are unsupervised?

Each trip is different, and each participant is different. You will need to think carefully about possible hazards at every step.

Minimise risks

What can you do to minimise the **risks** identified?

- Ensure contact details for all participants are available.
- Provide written and verbal advice, ensuring that procedures are in place and that everyone knows what they are. You or the party leader may need to do a pre-visit briefing.
- Use reputable organisations – for example, your school or college may have coach companies they use regularly.
- Visit any unknown venues to assess hazards and think about how they can be minimised.
- Ensure you have taken any special needs in to account. For example your teacher/tutor may do an individual risk assessment to help a wheelchair user.
- Make sure you have complied with all procedures and policies, such as staff/learner ratios.

Key terms

Hazard – anything that can cause harm such as loose wires, hot liquids, deep water.

Risk – the chance that someone could be harmed.

▶ Assess the level of risk

The hazards you identify may cause minor injuries such as cuts or bruises or slight distress. But more serious injuries such as burns, shocks, or even death might also occur as a result. Each hazard should be assessed as low, medium or high.

Low-risk hazards can usually be accommodated with measures to reduce or remove the risk. High-risk activities may not be able to go ahead.

▶ Recording actions taken to reduce risks

Risk assessments are usually recorded so that everyone knows what to do in a certain situation. The form should be completed carefully, updated and carried at all times on the visit by the group leader. Your centre may have a risk assessment form in use already. Ask your teacher/tutor if you can see an example. A note should be taken of any written and/or verbal advice provided. You should also be careful to use reputable organisations, such as a well-reviewed local coach company.

Case study

On a study visit to Disneyland Paris, the coach was delayed on the way to Dover because of a mechanical fault. This meant that the coach party missed the ferry they were booked onto, and would arrive very late at night at the Disneyland hotel. The coach company had a risk assessment which laid out the procedure for obtaining a replacement coach and re-booking a place on the ferry. All the important phone numbers were available in one place so this could be done quickly.

The party leader also had a risk assessment, which stated that the hotel should be notified of their late arrival, and that the college should be informed. The college then phoned the first person on the 'telephone tree' so all parents/guardians were also aware. The trip proceeded without further trouble and was very successful.

1 Can you think what might have happened if the risk assessment procedures had not been in place?

2 Can you think of another incident that might have occured on the trip, and the risk assessment procedures that should be in place so that everyone is prepared to respond in this situation?

Assessment activity 10.1   Maths

2A.P1 | 2A.P2 | 2A.P3 | 2A.M1 | 2A.M2 | 2A.D1

It is time for you to organise your own study visit or trip. This should be relevant to your BTEC First Travel and Tourism course, for example you might decide to visit a local tourist attraction to find out more about its services, facilities and how it appeals to different customer types.

Before the trip can go ahead, you have been asked to demonstrate how organised you are by preparing a presentation for the parents/guardians of those in your group, including:

- aims of the study visit or trip
- a detailed itinerary
- costs
- required resources
- risk assessment.

As part of this presentation, you should explore the following in detail:

- relevant legal factors
- health and safety considerations.

If you are working as part of a team, you must play an active role and demonstrate that you have individually met all assessment criteria.

Tip

When carrying out a risk assessment, remember to consider all risks and hazards associated with the venue(s) as well as those associated with travelling, personal safety and security. You will need to suggest ways that these can be minimised.

WorkSpace

▶ Elsa McBride

Corporate Travel Consultant

I work for a large international company. There is a team of us who arrange:

- travel to international conferences
- business meetings all over the world
- site visits
- hotels
- corporate hospitality
- travel and transfers.

I really love my job as every day is different. We spend a lot of time talking to people in other countries to find out exactly what the passenger requirements are. Our staff come from different cultures and we have to make sure they are comfortable with the arrangements. We have a number of staff with disabilities as well so we are used to making sure they have everything they need.

We have to be careful to keep accurate records so that any member of the team can deal with arrangements – we have many different things going on at the same time so have to rely on each other. Between us we speak four different languages so we can usually find someone to help.

We have budgets and processes we have to follow, so we all know what we are doing. I hope to work in other countries eventually, but at the moment I am really enjoying this job.

Think about it

1 What skills does Elsa need to do her job effectively?

2 What skills do you already have, and what skills would you need to develop?

3 Which units studied so far would be particularly useful in this job?

▶ Responsibilities prior to the study visit or trip

Introduction

You have already looked at your strengths and thought about how you can contribute to the visit. The decisions have now been made and you can start finalising documentation. What will you offer towards the final preparations? What can you do to help things go smoothly?

▶ Arranging documentation

It is essential that all the documentation required has been completed and returned to the organisers. How are you going to make sure all participants have sent their forms back? Do you have a checklist; a spreadsheet? Figure 10.2 shows some of the documentation you will need to check.

Consent forms will need to be signed by parents/guardians if the participants are under 18-years-old. The form will give permission for the learner to take part in the visit. This is important because the party leaders will be 'in loco parentis' – acting as parents/guardians could reasonably be expected to do.

Medical information will be needed in case learners become ill on the visit – group leaders will need to know of any allergies or prescription drugs so that they can inform doctors in case of a medical emergency as the learner may not be able to do this for themselves.

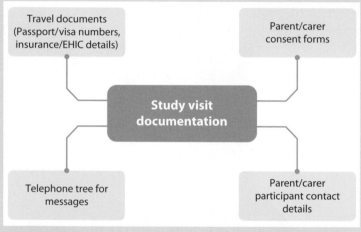

Figure 10.2 Why is it essential that all this documentation is checked?

Emergency contact details will be required if an accident should occur, or if there is a major unavoidable delay. They may also be required in the case of disciplinary action.

A 'telephone tree' will be useful to pass on information that is important but not urgent, such as a short delay. The group leader may telephone one person, who has agreed to ring five others, who in turn will ring five others each. This will avoid one person having to make dozens of calls, possibly from a foreign country.

Activity 10.4   Diaries, log sheets and observation sheets

Check you are completing your log sheets or diary as you go along – update them now if not. Make sure your teacher/tutor/team members are completing observation sheets as well.

▶ Providing visit information

Has the information booklet been completed and produced in hard copy and other formats? Is it available in large print for sight-impaired participants? Have you included information about clothing, possible weather and equipment needed? Have you arranged sufficient comfort and refreshment stops? Are they accessible to all learners,

Discussion point

In groups, discuss the contribution each person has made to the arrangement of documentation and how each individual can show what they have contributed.

and the coach driver if necessary? Have you arranged for specific dietary requirements, such as vegetarian or halal food? Is the itinerary finalised?

Now go and enjoy a safe trip, confident you have prepared well.

TOPIC   B2

Roles during the visit

Introduction

Now the preparation has been done, you need to change your role to support the team and participants on the visit.

How will you show you are an organiser? Will you wear different clothes/badges/carry a clipboard? How will you remain positive and in control even if things go wrong?

Personal responsibility

The most important aspect of personal responsibility is the health, safety and security of yourself and the other participants. Make sure you have contact details with you at all times, together with the risk assessment. Make sure the group knows how to contact the teachers/tutors. Obviously, your own conduct should be an example to the others.

Time management

Make sure you arrive early at rendezvous points, so you can assist if someone does not appear. Set the standard of behaviour. You may find that if you do not bother to turn up on time, neither will everyone else and a lot of time can be wasted. Those who have made the effort will also feel resentful about being kept waiting.

Working with others

You will need to support your team, the teachers/tutors and all participants, including any drivers. This could mean doing whatever needs to be done, whether it is picking up litter, providing a coach commentary or copies of itineraries. Hopefully you will already have allocated roles to the group for the things that can be predicted, but there are always things that can happen unexpectedly that need to be dealt with. Try to be the one who notices what needs to be done first.

Positive personal attitude

Remember the London 2012 volunteers? Their positive attitude and smiling welcome impressed the world. However you are feeling, make sure you smile and keep positive – it is amazing the difference it can make.

A London 2012 volunteer. Always smiling! What effect do you think a cheerful volunteer had on those attending London 2012?

▶ Keeping to the code of conduct

You should not only be a model of behaviour, but keep a look out for anyone not keeping to the agreed code. One or two people could spoil the trip for everyone. Remember the code of conduct you agreed when discussing the proposed visit – you may find it helpful to ask participants to sign that they agree with it. It would be helpful to photocopy the code and take it on the visit with you to remind people what is expected of them.

▶ Awareness of the needs of others

You should also show awareness of other cultures, whether it is those of participants or at your destination. For example, you must ensure everyone is in suitable clothing to visit a cathedral or mosque. You may have participants with particular needs – you might need to point out a sensory model of a building to a sight-impaired person, or ask for an induction loop if someone is hearing-impaired.

Remember

Complete your log sheets or diary every time you contribute something during the study visit.

Assessment activity 10.2   2B.P4 | 2B.P5 | 2B.P6 | 2B.M3 | 2B.M4

Whether you are working alone or as part of a team, you need to demonstrate your own role and the responsibilities in:

- organising the study visit or trip
- taking part in a study visit or trip.

You can do this by keeping your own diary or blog. You could also ask your teacher/tutor to observe you so they can document their thoughts on how you have performed.

Tip

Make sure you keep a record of how things went for you in terms of time management, working with others, attitude, personal presentation and consideration for others.

▶ Travel and tourism study visit or trip review criteria

Introduction

It is now time to review the success of the visit, using a number of criteria. Do you think the trip was a success? If something went wrong, were you able to change arrangements? How well did you cope with change?

▶ Meeting aims and objectives

If your original aims and objectives were well written, it will be easy to see whether they have been achieved. If not, try to find out why. Think about what you did to resolve any issues.

Suitability of destinations

Was the destination suitable for the age group? Were there opportunities to achieve the learning aims? Were the speakers/guides appropriate? Were participants able to obtain the information they needed? Did participants enjoy the visit(s)? Were some attractions/destinations preferred to others?

Travel arrangements

Did the travel arrangements work well? Was it comfortable? Did you arrive on time? Were any special needs catered for? Were there enough suitable comfort stops?

Could anything have been improved? Were there any complaints?

Itinerary

Did you manage to keep to the timings on the itinerary? Were the attractions/destinations suitable? Were any accommodation/food stops appropriate? Was suitable food provided?

Budget

Did the costs keep to the expected budget? Were there any unexpected bills? How do you know? Do you have a spreadsheet or a simple set of accounts? You may need to ask your teacher/tutor for help to see the income and expenditure figures.

Was your own personal expenditure what you expected? Why?

Duration of the visit

Was it too long? Too short? Just right? Why? What are the reasons given? Is there a particular group saying this, for example male/female; teachers/tutors?

Peer and teacher/tutor feedback

To review the experience properly, you will need to have feedback from the participants and the teachers/tutors; don't just rely on your own opinion.

One of the easiest ways is to use a questionnaire, which can be online or on paper. The questionnaire can be given out during, on the way back, or on return from the trip. During the trip you have the advantage of a captive audience, but they may be completed without much reflection. But completing the questionnaires after risks some events being forgotten.

If you chose to travel by coach, was the driver helpful?

Name:_____ Role:_____

Study Visit:_____ Date:_____

Circle the answers which apply (1 = excellent; 5 = poor) or tick the appropriate box.

1) Did the study visit meet your aims and expectations?

   1   2   3   4   5

2) How satisfied were you with the choice of visit destination?

   1   2   3   4   5

3) How would you rate the transport used?

   1   2   3   4   5

4) Considering the costs involved with the visit, did you feel the trip was:

  ☐ Excellent value

  ☐ Satisfactory value

  ☐ Poor value

5) How would you rate the duration of the visit?

  ☐ Too short

  ☐ Just right

  ☐ Too long

6) Do you think the visit was an overall success? ☐ Yes ☐ No

7) If you were to make one recommendation to improve the visit in the future, what would this be?

  [_____]

Figure 10.3 A post-visit questionnaire is a useful tool to gain feedback.

It may take some time to evaluate the answers, so keep the questions simple and where possible use multiple-choice answers rather than open questions. Open questions such as 'Tell me what you liked best' will give you many answers and are difficult to analyse.

You could also interview participants or teachers, and record the responses. Be aware that transcribing interviews takes a lot of time, so ask your teacher if they will accept a recording.

During the trip, you may have asked teachers and participants to complete observation sheets. You will need to have a copy of these and analyse the comments carefully.

In any case, remember that you cannot please all of the people all of the time and there may be negative comments. This is good – you will be able to recommend improvements for the future. It is also unlikely that everything went without a hitch – what matters is what you did to resolve the situation.

Do not avoid negative comments and pretend everything was wonderful – it is your honest review that is important, not an apparently perfect visit.

Remember

You should use a method of assessment such as a questionnaire – do not rely on your own opinion.

Activity 10.5   Analysing comments

Have you received responses from all participants and analysed them all – including any negative comments? What are the results of your analysis?

▶ Self-review

Introduction

You also need to review how well you met your own objectives. Look at your diary or log sheets – how well do you think you performed? Were there things which you now think you could have done differently? Did you identify the right strengths, or are there any others you demonstrated?

▶ Peer, teacher/tutor and observer feedback

Gather together as much information as you can from teachers/tutors and visit participants, using a set questionnaire, surveys, interviews and observation sheets. These, together with your own log sheets or diary, will give you a lot of information about how well you performed. You may also have some witness statements from others involved in the visit, such as guides or education officers.

Analyse this information, and extract some statistics from it, for example '70 per cent of participants were satisfied with the information booklet'. Try to obtain information about your own performance, for example '75 per cent of team members felt that I had carried out my duties with enthusiasm and all team members would like to work with me again'. You should be able to analyse every answer in this way.

Why do you think it is important to find out how useful the information you provided was to visit participants?

Again, be honest about your strengths and weaknesses. You may have dealt with a situation very well, but on reflection would do things slightly differently next time. Recommend improvements for the organisation of future visits.

▶ Personal and study visit or trip strengths and weaknesses

A good way to summarise the results of the feedback is to construct a chart showing strengths and weaknesses.

	Visit/trip	Personal
Strengths		
Evidence		
Weaknesses		
Evidence		

▶ Areas for improvements

From your chart, you can recommend ways in which the organisation of the visit can be improved. You can also recommend ways in which you might improve your own skills in certain areas. Make sure that you refer to the feedback evidence to back up your recommendations.

▶ Evaluation of achieving aims and objectives

Refer back to the original aims and objectives, both for the visit and your own skill improvement. Use the feedback received from participants and teachers/tutors to decide to what extent the objectives have been achieved.

Why do you think the objectives were or were not achieved? What would you have done differently? Do you have any recommendations for the future?

The lessons learnt from this process should help you develop your skills in the future.

> **Activity 10.6** Recommendations for the future
>
> In your teams, discuss how well the team worked together on the visit itself. Write a list of five recommendations for future visits. It is important to be honest – analysis is what is needed, rather than thinking it was all wonderful.

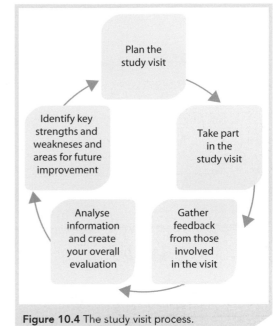

Figure 10.4 The study visit process.

> ### Assessment activity 10.3
> 2C.P7 | 2C.P8 | 2C.M5 | 2C.D2
>
> You have completed your study visit or trip. Your teacher/tutor asks you to prepare a report about the trip. You should think about everything that happened on the trip and use your diaries/logbooks to look back on your own role.
>
> You will need to find suitable ways to gather feedback from:
>
> - others in your group
> - your teacher/tutor
> - others that took part in the visit or trip.
>
> You should use this feedback to back up your own assessment of the success of the study visit. Are there things you might be able to improve on if you were to organise another trip in the future?
>
> #### Tip
> Think about different ways you might be able to present feedback from others. For example, you could consider producing bar charts or pie charts to present the data. In addition, you could include quotes from those who were involved.

Answers to Assessment Practice Questions

Unit 1, Assessment practice 1.1

Which of the following is an example of inbound tourism to the UK? [1]

Answer: B A woman from Africa attending a conference in Manchester.

Unit 1, Assessment practice 1.2

Study the information and answer the questions below.

Sector	Visitor numbers (m)	Spend (£bn)
Business	6.8	4.0
Leisure	11.5	6.6
VFR	8.4	3.6
Study	0.5	1.4
Other	2.4	1.2

Source: International Passenger Survey 2011

1 What does Gross Domestic Product mean? [1]

Possible answer: Gross Domestic Product can be thought of as the value of a country's economy. It measures the specific values of all goods and services over a specific time period (usually one year). Domestic and inbound tourism contribute to the UK's GDP.

2 Which sector contributes the most money to GDP? [1]

Answer: B Leisure.

Unit 1, Assessment practice 1.3

Give one advantage and two disadvantages of using non-serviced accommodation for a family with three children under 7 years old. [3]

Answers could include:

Advantage 1   Can prepare meals at any times

Disadvantage 1   Someone has to prepare food – just like at home

Disadvantage 2   You will have to clean the apartment/room and make the beds.

Unit 1, Assessment practice 1.4

A voluntary organisation such as the Youth Hostel Association provides accommodation primarily for young people.

1 Give two other products or services a voluntary organisation might provide. [2]

Answers could include:

- Advice, for example on sustainable tourism.
- Information, for example on walks.

2 Give two sources of funding for a voluntary organisation. [2]

Answers could include:

- Legacies from people who have died.
- Entrance fees to houses or gardens.

Unit 7, Assessment practice 7.1

A leading long-haul airline employing 35,000 staff operates with a traditional steep hierarchical structure. Explain one advantage of this structure for this type of organisation. [2]

Possible answer: There are many managers at each level, therefore senior management has a lot of control over the organisation.

Unit 7, Assessment practice 7.2

Identify three internal functions in a travel and tourism organisation. [3]

Any three answers from:

- Human resources
- Product development
- Finance and accounting
- Information Technology (IT)
- Customer service.

Unit 7, Assessment practice 7.3

Give three reasons why holiday makers might choose a staycation. [3]

Answers could include:

- There are no costs for accommodation.
- All the comforts and amenities of home are available.
- It provides the opportunity to see your local area in a new light.

Unit 7, Assessment practice 7.4

Explain two benefits of wireless technology to travel and tourism organisations. [4]

Answers could include:

- Customers can access websites and social media feeds from anywhere including at your resort. This gives the organisation the opportunity to provide guests with more information about their products or services.
- Travel and tourism organisations have developed wireless services designed to enrich the visitor experience, such as apps as tour guides or booking rides at a theme park on your mobile.
- Reduced costs in developing ICT networks and facilities as these no longer need to be hard-wired.

Unit 7, Assessment practice 7.5

Identify three common business objectives for organisations within the travel and tourism industry. [3]

Answers could include:

- increase market share
- minimise business risk
- create new products and services to increase profitability or react to competitors.

Unit 7, Assessment practice 7.6

Give three examples of how the government can influence demand in the travel and tourism industry. [3]

Answers could include:

- increase promotion of the UK abroad
- investment in infrastructure
- taxation policy and immigration policy.

Unit 7, Assessment practice 7.7

Identify and explain one advantage of vertical integration for an organisation within the UK travel and tourism industry. [3]

Answers could include:

- Better control over the components of the product and service.
- By owning more of the service delivery chain the organisation has greater control over the components of the product and service, i.e. if a tour operator also owns the airline then they can develop the airline to suit the needs of their customers.

Disclaimer: These practice questions and sample answers are not actual exam questions. They have been provided as a practice aide only and should not be assumed to reflect the format or coverage of the real external test.

Glossary

A

Ageing population – when the average age within a population rises.

Airside – the area within an airport after passport control.

Ancillary – additional products and services offered by travel agents.

Après ski – refers to the social opportunities offered by a ski resort – its bars, clubs and entertainment.

ATOL – is the Air Travel Organisers' Licencing. If an ATOL protected company goes out of business their customers would get their money back or be brought home if they are already on holiday. You can find out more through the Civil Aviation Authority's website, which you can find by visiting Pearson hotlinks. www.pearsonhotlinks.co.uk, and searching for this title.

B

Balance sheet – is a statement of the financial assets minus the financial liabilities of an organisation.

Banners – these tend to appear either across the top, bottom or down the side of a website.

Bespoke – means custom made or tailored to a buyer's needs and demands.

Bias – People often have strong opinions about certain topics. This is called 'bias'. Newspaper or magazine articles, or information found on the internet, may be biased to present a specific point of view.

Break even – the point where the business makes neither a profit or a loss.

C

Carbon off-setting – is where money is spent on renewable sources of energy, for instance wind farms, to offset the carbon used by aeroplane emissions.

Chain of distribution – means of getting the product or service to the customer.

Chronological – means in the correct order, starting with day 1 and working through to the last day of the holiday.

Consolidator – a consolidator is a company that groups together products or services from different companies in order to sell them.

Consumer loyalty – where consumer continue to buy or use a product or service.

Contractual – a binding agreement.

Credit crunch – is the term used to explain the difficulty of getting access to credit.

Culture – the way people behave; their traditions, music and food. Think of the Celtic culture, with its rich musical traditions and dress, poetry and food; a set of beliefs, values, behaviours, habits, traditions.

Currency exchange rate – also known as foreign exchange rate, is the rate at which one currency can be exchanged for another.

Customer – somebody who receives customer service from a service provider. A customer may be a person or an organisation.

Customer needs – are the requirements a customer has, e.g. children's meals at a hotel.

Customer service – The sum total of what an organisation does to meet customer expectations and produce customer satisfaction (this is the definition of the Institute of Customer Service).

Customer wants – are the requirements that the customer would like to have, e.g. a hotel with a beach.

Cyclones – mainly in the south western Pacific Ocean.

D

Demographic – a particular sector of the population.

Direct employment – jobs where employees are in direct contact with tourists and provide the tourism experience.

Discretionary spend – spending by consumers on things that they want to buy rather than on things they need such as housing or food.

Domestic – means operating within the UK.

Duration – the length of time that something lasted.

E

Economy of scale – the increase in efficiency of production as the volume of goods or services being produced increases.

Eco-tourism – resorts that have been developed in a sustainable way.

Equality – treating everyone fairly no matter what their background.

Ethnicity – being part of a group with a shared history, sense of identity, or cultural roots.

F

FCO – the Foreign & Commonwealth Office. You should check out their country travel advice at their website before you travel. You can access this by visiting Pearson hotlinks, www.pearsonhotlinks.co.uk, and searching for this title. If you travel to a country against FCO advice your insurance may not be valid.

Foreseen events – when events are planned in advance and so are expected.

G

Gateway – where passengers can access a country or area. Belfast is a gateway or portal into Northern Ireland because passengers passing through here can travel on to other areas of the country easily.

Great Britain Tourism Survey – takes place every year and gives information about tourism by residents of Great Britain. It excludes Northern Ireland.

Grey pound – refers to the economic spending power of pensioners.

Gross Domestic Product (GDP) – this can be thought of as the value of a country's economy. It measures the specific value of all goods and services over a specific time period (usually one year). Domestic and inbound tourism contribute to the UK's GDP but not all outbound tourism does as this involves outbound tourists spending money in another country.

H

Hazard – anything that can cause harm such as loose wires, hot liquids, deep water.

Honeypot – a destination that attracts thousands of visitors, like swarming bees, because it is so famous.

Horizontal – an organisation that owns companies within the same industry.

Hurricanes – tropical storms in the North Atlantic, Gulf of Mexico and Caribbean.

I

IATA – the International Air Transport Association. The three-letter codes they give to airports are used in civil aviation. Civil aviation covers non-military flights.

Independent travel agents – are often family-owned and may have one branch or a few branches. An example is Worldwide Escapes in Cheshire.

Indirect employment – jobs in companies that supply the direct employment companies such as aircraft suppliers and hotel laundry suppliers.

Indirect flight – when you have to change to a different aircraft to complete your journey.

Intangible – means not having a physical presence, i.e. a service. Intangibles may include service at an airport and on an aeroplane, welcome meeting or an experience.

International – means operating between countries.

Interpretation – a means of giving information to visitors to help them understand and enjoy what they are looking at.

Itinerary – this is the schedule of events throughout the holiday. It needs to have all the information laid out clearly for easy reference. Make sure you can spell this word as it is different from the way it sounds.

J

JAA-PPL – Joint aviation authorities private pilot licence.

L

Land of the Midnight Sun – towards the Arctic Circle, where the mid-summer sun never sets.

Landside – the area within an airport before passport control.

Latitude – refers to imaginary horizontal lines running parallel to the Equator.

Legacy – money or property left to someone in a will. An example is a historic house left in someone's will to the National Trust.

Long-haul travel – typically refers to destinations that take six hours or longer to reach by air.

Low-cost airlines – sometimes called no frills or budget airlines, they offer cheaper flights, but charge extra for meals, hold luggage, allocated seats, etc.

Ltd – is a private limited company and sells shares privately.

M

Market segment – a specifically defined group of customers that have similar needs and wants, that a product or service can be developed for.

Maternity – mothers' rights after having a baby.

Mission statement – the public statement many organisations work towards to provide a specific culture for their customers.

Multiple travel agents – are large chains of more than 50 branches all belonging to the same company. An example is Thomson.

Multiplier effect – the additional revenue, income or employment created in an area as a result of spending on tourism.

N

National – means operating within the UK.

National Air Traffic Services (NATS) – the organisation responsible for air traffic control in the UK. It is a public/private partnership between the government, several airlines, Heathrow Airport Trust and an Employee Share Trust.

NATS – National Air Traffic Services

NEET – refers to young people not in employment, education or training.

Niche market – a narrowly defined group of customers which forms a small, but profitable section of the market.

Non-serviced – accommodation without meals provided. For example, self catering apartment.

Northern Lights – spectacular natural light show in the night sky in North Norway. Check out some images on the internet.

O

Off-peak – the season which is less popular for the product or destination.

Online agents – sell their products and services over the internet.

Overcoming objections – this refers to addressing a customer's worries and concerns about a product or service. This may be done by explaining the product or service or even by offering a different, more appropriate product or service.

P

Pandemic – when an infectious disease spreads through populations across continents, for example the swine flu pandemic in 2009, which affected tourism, especially in Mexico.

Paternity – fathers' rights when their partners are having a baby.

Peak – the season which is the most popular time for a product or destination.

Plagiarism – If you are including other people's views, comments or opinions, or copying a diagram or table from another publication, you must state the source by including the name of the author or publication, or the web address. Failure to do this (so you are really pretending other people's work is your own) is known as plagiarism. Check your school's policy on plagiarism and copying.

Plc – is a public limited company and sells shares openly on stock markets.

Pop-up – a form of online advertising that literally just pops up when you first access a website.

Primary products and services – the main purpose of the visit, for example to see rock bands.

Primary research – original research – carried out for the first time.

Profit – is the money that businesses make from their sales after the costs of making their sales have been taken out.

Purser – the most senior cabin crew onboard a flight overseeing the other cabin crew members. The purser also completes the flight reports.

R

Recession – is where you have two three-month periods in a row where the country is producing less than it produced in the previous three-month period.

Resort – a town or village which is primarily a tourist destination. Some places may be on the sea but have a different main purpose; for example Southampton is by the sea, but is primarily a busy port and is not a holiday resort.

Risk – the chance that someone could be harmed.

S

Secondary products and services – add appeal and give extra revenue to the event organisers, for example T shirts, posters, refreshments, parking and camping.

Secondary research – using information already produced by someone else.

Serviced – accommodation with meals provided. For example, half-board hotel.

SMART objectives –
Specific – it must be very clear what needs to be achieved
Measurable – there must be a way to determine whether it has been achieved or not
Achievable – it must be possible to complete it
Realistic – it must be something that can be achieved
Timed – with a time limit.

Stakeholder – is anyone who has some interest in the business or project. This can include customers, suppliers, staff and even people who live locally to the business or project.

Statutory – a minimum entitlement in line with legislation.

Stopover – when you break up a long journey and take a short break en route, for example stopping over in Dubai en route to Australia.

Study visit – this is an excursion which has specific learning aims and objectives. It can be a day trip or a longer residential visit where you spend a night or more away.

Sustainable tourism – meets the needs of tourists and local communities while protecting the natural, historical and cultural environment for the future.

T

Tangible – means having a physical presence, i.e. a product. Tangible may include hotel accommodation and facilities, meals taken, tickets and souvenirs.

Turnover – is the money brought into the business through sales.

Typhoons – most common in the north western Pacific Ocean.

U

UNESCO – the United Nations Educational Scientific and Cultural Organisation. This is an international organisation and one of its roles is to recognise outstanding natural and cultural sites. There are over 900 UNESCO world heritage sites.

Unforeseen events – when events occur without any warning.

Unique selling point (USP) – is what makes your product or service different from other products or services in the market.

Unit cost – the cost to an organisation of producing and selling one unit of a particular product, such as a seat on an airline.

V

Vertical – an organisation that owns companies in different industries within the travel and tourism sector.

VFR – a term used for people who travel to destinations to visit their friends and relatives.

Visitor attraction – an attraction where it is feasible to charge admission for the sole purpose of sightseeing. The attraction must be a permanently established excursion destination.

(Source: Survey of Visits to Visitor Attractions 2011, VisitEngland)

Y

Yield management systems – are computerised reservation systems that are designed to help an organisation get maximum occupancy, while getting as much money from each booking as possible. If a particular flight is busy then the prices will go up, if the flight is not popular the price will go down.

Index

24-hour clock 132
3 Ps of customer service 144–5

A
ABTA (Association of British Travel Agents) 27
accommodation 18–20, 52, 114–15
  new types 201
  pros and cons 53
  providers 242
  technology use 34
  trends in 186–7
accounting department 180–1
accuracy of information 153–4
active listening 165–6
administration, study trip 267–8
adventure tourism 86
advertisements 222–3
advertising 181, 221
  cost of 226
  of job roles 254
  see also promotional materials
advice to customers 155
affluent empty-nesters 185
Africa 101
age-defined groups 152, 215
ageing population 93–4, 185
aims and objectives, study visit 264–5, 274, 277
air travel 18, 77–9
  disruption to 95
  price increases 94
Air Travel Organisers' Licensing (ATOL) 81, 88, 123
aircraft technology 77
airlines 18
  collapse of 91
  jobs 241
  low-cost 78–9, 87–8, 102, 185
Airport Passenger Duty (APD) 133
airports 102
  3-letter identification code 47
  consumer technology 33–4
  growth of 78–9
  jobs 241–2
  services 28
  in the UK 46–7
airside (air crew) 241
all-inclusive holidays 71, 184
alphabet, phonetic 167
ancillary services 240
annual leave entitlement 252
APD (Airport Passenger Duty) 133
application for jobs 254–5
apps 201, 220
après ski 106
'Arab Spring' uprisings 93
Arctic and Antarctic 101
arts and entertainment 24, 54, 114

Asia 101
assessment zone
  business environments 204–7
  customer experience 142–3
  development of travel and tourism 66–7
  employment opportunities 238–9
  international destinations 98–9
  promotion and sales 210–11
  study visit/trip 262–3
  UK travel and tourism destinations 42–3
  UK travel and tourism sector 36–9
  worldwide travel 126–7
asset management 213
assistance for customers 155
Association of British Travel Agents (ABTA) 27
Association of Independent Tour Operators (AITO) 27
ATOL (Air Travel Organisers' Licensing) 81, 88, 123
attractions see visitor attractions
Australasia 101
aviation regulations 81

B
balance sheet 146
banners 223
beach resorts 109
bespoke 70
bibliography, writing 61
billboard adverts 223
Bluetooth® technology 202
body language 167
BOGOF promotions 225
booking forms 160
booking systems, technological advances 202
bookings, downturn in 196
boutique/niche hotels 186
brand loyalty 172
branding 229
break even 212
broadband 219
brochures 222, 225, 235
  for study visit/trip 268
budget
  promotional materials 231, 233
  study visit/trip 267, 275
budget hotels 19, 187
bus travel, low-cost intercity 79
business environments 174
  business functions 180–2
  business ownership 176–7
  business structures 178–9
  destination trends 189–92
  economic trends 182–3
  new business opportunities 192–4
  opportunities and threats 195–202
  product/service trends 184–9
business structure

responding to changes 200–1
types of 178–9
business travel 5
business travellers 150
Butlin, Billy 69
Butlin's holiday camps 20, 58, 94, 186

C

camping 20, 114
capital cities, UK 44
car hire companies 27
carbon off-setting 186
career progression 256–8
categories of tourist destinations 44–6
celebrity appearances 224
Center Parcs 58, 88, 186
chain of distribution 31, 72–3, 218
Channel Tunnel 50, 75–6, 103
charities 176–7
chronological order 123
city breaks 107, 108
Civil Aviation Authority (CAA) 26–7, 81
civil unrest 92–3, 94
climate change 92
climatic conditions 128, 136–7
coach travel 49, 79, 186
coastal resorts 44–5, 69, 90, 109
    decline and rebranding 73–4
code of conduct 274
colour, use of 228
commercial partnerships 31–3
common ownership 31
communication with customers
    language use 166–8
    recognising unstated needs 160–1
    verbal requests 160
    written requests 156–60
competition 193–4
    competitor behaviour 195–6
competitions 225
complaints 172
computer reservation systems (CRS) 74
confidentiality 166
congestion charging 79
conservation tourism 6, 86
consolidators 16
consultancy 177, 181
consumer aspirations, changes in 195
consumer technology
    accommodation 34
    at airports 33–4
    e-ticketing 35
    mobile applications 35
    visitor attractions 34
    websites 35
contractual rights 252
Cook, Thomas 68
cooperative 177
corporate responsibility 214

costs
    cutting 202
    external 198
    promotional materials 226
countryside areas, UK 45
couples 150
Cox and Kings travel company 68
creative skills 232
credit crunch 189
cruise ports 104
cruises/cruising 71, 76–7, 107, 185
cultural events 197
cultural holidays/tourism 87, 199
cultural trends 187–8
culture 46, 116, 152
currency exchange rates 92, 183, 197–8
curriculum opportunities 265
customer 144
customer expectations 161–3
customer loyalty 213
customer needs 153–6
    changing 201
    responding to 156–61
customer service 140, 144–5
    department 180, 214
    environment 164–5
    first impressions 164
    good and poor, impact of 171–3
    knowledge 170
    personal presentation 164
    policies and standards 168–70
    role of technology 170–1
    skills and techniques 165–8, 248
customer types 148
    external 149–52
    internal 148–9
cyclones 128

D

'dark tourism' 6, 187
Data Protection Act (1998) 81
daylight saving time 131
demographics 93–4, 185
departments, business 180
design of promotional material 228–9
desires versus wants 153
destinations
    for study visit 265–6, 274–5
    trends in 189–92, 201
    UK, increasing appeal for 58–9
    withdrawal of 94
    see also international destinations
developments in travel and tourism
    coastal resorts 73–4
    different types of holiday 71
    historical aspects 68–9
    mass market and specialist holidays 70
    package holidays overseas 70
    technological advances 74

tour operators 72–3
travel agents 72
digital TV, sales channels 220
direct employment 12
direct mailshots 223
direct marketing 221
disabilities 152
discretionary spend 183
diseases and precautions 135–6
Disneyland/Disney World 88, 114, 187
displays, promotional 222
disposable income 83, 183
documentation, study visit 272
domestic 18
domestic tourism 4, 11
domestic visitor numbers 191–2
Dover Castle 266
Dubai 108
duration of study visit/trip 264, 275
dynamic packaging 74

E

e-marketing 202
e-ticketing 35, 202
earthquakes 138
east-west time differences 130
eco-tourism 6, 7, 186, 188
economic issues 91–2
   employment 12
   GDP (gross domestic product) 10–11
   infrastructure development 13
   multiplier effect 12–13
   recession 186, 189
   trends 182–3
economic responsibility 214
economies of scale 69, 202
electronic booking systems 34, 202
email 157–8
   as promotional tool 224
emergency situations 136–8
empathy 165
employment 12
employment benefits 246
employment opportunities 236
   career progression 256–8
   job roles 240–4
   job specifications 246
   new staff 256
   person specifications 247–50
   recruitment and selection 253–5
   rights and responsibilities 251–3
   working patterns 244–5
employment rates 183
employment rights 251–3
empty-nesters 185
English Heritage 30, 51
entertainment 24, 54, 114
   use of technology 34

environment of workplace 164–5
environmental issues 92, 199
   eco-tourism 7, 186, 188
   sustainable tourism 8–9
environmental responsibility 214
equality 251
Equality Act (2010) 81, 251, 267
equipment/resources, study visit 266
ethical issues 199
ethnicity 152
Euro currency, fluctuations 92
Europcar 80
European destinations 101, 105–7
Eurostar 50, 75–6, 103
evaluation
   of promotional materials 232–3
   study trip aims and objectives 277
events 24, 28
exchange rate fluctuations 183, 197–8
exhibition displays 224
existing customers 149
exit/entry requirements 133–4
expectations of customers
   exceeding 162–3
   meeting 161–2
external costs 198
external customers 149–52
external services 181–2

F

face to face sales 218
facilities
   improving appeal of 58
   international 115
   in the UK 52, 53
families 150
FCO (Foreign & Commonwealth Office) 137
feedback
   from customers 169
   promotional materials 232
   study visit/trip 275 6
ferries 47–8, 76, 104
festivals, UK 54
finance department 180–1
finance, study visit 267
financial objectives 212–13
first impressions 164
flat hierarchy 179
flexible working 83
foreign exchange rates 92, 183, 196
foreseen events 196–7
franchises 176
free entry attractions 190
fuel prices 91–2, 198
full-time staff 244–5
functions of a business 179
   external services 180–2
   internal departments 180

G

gateways	46
overseas travel	102–4
UK destinations	46–8
gender	215
geographical scale of operations	178–9
government intervention	198
Great Britain Tourism Survey	11
grey pound	93
gross domestic product (GDP)	10–11
ground crew	241
groups	150

H

halo effect	162
hazards	269
health and safety	154–5, 251
health alerts	155
health risks of travel	132, 135
study visit/trip	267
health tourism	6, 187
heritage attractions	22–3, 114, 191
heritage events	197
heritage tourism	6, 87
Hertz	80
hierarchical structures	179
historical destinations	46, 114
history of package holidays	68–9
hobbies	217
holiday brochures	225
holiday parks	58, 186
holiday planning, UK	61–3
holiday types	183
honeypots	46
horizontal integration	31, 73, 200, 257
hostels	19, 115
hotels	18–19, 114
use of technology	34
human resources	180, 214
hurricanes	95, 128
hygiene, personal	164

I

IATA (International Air Transport Association)	102
iconic structures/buildings	114
immigration policy	198
inbound tourism	4, 10–11, 190–1
independent travel agents	15
indirect employment	12
indirect flights	111
individual customers	149–50
induction of new employees	256
industries	14
accommodation	18–20
arts and entertainment	24
online travel services	16
passenger transport	17–18
tour operators	14–15

tourism development and promotion	25–6
travel agents	15
visitor attractions	21–3
information	
accuracy of	153–4
promotional material	227–8
sources of	60–1
information booklet, study visit/trip	268, 272
infrastructure	13, 198
insurance	28
intangible	180
internal customers	148–9
internal departments	180–1
internal tourism	191–2
international	18
International Air Transport Association (IATA)	102
international destinations	100–1
accommodation	114–15
culture	116
decline in UK visitors	189, 190
European	105–7
facilities and services	115
local attractions	114
major gateways	102–4
natural features	113
planning travel to	120–3
special interest tourism	116–17
travel routes	111–12
types of visitor	117–18, 121
worldwide	108–10
international events	196
international visitor numbers	191–2
internet access	74, 84, 219
interpretation	34
interviews, job	255
islands	109
IT (information technology)	
department	180
skills	247
itinerary	62–3, 122–3
study visit	267, 275

J

JAA-PPL, pilot license	257
job description	253, 254
job roles	240–4
job satisfaction	173
job specifications	246

L

Land of the Midnight Sun	107
landside (ground crew)	241
language	166–8
interpretation	34
in promotional material	228, 232
latitude, lines of	129
leadership skills	248
legacies	30

legal issues, study visit 267
legislation developments 80–1
leisure time, increase in 83
leisure travel 5
letters, writing 157, 158–60
lifestyle
  changes in 82–4
  segmentation by 215–16
listening skills 165–6, 248
local companies 179
log book/sheet, study visit/trip 268
logos 224, 229–30
long-haul travel 70, 71
longitude, lines of 130
low-cost airlines 78–9, 87–8, 102, 185
low-cost bus travel 79
loyalty 172
loyalty schemes 224
Ltd (Private limited company) 176
luxury hotels 201

M

market research 181
market segments 215
market share 192 3
mass tourism 70
maternity rights 251, 252
matrix structure 179
media influences, cultural trends 187
media, promotional materials 231
medication 136
merchandising 223
mergers 72–3, 200
message of promotional material 227–8, 232
'miniple' travel agent 72
mission statements 168, 214
mobile internet access 219, 232
mobile phone apps 220
mobile ticketing 202
mobile travel applications 35
monsoon season 128, 129
motivation, staff 173
multi-national companies 178
multiple travel agents 15, 72
multiplier effect 12–13
museums 51, 58, 114

N

national 17
National Air Traffic Services (NATS) 26–7, 257
national companies 178
national events 178, 196
National Parks 52
National Trust 30, 51
NATS (National Air Traffic Services) 26–7, 257
natural attractions/features 22, 52, 113, 190
natural disasters 92, 95, 138, 197
needs of others, awareness of 274

needs and wants 227
NEET 93
new business opportunities 192–4, 200–2
new competitors 195
new customers 149, 171
new markets, developing 201
new subsidiary companies 200–1
new technologies see technology
niche hotels 186
niche market 146
niche market holidays 85–7
non-serviced accommodation 19, 52, 242
North America 101
Northern Lights 107
novelty 229

O

objections, overcoming 218
objectives
  organisational 212–14
  of study visit/trip 264–5
off-peak (seasons) 188
oil price increases 91–2, 94
online agents 15
online bookings 34
online brochures 225
online resources 60
online sales 219
online services 16, 181
opportunities and threats 195–9
  business response 200–2
organisational objectives 212–14
organisational skills 248
organisations 146
  ancillary 27–8
  commercial partnerships 31 3
  common ownership 31
  private 29, 147
  product comparison providers 28
  public 29, 147
  sizes of 146
  trade and professional bodies 26–7
  types of 147
  voluntary 29, 147
Orient Express 103
outbound tourism 4
outsourcing 202
overseas destinations see international destinations
overseas health requirements 154
ownership of a business 176–7

P

P&O cruises 77
Pacific Ring of Fire 138
package holidays 14, 184
  dynamic 74
  history 68–9
  overseas 70

regulations | 81
paid for entry attractions | 190, 191
paid holiday entitlement | 82–3, 252
pandemics | 135
paper-based information | 60
part-time work | 244–5, 250
partnerships | 31–2, 177
  advantages and disadvantages | 33–4
passenger transport | 17–18
  operators | 243
passports | 133
paternity rights | 251, 252
patience | 165
peak (seasons) | 188
peer feedback | 275–6
Pendolino trains | 75
performance monitoring | 257
person specifications | 247–50, 253
personal behaviour | 144–5
personal presentation | 164, 249
personal responsibility | 273
personal skills | 248–9
phonetic alphabet | 167
physical disabilities | 152
physical resources | 213
placement, promotional material | 227
planning
  holidays in the UK | 61–3
  promotional materials | 230–1
  study trip or visit | 264–8
Plc (public limited company) | 176
policies and procedures | 168–9
political issues | 92–3
pop-ups | 223
ports see seaports
pre-wedding holidays | 87
press releases | 224
primary products/services | 24
primary research | 12
Prime Meridian | 130
private limited companies (Ltd) | 176
private organisations | 29
probation monitoring | 256
processes and procedures | 144
product development department | 180
product life cycle | 193
products and services
  competitors' | 196
  creating new | 193
  customer service | 144, 156
  growth/decline in sales | 95
  primary and secondary | 24
  travel agents | 72
  trends in | 184–9
  wireless | 189, 199
professional bodies | 26–7
profit | 212
profit maximisation | 193
progression opportunities | 257
project planning skills | 248
promotion and sales | 25–6, 208

  impact of new technology | 219–20
  organisational objectives | 212–14
  selling channels | 218–19
  target markets | 215–17, 226
promotional materials
  advertisements | 222–3
  assessment activity | 234
  celebrity appearances | 224
  competitions | 225
  creation of | 231–2
  design of | 228–9
  direct mailshots | 223
  effective features | 227–30
  emails | 224
  evaluation of | 232–3
  exhibition displays | 224
  factors affecting choice of | 225–6
  government funding | 198
  holiday brochures | 225
  information provided | 227–8
  logos | 224
  loyalty schemes | 224
  and needs of target market | 227
  online brochures | 225
  planning creation of | 230–1
  press releases | 224
  shop windows | 224
  special promotions | 225
promotional services | 181
promotional techniques | 221–2, 231–2
public limited companies (Plc) | 176
public organisations | 29
public relations (PR) | 221
purpose-built attractions | 22, 191
purser | 241

Q
qualifications | 247

R
radio advertisements | 223
rail transport | 75–6
  Office of Rail Regulation (ORR) | 27
rail travel | 17, 50
  train terminals | 103
Raitz, Vladimir | 69
rebranding of coastal resorts | 73–4
recession
  effect on tourism | 189, 196
  and unemployment | 93
record taking, study visit/trip | 268
recruitment and selection | 253–5
regeneration of seaside resorts | 90
regional companies | 178
religious sites | 114
repatriation of customers | 94–5
repeat and referred business | 172
resorts | 44–5, 73–4, 90, 109

resources
  human   180, 214
  online   60
  physical   213
  for study trip/visit   266
responsible tourism   188, 214
review criteria, study visit/trip   274–6
riots   137
risk assessment   269–70
risks   269
road tolls   79
road travel   17, 49
role allocation   266–7

S

safaris   86
safety issues   155
  security checks, airports   34
  see also health and safety
sales and customer service   171–2
sales promotions   222
sea transport   76–7
sea travel   18
seaports   47–8, 104
seaside resorts   44–5, 73–4, 90, 109
seasonal staff   245
seasonal trends   188
seasonal variations   129
second-home ownership   84, 186
secondary products/services   24
secondary research   12
security   155
security checks, airports   34
segmentation   215–16
self-catering   19, 114, 184
self-review, study visit   276–7
self-service check-in, airports   33
self-service machines   219
selling channels   218–19
sensitivity   166
serviced accommodation   19, 52, 242
shift work   245
shop windows   222, 224
shopping   115
sightseeing   54–5, 115
size of business/organisation   146–7, 178
SMART objectives   265
SMEs (small and medium enterprises)   178
social attitudes   199
social issues   93–4
social media   187, 189, 199
social responsibility   214
socio-economic groups   215
socio-economic trends   185
sole trader   177
South America   101
special interests   116–17, 150, 216–17
special needs   156
specialist holidays/travel   6, 70

specific groups, appealing to   59
spend per visitor   183
sponsorship   222, 225
sport tourism   85–6, 115, 187–8, 217
sporting events   197
staff performance   214
staff structures   179
staff turnover   173
stag/hen parties   188
stakeholders   232
standards of customer service   169–70
statutory rights   251–2
staycations   184
steep hierarchy   179
stopover   111
straplines   229
strategic objectives   213
strengths and weaknesses, study trip   277
structure, business   179, 200–1
study visit/trip   260
  planning   264–8
  responsibilities prior to   272–3
  review criteria   274–6
  risk assessment   269–70
  roles during   273–4
  self-review   276–7
subsidiary companies   200–1
summer sun holidays   105
superferries   76
sustainable tourism   7 8

T

tailor-made holidays   184
takeovers   200
tangible   180
target markets   226
  needs of   227
  segmentation   215–16
taxation   133, 198
teacher/tutor feedback   275–6
teamwork   168, 248–9, 273
technology   74
  aircraft   77
  consumer   34–5
  and customer service   170–1
  developments   199, 201–2
  and information accuracy   154
  internet access   74, 84, 219
  promotional materials   232
  and sales promotion   218–19
  trends in   188–9
telephone sales   219
television   220
  advertisements   222–3
terms of employment   246
terrorism   93, 137, 197
theatres, West End, London   24
theme parks   51, 58, 114, 187
Thomas Cook   68, 95

three-letter codes, airports 47, 102
three Ps of customer service 144–5
ticket office sales 218
time differences, calculating 131–2
time management 273
time zones 130–1
timescales, promotional materials 230, 233
tour operators 14–15, 72–3, 241
  collapse of 91
tourism development 25–6, 244
tourism types 4
tourist boards 25
tourist information centres 25
trade and professional bodies 26–7
train terminals 103
training
  career progression 257
  new employees 256
transferable skills 250
transport links, UK 55
transport methods 17–18
transport trends 185–6
transportation developments 75–80
travel agents 15, 240
  face to face selling 218
travel arrangements 266, 275
travel disruptions 95
travel insurance 28
travel types 5–6
trends 85–90
tropical storms 128, 129
tsunamis 138
turnover 146
  downturn in 196
  of staff 173
typhoons 128

U

UK Inbound 27
UK travel and tourism
  destinations 40–63
  development of 64–95
  sector 2–39
unemployment 93, 182
UNESCO world heritage sites 110
unforeseen events 197
unique selling point (USP) 227–8
unit cost 69
unserviced accommodation 19, 52, 242
unstated needs, recognising 160–1
uprisings 93
USA 23

V

vaccination 136
value of tourism 10–11
verbal communication 160

vertical integration 31, 73, 200, 257
VFR (visits to friends and relatives) 101
visas 133, 134
VisitBritain 26
VisitEngland 21
visitor attractions 21–3, 189–91
  jobs roles 242–3
  overseas travel 114
  technology used in 34
  in the UK 51
visitor numbers 191–2, 196
visitor types 55–6
vocational skills 247–8
voluntary organisations 29
voluntary work 6, 250
volunteer conservation holidays 6

W

wants and needs 227
wants versus desires 153
wars and riots 137
weather conditions 128, 136–7, 265
websites 35
  as a selling channel 219
  advertisements on 223
weddings overseas 115
wellbeing holidays 115
winter sports 106, 110
winter sun holidays 105–6
wireless products/services 189, 199
working hours and conditions 252
working patterns 244–5
Working Time Regulations 80
workplace environment 164–5
workspace
  airport passenger handling agent 139
  corporate travel consultant 271
  cruise line purser 151
  designer 235
  information assistant 57
  private business owner 203
  senior consultant, retail travel 259
  tour manager 89
  travel consultant 119
  visitor operations site supervisor 9
world heritage sites 110
world map 100
worldwide destinations 108–10
worldwide time 130–1
worldwide travel, factors affecting 128–38
written communication 156–60

Y

yield management systems 183
youth hostels 19, 115
youth market, declining 185